There's a Rhino
in the Rose Bed,
Mother

By Betty and Jock Leslie-Melville:

THERE'S A RHINO IN THE ROSE BED, MOTHER
ELEPHANT HAVE RIGHT OF WAY

There's a Rhino in the Rose Bed, Mother

Betty and Jock Leslie-Melville

Doubleday & Company, Inc.
Garden City, New York   1973

Excerpts from *Out of Africa,* by Isak Dinesen. Copyright 1937, renewed 1965 by Rungstedlundfonden. Reprinted by permission of Random House, Inc.

ISBN: 0-385-07233-3
Library of Congress Catalog Card Number 73–81419

Introduction

Our working title for this book was "Half and Half." Roughly half has been written by each of us. Given the fact that the title could be spoken aloud rather than read, "Half" could be pronounced with an American accent and "Half" with a British accent, reflecting our different backgrounds, and of course, half is by a woman and half by a man. Half of the anecdotes take place in Africa, half in the States. Half of the content is frivolous, half serious (half good, half bad, half true, half false . . .)

For married readers of different tastes, this book is quite a bargain. The first half is largely light adventures, kids, animals, and the second half dabbles in politics, emerging Africa, and problems on the continent, so you and your husband/wife can tear it in half if you like. We could go on and on.

Each of us wrote some frothy and some serious parts and made corrections and suggestions for each other's material, so some chapters are impossible to attribute to one or the other. However, at the beginning of certain chapters we have put "Mainly by Betty" or "Mainly by Jock" meaning just that.

Our publishers, the illustrious Doubleday & Company, Inc., thought that "Half and Half" was a rotten title. They suggested instead one of the chapter headings, "There's a Rhino in the

Rose Bed, Mother" as the title. We fought a rear-guard action for the following title:

"THERE'S A RHINO IN THE ROSE BED, MOTHER
(Or, Africa's political, sociological and tribal complexities)"

We lost that battle too.

So, here we are with a title. May you now have a happy safari through our book.

Betty and Jock

To my sister "Of,"
and
Dick and Jeanne

Contents

Me Tarzan, You Betty

Time and time again people say, "You live in Africa, Wow! What's the most harrowing adventure you've ever had?" Our most harrowing adventures have been, without any doubt, on the New Jersey Turnpike and in Tulsa, Oklahoma. However, we have had some harrowing adventures in Africa, and it *can* be very dangerous for travelers. I mean, they might be molested by Jock, for instance:

One Friday Jock was having lunch in the upstairs dining room of the New Stanley. Every Friday there is a magnificent smorgasbord and the place was very full.

For some reason the conversation turned to basic training in the army, and Jock told his friends about an incident that had happened when he was at Sandhurst, the equivalent of our West Point.

It seems that they were having a rehearsal for a dress parade and were all decked out in fancy special uniforms and were drilling with old-fashioned rifles which had long bayonets—used only for ceremonies. On the command "Right Dress!" all the cadets had to look squarely to their right and at the same time punch their left arm out sideways so that the next cadet could measure off and stand the exact distance away, just touching the outstretched arm. On the command "Eyes Front!" they had to look to the front and return the outstretched left arm smartly to the side, thus resuming a position of Attention. The cadet to

Jock's left was half asleep in the hot sun and had allowed his up-right rifle and bayonet to lean away from his right side, so that when Jock dropped his outstretched left arm back to his side, he cut his middle finger badly on the projecting bayonet. Months of rigid training overcame all other instincts. He stood motionless and silent, listening to the dripping of the blood. The next com-mand was "Unfix Bayonets!" which means that they unscrewed the bayonets from the rifles and returned them to the scabbards on their belts—and for this purpose they were allowed to look down.

Jock saw that there was a pool of blood the size of a dinner plate at his feet and a couple of drops had splattered his uniform. Since they had to clean their own uniforms, and since the biggest parade of the year was next day, he was anxious not to get more blood on the pants, so he held his hand very slightly away from his body. The movement was enough to attract the attention of the Sergeant Major, even though he was nearly a quarter of a mile away and there were two thousand other cadets on the vast square. "The third gentleman in the front rank of Normandy Company is standing with his hand out like a queer!" he bellowed. "Take his name!" That meant Jock would be punished later, but he still stood there with his hand out.

Incensed, the Sergeant Major strode over. Jock knew that when he saw what had happened he would give him a Purple Heart for being wounded and brave—but not a bit of it. He glared at the pool of blood, appalled.

"Look at you!" he yelled at Jock. "Look at the mess you are making on my square!"

He ordered Jock to march himself to the hospital a mile away, and when he arrived the doctor put five stitches in his finger. He has quite a scar to this day.

Anyhow, Jock was telling this story at the smorgasbord lunch in the New Stanley and when he got to the part about "Right Dress!" he jerked his head to the right and punched his left arm out sharply in the approved manner to demonstrate. He was sit-ting at the table and his left fist was, therefore, exactly at the right height to catch an enormous Swiss man on safari an agonizing blow in the privates. The Swiss was returning to his table and had a plate laden with every kind of smoked fish and Scandinavian delicacy, all of which he dropped as he clutched himself. People came to their feet at neighboring tables, waiters rushed to help and to mop up and Jock tried to explain to the visitor, who barely understood English, that he had not molested him deliberately, and that he had been telling a funny story ha! ha! Jock, who is inclined to be shy anyway, says that it was one of the worst moments of his life. It probably was for the victim too—so the first thing to beware of in Africa is someone hitting you in the balls in the New Stanley dining room.

In Africa we've been charged by rhino and elephant while in cars in the game parks, and so forth, but these experiences are not harrowing; they're filled with excitement and are what you expect will happen and why you go on safari—like visiting the spook house at an amusement park—you expect a thrill or two. "Harrowing," according to the Oxford Dictionary, means "distressing" and distressing is breaking down in ten-degree weather on the New Jersey Turnpike, just a few miles outside New York on a Friday night.

It was during the Rolls-Royce period of our life, which lasted about three weeks. We had bought this twenty-year old Rolls in Kenya for $1,500 and shipped it to the States where we were driving it everywhere because it was our only car. As Jock concluded, "It is a nice car to visit your mother-in-law on Sundays, but it is not the kind of car you need for traveling five hundred miles a day"—which we frequently do on the lecture tours we undertake each year in the States. It had many faults. Number one fault from my point of view was having no radio, because as long as a car has a radio I'll push it. Number two fault was having no heater. Numbers three to ten were not being able to get parts—we even had to use small truck tires because no others would fit. The car had a trunk designed to hold two top hats and a briefcase because the luggage, naturally, would follow behind in another car

with the footman. It had a right-hand drive, and wouldn't run 90
per cent of the time, but other than that it was grand.

We usually travel like gypsies. We never go anywhere, it
seems, without lamp shades, kids, friends of the kids, and the
friend's cat which has to be bred with another cat in Washington,
D.C. We also always seem to have a rusty stove and small refrigerator, which do not work, and which were destined for the Salvation Army, but which my newly married niece has asked us to
hijack en route—her husband will fix them. He never does, but we
always take them just the same. We never travel without yoghurt
and other food even if we are just driving to mail a letter at the
corner. Jock, the children and I are all sloppy and are not types
who put tops back on toothpaste, but we do have a hang-over
from "Keep your Country Clean" and we never throw anything
out of the window. Unfortunately, we don't throw it out when we
arrive at our destination either, so our car always smells like
tangerines and looks like a garbage truck, with egg shells, sticky
plastic spoons, masses of rattling Coke bottles, crunched waxed
paper with one bite left of a roll stained with mustard, and a
quarter of a tuna fish sandwich. This caused a friend of ours,
upon getting into our car once, to ask if we had cockroaches.
Maybe we will be the first people to be picked up in our car by
the health department instead of the police department.

Anyway, on this particular Friday night, in addition to Jock
and me and our daughter, Dancy (wearing bedroom slippers because she forgot her shoes) and our son McDonnell, who had
a temperature of 101° and was about to throw up, and Mary
Mary, our eldest son Rick's girl friend, who wanted to ride to
Baltimore, and all our collective luggage, we had two retread tires
in the back seat, there being no room in the trunk which was already filled to capacity with six yoghurt cups.

Accustomed to the discomfort, we set out cheerfully for our
five-hour drive to "Bawlamer" (as native Baltimorians pronounce
it). But twenty miles out of New York we broke down. (We had
broken down earlier that month in the Lincoln Tunnel—an excellent place to have trouble. Within seconds someone comes in a

truck and hauls you out and dumps you right by a telephone booth at the end of the tunnel. They never say a word to you and there is no charge.) This time the gods must have been angry because we flew white handkerchiefs out of the window but nobody stopped. We calculated that the nose-to-tail stream of cars on three lanes amounted to 3,600 cars in the first hour, so the odds of having one stop within the next week or so were, therefore, not very good. It was 10° with a howling wind and with the engine stopped there was not even faint heat. We huddled under the tires, and as we became seriously cold I remembered stories of people dying in the cars in snowstorms and understood why.

I foresaw the headlines: "Five Freeze to Death in Hackensack" or wherever we were. Jock spent forty minutes under the car trying to fix it and he nearly froze to the exhaust pipe. Then he stood outside waving people down. They all sped past, but finally a policeman did stop. We cheered. He said he'd call a tow truck and be right back. We never saw him again or a truck. The situation was really getting serious with the high winds and intense cold and no heater, so Jock said he was going to climb the fence on the side of the highway and walk toward some lights we saw in the distance. No, he would go alone. In a few minutes we heard a feeble, "Help, Help!" and we all clambered out of the car and ran to Jock who had dislocated his good arm in scaling the fence. (I say good arm because he had polio when he was twenty and his right arm is completely paralyzed.) He had dislocated his left shoulder and could not move from astride the top of the fence. I got to him first, and followed his instructions of pulling his arm hard so that it would go back into place. The pain was so great he almost fainted, and we had to help him back to the car. He was now in no condition to go anyplace, so McDonnell and I decided we would be the next team to go for help while Dancy and Mary Mary stayed with Jock. We got over the fence but found ourselves in a garbage dump—empty tin cans and broken bottles were sticking out of the old snow and cutting our ankles. We kept falling down and crawling through brambles and goodness knows what else. In about ten minutes we arrived at a huge factory. We went in and I said, wobbling on bloody ankles, "Could you help us?" A group of three men sitting with their backs toward us jumped a mile—they were scared to death! "How did you get in here?" they asked, astonished. We explained we had climbed the fence from the highway where we were broken down in our car, and they told us the factory was supposed to be heavily guarded. It looked like a trucking depot and they must have been shipping guns to Vietnam—I didn't know, nor did I care. They gave us hot chocolate, and a radiator to sit by and a telephone to use. They told us we were about fifteen miles from New Brunswick. New Brunswick!—my nun friend was in the convent there before being sent to Rome. It was now after midnight, but I telephoned and awakened her, and Sister Helen promised that she and another nun would rescue us immediately. I explained to the truckers that my friends would be over soon to get us, but I neglected to say they were nuns.

"What kind of car youse got?" one of them asked, very friendly, as we waited.

"A Rolls-Royce," McDonnell answered, embarrassed.

"One of them new ones?"

"Oh, no, a 1947," explained McDonnell quickly, anxious not to appear to be a filthy capitalist.

"Where youse from?" asked another.

"Nairobi," I answered.

"Nairobi, New Joisey? Don't think I know it."

"No, Nairobi in Africa."

"Africa! Jeez. Hey, from Africa. Wow—about them elephants . . ." he started when the intercom clicked on and from the main gate we heard "We got two dillies out here who says they is nuns."

McDonnell and I tried to explain to him that they were not Al Capone types dressed up as nuns but were genuine and were our friends. Finally, he let them into the factory, and we had a big reunion with Sister Helen and a French nun who had come with her. The French nun spoke no English, but since she had lived in Africa we spoke to her in Swahili. We thanked the truckers, who

had suddenly become very suspicious of us again, and left them
wondering if they had been hallucinating all evening.

Helen drove us to the highway where we hoped to find no Rolls-
Royce—that it had been towed to the first gas station on the
next exit. But it was still there, so Jock, Dancy and Mary Mary
got into Helen's nice warm car too and we all went to a Howard
Johnson's where we had lots of laughs over hot chocolate and
telephoned Rick in Baltimore who got in his car and drove to New
Brunswick immediately. We spent the night there and the next
day sorted out the "Royce-Rolls," as George Scott called it in *The
Yellow Rolls-Royce.*

So now you know that if you ever break down on a turnpike in
the States, call the nearest convent.

Number two harrowing adventure you will probably think
more harrowing than number one. Perhaps you are right, but on
the New Jersey Turnpike two of my children were along and I
was concerned over them as well as Jock and myself. But this
time there was only Jock and me. We got trapped in a hotel fire
in Tulsa, Oklahoma. We were on the top floor of the brand new
fireproof hotel which was having its fifth fire (we discovered
afterward).

We went to bed about midnight, exhausted after a lecture followed by a luncheon party, followed by another lecture followed
by a dinner party, and so on, and at what turned out to be 3 A.M.
we both woke to hear running feet and shouting. "More drunks,"
we thought. But then we smelled that acrid burning smell of plastics and "fireproof" curtains and carpets. Rushing out into the corridor we were confronted by smoke so dense that really and
truly, just like the cliché, you couldn't see your hand in front of
your face. Out of the non-opening plate glass picture window,
our picturesque view was billowing smoke and flames. Later we
learned our room was directly above the one on fire. I flung on a
bathrobe and shoved my bare feet into some nearby shoes but
didn't bother to buckle them and started for the door. I turned to
make sure Jock was following me, and do you know what he was

doing? Putting on socks! We never fight, but we had a screaming row then.

"What the hell are you putting socks on for?" (An ungrammatical fight at that—I always say "what for" instead of "why" in fires.)

"It might be chilly outside. Take something warm," he answered as he put his stockinged feet into his boots and turned to look for his undershirt.

"Undershirt! Are you going to wear a TIE?"

"I am going to be warmly dressed outside," he said emphatically.

"What makes you think we are going to *get* outside?" I shouted.

"Now get some wet towels," he instructed calmly. (It still makes me mad to think of it . . . socks, calm—damned British.)

When I returned from the bathroom in noisy desperation with the towels, he had a sweater, an overcoat, and our irreplaceable lecture film. I shoved a towel at him, kept mine, and we left the room and turned to the right as we had always done to leave the hotel room. I knew you were supposed to do something with the towel, but I didn't know what, so I wrung it in my hands as we tried to get through the smoke to an exit. The smoke was too thick. Then I wiped my sweating brow with the towel and decided that this was it—what an embarrassing place to die— Tulsa, Oklahoma. The smoke was choking us to death, there wasn't a hope we could make the elevator bank and the adjacent stairway, so I wrung the towel in my hands some more, and we barely got back to our room which mercifully was still relatively free of smoke. (Yes, Jock had shut the door and brought the key.) The smoke was coming in under the door, and I did not know then that what you are supposed to do is to shut yourself in the bathroom and turn on the hot shower—something about bringing oxygen into the room. Jock said, "Perhaps if we go to the left we'll find another exit, and you're supposed to *breathe through* the towel."

Jock also knew from having done fire drills with dense smoke at school that if you crawl very low—even on your stomach—

there is usually a layer of clear air. We crawled along and soon found an exit door, we opened it and there was an outside fire escape! As we stood gasping in huge breaths of clean air, it was like being handed a new life. I started down the stairs but Jock went back in to wake up other people. I think this was very brave, but he insists that it was not—that being certain of his escape route he never ventured farther than a deep breath would last him from the exit. He woke more than a dozen people and I still think he was very brave.

Meanwhile, on the fire escape I passed two young blacks who were running up as fast as they could go. I assumed they were firemen who had not had time to put on their uniforms but were trying to rescue people. I mentioned the fact to a bystander, who assured me, "Then they weren't firemen, they always wear their hats and uniforms." Curious, I went up to a fireman who was playing a hose through an open window and asked him, "Do you have two American blacks in your fire department?"

"We have *eleven* of them, lady, *eleven!*" he snapped back, as if I were an office bearer of the N.A.A.C.P. We never discovered who they were.

Outside the scene was terrific. People who thought they were trapped on high floors were smashing the picture windows from the inside with chairs and were coming down on sheets tied together, just like in the funny papers. In some cases the sheets were not long enough and the firemen were hollering at them to stand on window ledges while they maneuvered ladders into position and plucked them off like apples. More than forty people came down on the ladders. Then suddenly it was all over and the fire was under control. Although seven people were taken to the hospital, fortunately, nobody died or was even seriously hurt.

Inside, the scene was very funny. The Red Cross and the Disaster Squad were there, as well as the Fire Department. I always thought the Red Cross gave out doughnuts and I was looking forward to mine, but no one ever got a doughnut. In the lobby, which had not burned, airline pilots were standing around in their undershorts; lanky members of a Memphis basketball team were wearing the nearest thing they had been able to grab—one in a girl friend's nightgown—and the drunk conventioneers in blue-striped pajamas were starting up again, toasting one another from flasks. Most collected their smoked or charred belongings and drove to other hotels. We had no car so we were transferred to a room in another wing, on the ground floor, where we now prefer to stay whenever possible.

Incidentally, never use an elevator in a fire. The shaft acts as a chimney, the power can be cut at any moment trapping you, and the heat-responsive push buttons to summon the elevators on each floor will ensure that you are promptly delivered to the heart of the inferno. Elevators in fires are verboten.

People ask, "What would you take in a fire?" Afterward I found that quite unconsciously I had grabbed only a bracelet Rick had made for me and my address book. I had no thought of money or driver's license or air tickets—but how could I call everyone and tell them about the fire without my address book? The classic question is, "In a fire, if you had time to save a Rembrandt or a cat, which would you save?" The answer I like best was from the person who said of course he'd save the cat, then set it free. Fortunately, there was no cat or Rembrandt in our room in the Tulsa hotel, so we had no such decision to make —but it wouldn't be hard. We'd save the wretched cat too, even knowing that a Rembrandt is more valuable, lasting, and would give more joy to thousands. But the cat is alive. We'd probably leave the Rembrandt and save a cockroach.

But the terror of the fire lasted only ten minutes in all—until we knew we would be safe. If it comes to a choice of ten minutes of panic or twenty-four hours of grimness, I'm not so sure I wouldn't choose the terror of a fire.

Once, we finished lecturing in Cicero, Illinois, at 5 P.M. and had to be in Binghampton, New York, lecturing the next day at 3 P.M. There were no planes that could get us from Chicago, or anywhere near it, to Binghampton by the next afternoon, so the only way for us to go was to drive. There was a terrific snowstorm to cheer us along our 1,003-mile drive. We passed a sign that read "Niagara Falls—5 miles," and though neither of us had ever been—and still haven't—we couldn't stop. We delayed a few minutes at a roadside diner to eat, and 150 miles farther spent two hours in a motel for Jock to throw up because he had eaten something that made him sick. That enhanced the trip too. Finally, at 2:30 P.M. we arrived in Binghampton, exhausted, but we had no time to find a hotel to have a bath and dress. We went to the municipal garbage dump, for privacy, and changed our clothes there, in the car, and when I stood at the lectern, the entire audience moved, just as the road had been doing for the last twenty-four hours and I had to hold on to the podium for balance. I remember a midget in the audience—it was all like a Fellini film. I'll take the fire.

Another time in Boston during the first terrible tour when I was lecturing alone, I was getting dressed for the lecture, and as I leaned over to step into my shoes I laughed at something Jock said and sneezed simultaneously and pulled my back. There I was, bent over at a right angle, unable to stand upright, and that is just how I walked onto the stage half an hour later. I lowered the microphone to waist level, which was the same level as my head—and gave my speech in that position. Then I went to the hospital and had a brace put on my back and stayed in bed unable to move for two days.

But now that Jock and I lecture together it isn't as nerve-racking. Once I swallowed a fly on stage, and while I choked and people ran to me with glasses of water, Jock carried on. Once or twice our film has broken—it is inevitable when you show an hour film each day in a different projector that one projector is going to chew it up, and there is no way to find out until you get to that part the next day. So, if the break happens Jock deserts me and goes to fix the damaged film, while I carry on with a little tap dance routine on the stage all by myself! Oh, the lecture business is lots of laughs. It is actually show biz—one night stands. Time is the main problem. You lecture in one city in the morning, go to the luncheon afterward, do a TV show after that, then a newspaper interview, fly to another city five hundred miles away, and there the new people are waiting for you at the airport. "We have invited ten committee members to meet you in the cocktail lounge—just a small welcoming party."

And so it goes every day. When do you ever get to wash your underwear? On the plane? Do you know that once I had to go to the dentist—not that I could afford such a luxury as the dentist on a lecture tour, but my tooth was falling out, so I had no choice. I simply had to wash my filthy hair that day, so where did I do it? In the dentist's little sink with that dopey curved spout. If you have ever washed your hair in the dentist's office, you will know there are no taps to make the water run. You have to step on "hot" and "cold" pedals on the floor, which is as difficult as rubbing your head and patting your stomach. The dentist, who was a stranger, thought it was peculiar when I said, "Would you mind if I washed my hair here?"

He thought I was talking funny because of the Novocain and that he had misunderstood me, so I repeated it, and, well, what could he say—"No"? So he said, "Ha ha, um—of course, of course."

And everyone says what a "glamorous life" we have and think of us jet-setting round the world playing Tarzan and Jane, doing TV shows, living in hotel luxury and having Sassoon do my hair. "You're so lucky," they say.

That's right, and the harder we work the luckier we get.

It is mostly hard work and we are not members of the jet set— we are members of the propeller set—or turbo-prop set at best. In January or February many people spend their weekends skiing —not us. We run for planes in Chicago airport all weekend, and I am sure we get more exercise than the skiers. Many are the nights we spend in grotty hotels or worse—airport motels. If you can read lips airport motels are fine, but otherwise they are just too noisy for conversation—and noise usually does not bother me—the only thing I ever really hear is silence. Our house in Africa is so quiet—no traffic, no neighbors—that sometimes I feel as if something is wrong. Then I realize it's the silence—so I put on a loud record and relax. It is not the actual noise of an airport motel I dislike, but the fear brought on by the fact that every plane sounds exactly as if it is about to crash into our bed.

Late one night in a quiet motel on some obscure highway in the middle of Arkansas we put our quarter in for the "Magic Fingers" treatment—fifteen minutes of gently relaxing vibration of the bed—and after about half an hour when it hadn't clicked off we began to suspect something was wrong. After an hour and a half we knew it. It was stuck and was beginning to be annoying —not full of relaxing joy any more. So Jock got out and tried to disconnect the plug, but it was not the kind you could just pull out—it was hooked in the socket for good. We got under the bed and fooled with wires there—to no avail. Finally, unable to stand the magic any longer, we hauled the mattress off the bed and lay on it on the floor listening to the springs clanking away all night long.

Once, after an evening lecture in Indianapolis, we went right on to Denver so I stayed in my evening clothes. The next morning we had a 10 A.M. lecture, and at 9:30 A.M. I realized I had left my daytime shoes in Indianapolis. With my suede pants suit I was wearing for the lecture I had a choice of either sparkling silver evening sandals or Jock's boots. I chose Jock's brown boots and shuffled out on the stage in my clown's feet and stood there looking like a female impersonator. You can imagine the problem clothes can be, packing and unpacking and quickly moving from one city to another every day. Half of what I start out with is left, forgotten and strewn out from coast to coast. There must be a bathrobe of mine or Jock's on the back of a hotel door in every state. We always take our summer clothes to the States in the winter and our winter clothes in the summer, because we freeze to death in the air conditioning in the summer and roast from the central heating in the winter.

Another time we were leaving Baltimore, having stayed with my sister, and were starting out on a new leg of the tour, from Friendship Airport. We checked in at the curb checking-in place and Jock handed me some letters he wanted to mail. While he collected the baggage stubs, I walked over to the mail box and put the letters in. Carrying a six-foot high wooden giraffe we had dragged all the way from Kenya for an ex-friend in Denver—we were afraid it would break if we checked it with the bags—we went inside the airport and looked at books and people to kill the remaining minutes before final call.

Jock then said, "Give me back the tickets."

"What tickets?" I asked.

"Our air tickets, the ones I just gave you to hold."

"Oh, dear, how awful . . . I must have mailed them."

"You what?!"

It was the last flight out of Baltimore to Denver, we *had* to make the lecture and therefore we had to be aboard the plane which was taking off in ten minutes. We went to the United Airlines counter and said,

"We mailed our tickets."

"I beg your pardon?"

"We mailed our tickets—just now, outside."

It was impossible to rewrite them in that short time because we had onward reservations for the next week to Witchita, Tulsa, Dallas, Bismarck (we are very big in Bismarck), Salt Lake City, San Francisco, Los Angeles, Des Moines, Houston, St. Louis, Louisville, Danville, Chicago and Milwaukee—to mention a few. The United man called the Post Office Department at the airport, and a policeman—evidently you have to have a policeman there if you are going to open a mail box other than at 7:10 A.M., 10:57 A.M., 1:54 P.M., 5:25 P.M. or 8:45 P.M. The efficiency was beautiful. Both the mailman and the policeman arrived on motorcycles in what seemed like two seconds instead of the ages those things usually take. They opened the box, handed us the tickets—with a smile—and we ran with the giraffe shouting thanks at them, and got on the plane just as it was about to taxi to the runway.

We have missed plenty of planes, but somehow never the last one to get us there on time. How we have never missed a lecture, I don't know. Once we were the *only* people at one of our lectures.

There was a major snow storm—a blizzard really—and the pilot said as we landed in Boston, "Welcome to Siberia."

Following the instructions to get to the museum, we took the local train, then a cab. The train got halfway to where it was supposed to go, a cab got us a little farther, and then Jock and I staggered a few blocks through the snow—climbing over mountainous drifts like Julie Christie and Omar Sharif in *Dr. Zhivago*—and finally arrived at the auditorium—but no one else did.

Nor have we ever taken a wrong flight. Someone we know said he and two business friends were going from Sacramento to San Francisco early one morning for a business conference—about a fifteen-minute flight. They all walked toward the plane together, when one of them realized he needed cigarettes. The other two didn't smoke so he ran back to the terminal to get a pack, while his companions boarded the plane. He didn't arrive back in time and the plane took off without him. The others chuckled and expected a call when they arrived at the meeting, or at least at the hotel at lunch time. Nothing. They began to worry because they had assumed the doors had been closed seconds before he got back and he would simply get the next shuttle, but now they were beginning to wonder if he had had a heart attack or something. At 6 P.M. that night, the phone rang.

"George, this is Phil."

"Where the hell are you, Phil?"

"St. Petersburg."

"St. Petersburg, *Florida?*"

"Yeah, but I might just as well be in St. Petersburg, Russia."

He had run back to the boarding gates with his cigarettes and right onto the non-stop flight for sunny St. Petersburg—just as it drew away from the ramp.

John Reddy, Jr., son of our great friends John and Nora Reddy, was flying to New York from Washington, D.C., to see his parents, and after he had been airborne a few minutes he noticed the men next to him changing the time on their watches. This he thought was strange, but when the stewardess announced over the loudspeaker that the movie would be shown after lunch, he got really suspicious, and quietly went and asked her the embarrassing question of where the plane was going. Los Angeles. Non-stop. After the five-hour ride he was whisked immediately into another non-stop flight from Los Angeles to New York. He saw the same movie twice and had four dinners.

In the days when airline captains used to put out a circular in mid-flight, giving altitude, time of arrival, weather conditions on the ground, and so forth, and the passengers passed the sheet back down the cabin to one another, a friend of ours used to collect the sheets and store them away. He frequently traveled internationally and the big joke was to select one of his old flight sheets and pass it back instead of the real one. On a London to New York flight he would circulate one that read London to Zanzibar and then he would watch the consternation of passengers calling for the stewardesses and panicking about being on the wrong flight.

In Akron, Ohio, I got locked in the bathroom of the Holiday Inn. For hours! I found this really unpleasant. And embarrassing —here we are, safari biggies supposed to be able to get people out of the jaws of a lioness or other awkward situations, and I couldn't even get out of the bathroom in Akron, Ohio. Jock and I tried for about a half hour jiggling the handle, pulling up on it and pushing it down and all those things everyone does, but nothing would give. I hadn't in fact locked the door, I had just closed it and it had jammed. Jock finally called the assistant manager who said he was alone on duty and could not leave his post, and no, there was no resident engineer. Good-by.

Although I am not claustrophobic, I have the interest span of a two-year-old and there was nothing *to do* in there. If I had had my shower cap, I'd have taken a shower, or if I had had my shampoo I'd have washed my hair, but I was getting hysterically bored. Jock tried to shove a magazine under the door for me, but the only one slim enough to fit was *The Holiday Inn Magazine,* which extolled the facilities and efficiencies of Holiday Inns the world over. There was no window in the bathroom, and I wondered what a person traveling alone would do—there would be no Jock to holler, "I can't get out of here" to. After Jock had tried unsuccessfully to shoulder the door, and I had been in there almost an hour, he told me, for occupational therapy, to compose a mental letter to the president of the Holiday Inns, and he walked to the desk, grabbed the young assistant and marched him to the room.

Jock said, "Get that door open. Call the fire department or *somehow* open that door or I'll batter it down myself."

The assistant manager advised against battering the door down "lest the manager get mad," and this made Jock so mad that he aimed a tremendous kick at the steel door, which to his astonishment flew open and nearly knocked me into the toilet. We sent a nice letter to the president suggesting there should be a bell or something for people who get locked in, or sick, or any grisly thing, since a lot of those motels are often almost empty in the winter and sometimes one is put at the end of a wing far from the desk or other guests. We got the "bed bug" letter in reply.

Don't you know about the bed-bug letter?

On British Railways some years ago, a passenger who traveled on the night train from Inverness to London was bitten by bed bugs. He wrote a letter of complaint to the management and a week later got a reply. British Railways were appalled. Never, they wrote, had any passenger had cause to complain about bed bugs. They had traced the bed roll supplied to his compartment back to the laundry and had placed their laundering contract elsewhere. Further, they had withdrawn the entire coach from service, had isolated it in a siding and had a team of twelve men fumigating it. They were so glad, they went on, that he had immediately drawn this devastating matter to their attention, and they would be most appreciative if he would refrain from mentioning the experience to anybody since it was an isolated instance, and they had, after all, taken drastic remedial action. They remained his obedient servants, etc., and hoped to serve him on future occasions.

He was grudgingly impressed with their letter and the steps taken, but then he noticed a hand-written memo still clipped to the back. It read, "Send this gink the bed-bug letter."

After a lecture in Florida once, Jock and I visited our friends Henry and Ewell Stewart in Duck Key for a few days. The first evening there we decided to go bicycling. I raced ahead showing off, and came to a little arched bridge, which I didn't know, until it was too late, was covered with loose gravel. The bike started skidding all around, I had no control over it whatsoever, and down I went flat on my face—with a very hard bang indeed. I put my hand up to a mass of blood and felt to see if I had any teeth left. They seemed to be there. Jock said my face was such a bloody pulp that he thought I would be disfigured for life. I was quickly driven to the emergency room at the local hospital where they discovered it was skinned more than anything. They cleaned my face and wrapped my entire head in bandages with just my eyes, nose and mouth sticking out so I looked like a war hero. My legs were bandaged too—I felt like a kid again with scabby knees—and I still carry quite a bit of Florida's gravel around in one kneecap. We went back to our friends' for dinner, and it was difficult to eat through the bandaged slit. Three days later Jock was removing the bandages as he had been told to do and suddenly he stared at my chin. I could see a worried look appear. The doctors had told us my face would be fine, but evidently there was something grotesque. I grabbed a mirror and looked. To say that my chin had "festered" would be an euphemism—it must be gangrene at least. A terrible green mass. I was terror struck. Face amputation? I looked again carefully and then realized it was the spinach and cheese casserole we had had for dinner the night of my fall! Some of the spinach had fallen into the bandage and stuck to my chin. Actually skinning my face must have been something like having one's face sandpapered in Paris but much less expensive. My skin looked better than it usually did. But while I was waiting for it to heal there I was back at the lectern looking as if I were about to tell some marvelous African adventure story, and it was very disappointing to admit I had only fallen off a bike in Florida.

When I was about twelve years old I ate poison ivy. Did you ever pick leaves off hedges and chew on them when you were a kid? I didn't know it was poison ivy, and I ate a lot. In addition to having it in my throat, it must have gone into my bloodstream because it all "came out" on my hands. I had thirty-two blisters about the size of a pickle on one hand and about twenty-five on the other. I had to hold both hands up all the time—the pain was too great if the blood ran down into my fingers. My mother had to feed and dress me for days. Finally my hands turned black from the medicine and everyone in the supermarket would stop me and say, "Oh, little girl, what *have* you done?"

I felt goofy saying, "I ate poison ivy,"—and besides, I wanted sympathy from them not a smile, so I started to lie. There had been quite a serious circus fire in Baltimore just about then, so I told everyone I had been in that, and no one was disappointed because I hadn't let them down from their most horrid expectations. Eventually the skin all peeled off and the new skin was as tender as a baby's. This was the most humiliating part of the ordeal because at Ocean City, New Jersey, where my mother took me that summer for our vacation, there were lots of *boys* on the beach, and what did I have to wear with my bathing suit? Gloves! And boy, did I look stupid. However, I never got poison ivy again—ever—so if you want to become immune to it, eat it. You could have all the kids in the neighborhood in for a poison ivy dinner party.

My affliction, of course, was temporary, but Jock has a permanent problem with his arm in a leather sling. "Jock's strap," we call it. He can use his fingers, and the sling holds his arm at a good height, otherwise it would just dangle at his side. But of course everyone thinks, understandably, that it is a current and temporary ailment. They ask, "What'd you do to your arm?"

Then, depending on which part of the country we're in, we often get their guess. For example, in Colorado, "Hurt your arm skiing?" In Wyoming in a lonely highway diner, "Somebody shoot ya?" And, of course, anyone knowing we're from Africa conjures up marvelous images with rhino, elephant, and lion. Everyone is always slightly embarrassed at his, "I had polio" answer, except Jock, who knows it is a perfectly obvious question to ask and after twenty years is quite used to it. He is often tempted to lie and tell everyone how he rescued me from this ferocious leopard . . . I love the sling; for one thing, it is so easy to identify him. At the Pan Am counter in New York, for instance, where 247 other people have also just checked in, I ask, "Pardon me, but did a man with his arm in a sling just check in?"

"Yes, five minutes ago."

They always notice. In a movie theater when I am late meeting Jock and wonder if he got tired of waiting for me and went on in, I say to the ticket taker: "Did a man with his arm in a sling go in?" (With the 689 other people?)

"Oh, yes, he said to tell you he's in the last row on the left."

Now how many other people can do that? How else would you go about it—"Did this tall guy with blue eyes, hair down to here, a yellow sweater . . ." Do you think they'd answer you? And besides, Jock's sling is very sexy.

The only time he has had even a slightly unpleasant experience over it was at a dinner party when an actress sitting next to him, whom I hope was slightly drunk instead of just plain mean, asked him what was wrong with his arm and he told her he had had polio and his arm was paralyzed.

"I don't believe you need a sling," she said. "You probably just wear it to get attention."

Jock said that for once in his life the answer came to him that you always think of lying in bed later on that night and wish like mad you had said at the time—so much so that you re-create the scene mentally and there you are, devastatingly giving the clever retort, quickly and with great confidence. But that wonderful Walter Mitty answer came to him immediately and he was able to reply, "No, if I had wanted to get attention, I would have become an actor."

A friend of ours is in a wheel chair permanently. He is extremely bright, and he says the worst thing about being in a wheel chair is that everyone assumes because he is physically paralyzed he must also be mentally paralyzed, and that when, for example, he is going into the theater or into an airplane, ticket collectors always ask the person pushing him, not him, "Do you have his tickets?"

He is perfectly capable of saying whether he has his tickets or not, but no one ever asks him. I was so glad he told me that because I know I am guilty of having done the same thing many times before, and from now on I will talk directly to the person in the wheel chair.

"Do you have your tickets?" I will say, looking him right in the eyes. And he will reply, "Ughhhhhhhhhhh, oooooooooooog, uuuu-uuuuuugo."

But back to harrowing adventures in the States. In Corpus Christi we mentioned at the luncheon after our lecture that we had never been to Mexico, and one of the ladies said, "Why don't you go now? It is only a short flight to Brownsville, and to go on to a border town you don't need a passport."

What a good way to spend our free day, we reasoned, and off we flew to Brownsville where we rented a Volkswagen beetle at the airport. As we left the States we paid our twenty-five cents to the American sentry in the little box at the border and drove over the bridge to the Mexican side.

"Where were you born?" the Mexican official asked me.

"Baltimore, Maryland."

"And you?" he asked Jock.

"London."

"Where's your passport and visa?"

"I don't have it with me."

"Then you can't come in here."

"Why not?" I asked. "I was told I didn't need a passport to go to a border town—that's the only place we're going."

"That's for American citizens *only*."

Stupid lady, he thought.

"Now listen, officer," Jock lied, placating him, "we came all the way from *Africa* to see your magnificent country."

"Then why don't you have your passport with you?"

"I left it by mistake in Baltimore."

Stupid man, he thought. He looked at us with distaste but finally he took pity on us and told us that he was sorry but he really could not let us in, but if we went back and drove to another little bridge about two miles up the river, the Immigration officials there were lenient and would probably let Jock through. We thanked him anyway and turned around.

The Americans stopped us on the other side of the bridge where we had been five minutes earlier.

"Where were you born?" the American official asked me.

"Baltimore, Maryland."

"And you?" he asked Jock.

"London."

"Where's your passport and visa?"

"I don't have it with me."

"Then you can't come in here."

"Why not? I really haven't left here. I just this minute went to the Mexican side but they wouldn't let me in there without my passport, so I have just now turned the car around and come back."

"That's what they all say when they try to enter the States illegally."

"But it's *true*," insisted Jock.

"Yeah? How do I know that?"

Leaning over Jock I looked up at the Immigration man and said, "You can ask that sentry over there in that little box—we *just* gave him a quarter."

"I'm not talking to you, lady," he replied, turning to Jock.

Bastard, I thought.

"You are trying to enter the States without a passport. It cannot be done."

"If I am not in the United States but trying to enter them, and if I have not been in Mexico because they would not let me in, then where have I been?" asked Jock logically.

"No man's land."

(Do they have post cards you can send from no man's land?)

Jock pulled the little car over to the side, and we went into the Immigration building to argue—which we did for about two hours and got nowhere."

"What must I do?"

"Get your passport."

"As I have told you at least fifty times, it is in Baltimore."

"Then your wife better go get it and bring it here."

"There isn't time. We have to be in Salt Lake City tomorrow night to lecture."

He shrugged. We all have our problems and this was ours. One of the American officials told us with relish about a German professor who had lived and taught in the States for thirteen years without regularizing his status, and who had gone into Mexico without a passport—I guess they just hadn't asked him where he was born—and when he tried to get back into the States, he couldn't. He didn't even own a passport and by the time he wrote to Germany and sorted out all the red tape, he was there in no man's land for six months.

"Six months!"

"Yeah. We have a jail here."

I decided to smoke a cigarette, which I usually do only at night or when I am nervous. I was nervous. As I pulled my cigarettes out of my bag, the newspaper clipping the hostess at the lecture had given me fell to the floor. Jock picked it up and said, "Look, this *proves* I was in the States earlier today. Here is my picture with my wife. Here is the date . . . right at the top of the page. Here is the article."

They let us through.

Driving back through Texas to catch the plane in Brownsville again, the folksiness of the "Drive Friendly" signs irritated us. We stopped to ask directions to get to the airport and were told to drive about three miles on up the highway until we came to "Nanny," where we were to turn right, and that road would take us into the airport. We could not find Nanny. We looked and looked and drove up and down and up and down until we realized that Nanny was their pronunciation of Route "90."

We flew from Brownsville into the Bible Belt. At a dinner lecture there, the lady sitting next to me at the speaker's table turned to me and asked, "What denomination are you?"

"An Episcopalian," I muttered, giving her a false impression of myself, since I am not a practicing Episcopalian, nor even a lukewarm one if you want to know the truth. She lapsed into silence, so I cautiously asked, "What denomination are you?"

"Disciples of Christ!" she declared emphatically.

Since I had never heard of the Disciples of Christ, I asked if they were similar to the Baptists? She said only in that they both christened. Defensively, I immediately said, "We christen too."

"You only *sprinkle,*" she said—mad as hell.

Then she went on and told me how Christ was a cannibal. I thought it was really a very strange religion until I finally realized that she was saying Christ was "accountable" (presumably by being old enough to understand what was going on when he was baptized), but with her Southern accent it came out as "a cannibal."

But I can't blame the Bible Belt for imposing morals on us. When Jock and I were first married I lectured alone, and Jock traveled with me. I had signed up for the lecture tour before I met him, and since you pay your lecture bureau 35 per cent of your fee, whether you lecture or not (wisely, they do it to make sure their lecturers show up), I simply could not afford not to do the tour. I had signed under Betty Bruce, which was my name before Jock and I were married, but naturally checked into hotels as Mr. and Mrs. Leslie-Melville, but because the people I was lecturing for had heard of me only as Bruce, Jock would say to the desk clerk or manager, "If anyone calls for Betty Bruce, that is my wife's professional name—so just put the call through to our room."

Every time in the Bible Belt he'd get a wink and a, "That's O.K., Mac." Jock said it had never before been an embarrassment to him to *be* married.

On a flight to Fargo, North Dakota, Jock joked that perhaps they would be having a heat wave so that the temperature would be up to zero. We took a cab from the airport to the hotel. It had been 30 degrees below zero in Fargo the day before (60 something below with wind chill factor), so we asked the driver what the current temperature was. Jock's wish had come true.

"It's zero now, but it tends to cool off at night," he replied, just as if we were on the equator in South America and it was 127 degrees but "tended to cool off at night."

We were driving to Philadelphia one evening after a lecture at a museum in Scranton, Pennsylvania, which had lasted until midnight, when we ran into a snow storm. It was heralded by radio warnings that the highways should be used only for emergencies, so we found ourselves virtually alone with the snowplows on the road. About forty-five minutes out of Scranton, our car just stopped—as if it were out of gas, which it wasn't—and refused to go. So we sat there—Jock in his black tie and me in my long evening dress. The snowplows did not stop and pick us up and it was getting colder and colder, and there were no lights anywhere, not even in the distance. We were in the beautiful hills of Pennsylvania, but they seemed much lonelier and less friendly than the green hills of Africa. The difference, of course, is that when you break down in Africa it is never cold—you can sleep in the car in great comfort and no matter how far you are from a city, *some* person will always appear out of the bush and come up to you, willing to help. He will feed you, even though you don't like goat meat, and he will give you shelter even though you don't like sleeping with his camels, but you know you will not perish. On the Pennsylvania Turnpike at 2 A.M. in a snow storm with no heat and no cars coming by and no place to walk to, what are you to do? Sit there and worry, which we did. But finally a big truck came down the turnpike. Jock got out and waved it down, and it took half a mile to stop. We ran down the highway in the snow in our evening clothes and Jock shoved and the driver pulled me up into the truck. The cab was very comfortable, warm, spacious and with a good radio.

The truck belonged to Hertz and was empty. The driver told us he had flown that morning from Wilmington to Cleveland to "bring it back" and he gave us the following very useful tip.

If you want to move your household belongings, or anything else, over a distance that would cost you more than fifty dollars by hiring a truck, this is what you do. *Steal* a self-drive truck —having hired it by paying the fifty dollars deposit. Then drive from Tampa, Florida, to Whitefish, Montana, where you unload your belongings and park the truck carefully in a neighboring town or, if you live in a city, drive it round the block and leave it. Now, wasn't that easy?

All the rest is done by the police and dear old Hertz. The police find the truck, or notice it sitting there, and call Hertz who check their list and find that a Tampa rental is missing. A special man (our kind truck driver was just such a person) now flies or takes the train from a nearby Hertz depot and picks it up. It is a life's work for many, ferrying "borrowed" trucks around the countryside. By doing your household moving this way you are actually helping to create jobs and to provide opportunities for those who would otherwise be out of work.

"Doesn't stealing a truck involve a certain element of risk?" you may ask. The simple answer is that it costs more to hire lawyers and bring a case to court than it does to send somebody to collect the thing. So all you need to do is to give a false address or borrow a friend's driving license when you fill out the Hertz form and you are in business—and they won't even trouble to track you down later. But if they do . . .

Actually, we wondered about including this story in our book lest you think we really approved and tried the idea. But then we figured that people who steal things do not read books, and in that knowledge we thought we might just as well tell you how those other people do things.

Anyway, it was about thirty miles before we saw a motel on the side of the highway and we told him not to turn off, he would have had to hassle a lot to get back on the turnpike, and the motel was just a few hundred feet away. We insisted on walking. Thanking him and waving, we trudged toward the motel. Only when we were upon it did we see the ten-foot steel mesh fence that had been invisible from the highway through the falling snow. Unable to climb it, we plowed back through the snow to the highway and waited again for another car. It was now about 4 A.M. and a milkman picked us up. This time we let him leave the turnpike to take us to the front door of the next motel. Like two drowned rats, we leaned on the front desk, and Jock asked for a double room, please.

"Where's your luggage, Mac?"

So it was not in the Bible Belt we were questioned about our morals. Finally he did let us have a room, and the hot bath never felt better, but it would have been nice to have had a toothbrush. The next morning we put on our soaking wet evening clothes and Jock, unshaven in a tuxedo at 9 A.M. telephoned for a taxi which took us thirty-seven miles to Philadelphia. You can imagine what it cost, and our car was still near Scranton.

And so life goes on in the lecture business. Oh, it's fun eating out of suitcases for five months of every year and reading the matches in your hotel room each morning to see which city you're in, but despite the harrowing adventures there are more good times than bad, or we wouldn't do it.

We laugh a lot at the funny things that happen to us, and our friends help to keep us amused as we reunite with them in different parts of the States as we travel.

In New York Jock and I were sharing a taxi with our dear, funny friend, Ed Keyes. We got out at Fifty-seventh Street and Seventh Avenue and Ed was going on somewhere else. We had been talking all the way and the driver must certainly have noticed Jock's English accent in contrast to Ed's Brooklynese. Because the meter was to be kept running, as Ed got out of the taxi to let us out Jock handed him a couple of dollars to cover our part of the fare, but Ed didn't want to accept it and neither of them would give way. Suddenly Ed, a master of outrageous jokes, held out the money and started shouting at Jock.

"I don't want your money!" he hollered, right there on Fifty-seventh Street. "That's the trouble with you foreigners—always coming to this country trying to tell us what to do! STUPID FOREIGNERS."

A crowd was beginning to gather and the cab driver looked very upset at the unprovoked attack and started to come to Jock's rescue. I was laughing so hard I had to hold onto the lampost and Jock just grinned and looked embarrassed—he is not used to noisy street scenes. Ed stood there shaking his fist at him and yelling, "STUPID, DAMN FOREIGNERS!"

Everyone who comes to East Africa and decides he or she wants to stay here, complains because it is difficult to get a work permit. Jobs are for citizens first, which is right and how it should be, and most countries in the world have the same policy. In fact, America takes the toughest line of all on this subject. If Jock wanted to get a job as a butler, and I think he would make a terrific butler, he would not be allowed to. Nor could he work in a gas station or a department store part time in the United States.

As a non-American, Jock has no trouble getting a visa to visit America. But lecturing is work for money and an entirely different visa is needed. He has to show that he is doing a job that could not be done by an available American and is not blocking an employment opportunity for anyone else. It takes weeks of form filling, letters of authority and rubber stamping, and he had to reapply each year.

By taking out an Alien Immigrant card he found that he would never need a visa again. To get such a card takes months. First you must be married to or have an immediate relative who is an American citizen (I always knew he married me for my passport). Then starts an unbelievable probing. Police records, or proof of the lack of them must be obtained from every country where you have ever lived for more than six months. *Original* versions of divorce certificates, mine and his, must be produced and verified. Fingerprints, birth certificates, chest X-rays, a full-scale medical with urine and blood samples and heaven knows what else must be obtained and endured. Military discharge papers, oaths, interviews with the consul—it was endless.

Finally all was set. Clutching a bulky envelope of documents and an enormous X-ray picture, Jock and I landed at Kennedy and Jock was ushered through a special door. Everything was double-checked once more and at last, the summation of the months of rigmarole, an insignificant little blue card, looking rather less impressive than a plastic laminated driver's license, was handed to him. The man patted him on the shoulder and said, "Welcome to the United States. Report to your draft board on Tuesday."

Jock met me in the baggage hall. He didn't think he was eligible because of his age and his arm, but he imagined it might just be possible that he had just that rare military training from his experience in the Coldstream Guards, a crack regiment of the British army, that was needed in Vietnam.

On Tuesday he drove over to Catonsville—where the Berrigan brothers had their little shindig. Jock had been drafted before in England and knew what to expect. Tough sergeants bellow at you and stamp their feet and it is neither jolly nor welcoming. But at Catonsville there was a nice granny with gray hair and spectacles. She was gentle and kindly and Jock started filling out the forms. She glanced up, "How old are you, dear?"

Jock told her.

"Well then, you don't have to worry about a thing."

It was a relieved husband who drove back half an hour later.

Little Lulus

Somehow dangerous involvement with wild animals or nature is the stuff of which headlines are made. Traffic probably poses more actual danger than animals in Africa, and even here the majority of injuries are sustained in the home, as is the case in the States. But when something goes wrong in the bush one always hears about it.

For instance, there was the report of an unfortunate German tourist who had taken a day trip to Tsavo Park and after his picnic lunch had decided to try what the brochure suggested, "fish a little." He was standing on a rock in the narrow Galana River, slipped, fell off the rock, was carried downstream and was never seen again—he had been taken by a crocodile.

A few weeks later a local English couple took their six-year-old son, Mark, on safari over Easter weekend and while swimming in Buffalo Springs a crocodile seized him. His mother, Mrs. Carole Radley, saw this hideous happening and hollered at some other holidaymakers nearby. They formed a human chain and heaved and hauled Mark and the crocodile out of the Springs. It was then that Mark's father, Dr. David Radley, leaped on the reptile's back, took hold of its head and tried to prize open its massive jaws. It would not release its victim. Other onlookers ran with pangas (machetes) and began slashing the eight-foot long crocodile, and finally it let go of Mark and slithered back into the water. The tug of war between the croc and the Radleys with Mark in between those wicked teeth did a lot of damage to the boy. They feared he would never walk again. The Flying Doctors flew in immediately and took him to the hospital and miraculously within a few weeks he was swinging his cricket bat again—the teeth had just missed vital organs, and other than a slight limp, which will eventually disappear, Mark is now fine. There is no sign at the Springs warning visitors not to swim, and the next victim might not be as lucky as Mark.

It is indeed comforting to know that doctors can fly to one's help on safari if necessary.

Two friends of ours are sky-diving nuts. One is Dr. Charles McCaldin and the other is a professional hunter. Charles is young and attractive and cleverly arranged to have himself appointed as personal physician to Miss World when she was on holiday here. She was blooming with health, but he was to be available just in case she might need a doctor. Off she went on safari to Amboseli National Park near Mount Kilimanjaro, and what do you know? She caught a cold and was anxious that it should not turn into flu and spoil her holiday. The radio call went out to Charles in Nairobi asking if he could fly down in a light aircraft to the little landing strip.

The first thing he did was to get hold of the hunter to discuss this great idea he had just had. The two of them piled into the little plane piloted by a friend and off they went. They donned their gear, strapped on their chutes, and with Charles clutching his black doctor's bag under one arm they baled out at about 12,000 feet over Amboseli. The Maasai who live there nearly went out of their minds. Just when they have become used to planes, the crazy people start arriving silently out of the sky without notice.

Miss World was pretty damned impressed as well. Some house call!

On one safari Jock and I were taking a family from Texas—a mother, father and two children about ten and twelve years old. Our eldest son, Rick, was along too, which made us seven altogether. One morning we had four flat tires. The fourth and final

one really finished us off because there were no more tubes, so
Jock insisted on walking through the buffalo and elephant country to the lodge about five miles away to get another tube. I was
worried about him because once he had had a very frightening experience with a buffalo. When he was on safari in the Mara Triangle in Southwest Kenya, the Land-Rover broke down several
miles from the camp. Leaving his party he set out to walk back
for help. The area is well known for its large prides of lion, and
Jock's main preoccupation was that he should not stumble into
the middle of a sleeping pride in the long grass. Though it may
sound hazardous, someone with experience and sharp eyes can
actually proceed unarmed with relative safety through game country. Practically all animals, including big game, will simply move
quietly away as you approach. They are not looking for trouble
and you are at pains to avoid it.

For this reason Jock did not pay more than fleeting attention
to a lone buffalo standing under a tree about quarter of a mile
away until it started moving purposefully toward him. Usually
there is a tree or a pile of rocks or a large fallen log wherever you
go in the bush and as you walk you keep these little refuges subconsciously in mind, but as the buffalo approached, Jock found
himself in the middle of an open grassy area. The great black bull
accelerated from a trot to a canter and Jock, who has very long
legs, ran for his life. The buffalo altered course to cut him off and
came thundering at him in a full charge. At the last minute, when
it was upon him, Jock slithered to a stop to face it, certain that he
was about to die. For some unknown reason, perhaps because
Jock turned unexpectedly at the last second, the buffalo veered
suddenly, went crashing past, and loped away leaving a trembling
and breathless Jock to make his way back to the camp. You can
never really tell with animals. Old male buffalo living alone get
sort of crazy sometimes and may act unpredictably. An animal
that has once been wounded may develop a special hatred for
man, but when that is the case and they launch an attack, the
odds are that they will go through with it. Jock, who is not a
hunter but has spent much time walking through game-inhabited

areas, says that this is the only really dicey encounter he has ever had. (To put the thing in perspective, he points out that if he had grown up in a city he probably would have had equally narrow squeaks from being run over by a car or being mugged on a dark night.)

But, worried as I was that Jock was having a similar experience, I kept telling cheerful little stories to distract our clients. Much to my relief he appeared soon with another tube, so we spent a delightful afternoon and night at Ngorogoro, and set off to cross the Serengeti plains the next morning equipped with yet another spare tube and wheel. Again a flat tire. And again. And again. (We discovered later a distorted wheel rim was causing the flats.) This time we were really stuck with no spare anything and were not in walking distance of the lodge, which was about ten miles away. There were a lot of lion about, it was growing late, and the Texans were all getting nervous. We had no food, nothing at all to eat or drink with us, and spending the night with seven people in a Land-Rover in the middle of a million animals was not anyone's idea of fun, nor what they were paying $100 per day per person to do. Our only hope was that someone would drive by and save us. After about a two-hour wait with no one anywhere within sight, we saw a mini-bus approaching. What joy! Jock and the others stood on top of our car and shouted and waved and I ran toward it and was the first one to reach it. I was relieved to see it wasn't full of people—there was just one couple in a bus which holds eight so we could all pile in! "Are we glad to see you! We've been broken down about three hours," I shouted gleefully.

The African driver had a big grin, he looked as happy as I. The woman translated what I had said to her husband, and it was then I realized they were German. His answer, I thought, was, "Americans, *nein*," but perhaps I was wrong. So I told them again about being broken down. "Americans, *nein*," he repeated. I was right. By this time Jock had arrived at the bus, and neither of us could believe our ears. We explained over and over again how we had children with us and all we wanted was a ride back to the lodge. "Americans, *nein*." They had rented this bus, his wife tried to explain, to photograph the le-o-pards (like "leotards" she pronounced it). We said all right then, they could pick us up on the way *back* from photographing the le-o-pards. *"Nein."* The driver was in a state of shock, but we asked him in Swahili if he would tell someone when he got back that we were stuck out here, and naturally he agreed. Off they went, leaving us utterly alone again. Within minutes of the Germans' refusal to take us, two more cars appeared from the opposite direction and they both stopped immediately. The people jumped out, offered help, and tires, food, drink—everything. We decided to abandon our car and worry about it tomorrow, like Scarlett O'Hara, and divided ourselves up between the two cars. I noticed they had Tanzania tags, so I thought they were tsetse control or game department people, but I couldn't place their accent.

I asked, "Where are you from?"

"Sewviettiyuyoni."

I had never heard of that place in Tanzania. Italians I wondered?

"Where?" I asked again.

They repeated the place I had never heard of, so I said, "Oh I don't know that"—after all, one doesn't know every nook and cranny in Tanzania.

"You don't know where the Sewviettiyuyoni is?"

"No idea."

He looked totally unbelieving and hurt. Then I had a terrible suspicion. The Soviet Union? Yes. They were three Russians on a holiday who had borrowed a friend's car. When we got to the lodge they broke out a bottle of vodka they had brought with them from Russia, gave the children little Russian dolls, and turned out to be the nicest and most friendly and interesting people we'd met for a long time. One was a palaeontologist, and we asked how he had enjoyed Olduvai Gorge where Dr. L. S. B. Leakey made his famous discovery.

"Where is it?" he asked, all enthused.

Without knowing it he had driven two miles from the famous

excavation site. We began to discuss how Dr. Leakey had found Zinjanthropos and how the skull fragments were about 2.5 million years old. The Russian said, "Of course we Russians have the remains of man 5 million years old!" and added with a twinkle, "but of course that is Communist propaganda," and we all laughed with him.

Rick, who was studying his first year of political science at Georgetown University in Washington, D.C., and the Russian politician had marvelous discussions all night too. The Germans were nowhere in sight. It was a good evening. The next morning, Jock was at the garage sorting out the tire troubles when I saw the Germans leaving the lodge and walking toward their car. I hate to do unpleasant things and normally Jock handles all the firing of people and those other nasty things I loathe, but there was no one except me this morning, and I thought it was absolutely necessary to reprimand them. I was still angry. I called to them to wait and asked, "Have you ever been in East Africa before?"

The woman, trying to be pleasant, said, "Vunce before last year ve came—"

"You'd never know it, and I don't think you'd better come again unless you can act like everyone else here. We have an unwritten rule that everyone stops and helps anyone who is broken down. I have lived here fifteen years," I exaggerated, "and I have NEVER known anyone to act as despicably as you," and with that I turned on my heel and marched away—just like a German.

One of the most unusual experiences I have ever had started in Ethiopia.

When my mother died she left me a little bit of money. Instead of just frittering it away on bubble gum, I decided to buy one good thing as a keepsake. I was in Ethiopia at the time, and in a store window I saw a black leopard coat which I fancied, although I can't imagine why. I don't really like fur coats at all, but this was so different it grabbed me. (This was also ten years before I was ecology or conservation conscious.) I went into the store and talked to the lady there who convinced me I had to have such a coat. What I really wanted was a trench coat style, and she said yes, they would have to make it and it would take a week. Since I was leaving the next day I said, "Fine. I'll give you my address and you can send me the coat."

"Oh, no," she exclaimed emphatically, "the duty would be outrageous. If you *wear* the coat into the States you won't have to pay duty on it. You must wait."

I had never bought anything of value before, but I thought that made good sense, so I cabled Baltimore that I would arrive a week later.

The week passed and the coat was beautiful—it looked like ranch mink, yet when the sun hit it you could see the black spots. I paid the $1,098 by check, turned the collar up, tied the belt tight, and sauntered off to Spain for a few days before going on to New York. On the States-bound plane I declared the other little things on the form they hand out but not the coat, since I was and had been wearing it. After going through everything the Customs man at the airport said, "Do you have anything else to declare?"

"No," I replied and went on.

Two steps past the customs counter I felt a hand on my left shoulder, another hand on my right shoulder, and I saw a badge in front of me.

"We are Customs officials. Where did you get that coat?"

"Addis Ababa," I answered bewildered.

"You're under arrest. Come with us."

I was led into a little room, just like in the movies, and a woman was brought in to search me. They went through everything in my purse, even my address book page by page, and I felt frightened.

"Why didn't you declare the coat?"

"Because the woman in the store told me if I wore it I didn't have to declare it."

"Didn't you read your Customs form on the plane?"

"Of course I didn't *read* the Customs form on the plane—you just fill it out, you don't read all that small print on the back."

"You gotta declare everything, lady."

"But," I kept repeating, "the woman in the fur shop told me if I wore the coat I would not have to declare it."

"If she told you to jump out of a twelfth floor window would you do that too?" (I was reminded of my mother who always used to say things like that.)

"No, but I know better than to do that. I've never brought anything valuable into the country before—I didn't know anything except what she told me."

"Sure she told you that. She is the one who turned you in. That's how we caught you. She warned us you would be coming in with the coat—undeclared."

In stunned disbelief I asked, "Why?"

"For the ten per cent of the value of the coat. They all get a ten per cent kick back from us. How do you think we pick people up? We'd never catch half of them if someone in the shops at source didn't tip us off. A lot of women buy valuable diamonds then have them put in ten cent store settings, and the jewelers who make the sales tell us."

"May she rot in hell," I thought silently, and swore to seek revenge.

"If you report people who cheat on their income tax you can get ten per cent too," he added, and I hoped she cheated on her income tax so I could report her.

Finally they decided I was stupid, not evil, and although they kept the coat, they let me go until the date of the trial which was to be set later. In a little silk dress in the middle of winter, I arrived in Baltimore, upset, scared and freezing cold.

At the trial, four months later, who do you think appeared as my witness? The Customs man! He testified on my behalf. I had been told all kinds of bad things could happen—huge fines, even my passport taken away, but the judge believed the Customs man and me—that I was not a smuggler, just dumb, so I was fined $500 and my coat was returned. It was July, and a leopard coat was not what I needed then in Baltimore, so I put it away, and the following winter returned to East Africa where I would not need the fur coat either. It came to pass that I met and married Jock and moved to Nairobi, where I would never need the fur coat, so it remained in storage.

A year or so later my special friend, Colleen Harrity, from Philadelphia wanted to come and visit me but she didn't have the money. I was dying to have her come to Africa and finally I had an idea . . . sell the leopard coat! I had paid $1,098 plus the $500 fine, and if I could get that much back she could have the rest, which should be more than enough, for carfare. I wrote suggesting this to her and she agreed to try to peddle the coat. She got it out of storage and lugged it around to stores, none of which were interested because they all said, "It's dyed fur."

"It's not dyed. It is *black* leopard."

"What kind of black leopard?"

She didn't know the answer to that question, so she wrote me and I didn't know either. She decided to find out.

Lecturing in the States at this very time was our mutual friend from Nairobi, Gaby Sheikh. Colleen asked him if he knew what kind of black leopard the coat was, and he said no, but he was going to Washington the next day where he was to have lunch at the zoo with Dr. Roth, a renowned zoologist and why didn't Colleen come with him and bring the coat, since Dr. Roth was an expert on furs. Colleen winced at lunch at the zoo—hot dogs and balloons—but O.K., why not? So she tossed the "leopard rug," as it had come to be known, on the back seat of the car, and drove to Washington and actually had a very elegant lunch in a private dining room at the zoo. After lunch, Dr. Roth took them to a closed building where a white tiger had just arrived and was being televised. (Later Gaby, not knowing American slang, informed all the ladies attending his lectures that he had spent the afternoon in a cat house the week before and that he was televised there too!) It wasn't until they were saying good-by and climbing into the car that they even remembered to show

Dr. Roth the coat. He looked at it very carefully, and rubbing the fur asked, "Where did you get this?"

"Addis Ababa," Gaby and Colleen replied in unison.

He took them inside and examined a hair from the coat under a microscope. He wouldn't say anything about it. Then he drove them to the Smithsonian Institute where he mysteriously disappeared for a half hour. When he finally returned he said, "I thought so. This coat is a collector's item. There are only two skins like it in the entire world, and they have been in a museum in Russia since 1898." The Emperor of Ethiopia, he explained, had scouts out constantly looking for this rare type of black leopard. The ordinary person couldn't tell, but it is quite different from the usual melanistic black leopard.

"Your coat may be worth $100,000," said Dr. Roth, and giving them a note stating the name of the species he left the two dumbfounded people stammering thank-yous.

The leopard rug took on a new light. No longer was it tossed in the back seat but held lovingly next to their hearts. Colleen wrote to me immediately and had the coat insured for $80,000. Dollar signs grew in our eyes. She wrote to the Shah of Iran who collects furs, and Jock and I turned down previous offers for $5,000 and $6,000. When we went to the States, we took the coat to the Museum of Natural History in New York who craved it, and wanted us to donate it to them saying we could have an $8,000 tax deduction, but since we didn't even make $8,000 a year in the States it wouldn't do us any good at all, nor would it pay for Colleen's carfare. We continued to peddle the coat, but in its new light and for a fancy price. Three months passed, a lot of interest, but no big buyer yet. The man who had insured the coat told us that he had a friend who was a theatrical agent and the agent, whom we shall call Fred the Fence, to implicate him, had told Barbra Streisand about it and she was very interested and wanted to see it. She was my size, loved furs and had lots of money. We delivered the coat to him the next afternoon and noticed with alarm that the insurance had expired. Since we were on our way to the airport to lecture in a series of exotic places like

Terre Haute, Indiana, we told the agent to get in touch with the mutual friend who had introduced us and who had arranged the insurance in the first place so that the policy could be renewed. He promised that he would do so at once. He was eager to sell it because we had made him an ultra generous offer in the event that he found a buyer—he stood to make about 30 per cent.

Every day we called the agent for the news that we were all rich. Every day we were disappointed. When we returned to the East Coast we telephoned him, and he replied, "Sit down, I have something to tell you." We sat, knowing that the shock of $100,000 would be too much for us. "I don't quite know how to tell you this," he began, "but the coat has been stolen from my office."

"Wonderful," we thought, wondering how he had arranged that, "$80,000 to be split according to our formula."

"I, er, well you see . . . that is . . . I . . . I never renewed the insurance."

It seems that Fred the Fence has an uncle who is in the fur business and who has a vault. Being pressed for time he decided to store the coat in the vault and take care of the insurance the following day. Being further pressed for time he stuffed the coat into a filing cabinet in his office on Broadway, planning to vault and insure it all later, and that night his office was broken into and the coat, as well as typewriters and adding machines, was stolen. The police and the F.B.I. (who were called in because more than $5,000 was involved) grilled Fred and in the absence of any significant lead concluded that it was a typical dope addict robbery and that the coat would probably turn up in a pawn shop since no layman, nor indeed most experts would have any idea of its value.

Fred was a wreck. He told us he had had nervous diarrhea for a week and that he hardly knew how to face us. He said he accepted the responsibility, admitted that he had been lax, and he looked so forlorn that we felt sorry for him. In the end we agreed that he would repay the cost of the coat to me—the original $1,098 plus the $500 fine—and that he would do this over a period of a couple of years since he was so broke and struggling to be the successful agent. He was grateful to the point of being obsequious that we were so understanding and had not been mad and that we accepted the idea of monthly payments.

We returned to Africa and a year later were back in New York. Fred had been unable, because of his struggles with his business, to make even the first payment—but not to worry, he would surely make a lump sum available soon . . . We returned to Africa and a year later were back in New York. Again, he was so sorry, he was chagrined to think how long he had been, in fact he didn't realize how long it had been—the time had gone so fast— but things were looking up and by May . . .

We returned to Africa and a year later were back in New York. Jock called Fred (we were very broke ourselves at this point and really needed some cash) and went around to see him. His offices had expanded and there was a feeling of modest prosperity. A cocky, tougher, Fred the Fence greeted Jock and announced that he had decided that he was in no way responsible, that he had changed his mind about any moral obligation, and that there weren't going to be any payments.

Until this moment we had treated Fred as the friend of our friend. We now went to a lawyer who shook his head in disbelief at our naïveté. Almost to a day the three-year New York Statute of Limitations had passed, and with it our last hope of any legal recourse. They say that suckers are born every minute and maybe that is true. There are also other remarks about people who are devious and who will boil in oil and hopefully that is true too.

Do you think that maybe the black leopard coat has some kind of hex on it? Has it been sold for $100,000 to the wife of an Eastern potentate? Is some lady in the Bronx who paid fifty dollars for it in a second-hand shop wearing it to go to the Food Fair? I subconsciously scrutinize every dark-colored fur coat I see.

Our saddest adventure began one evening just back from safari with four houseguests. We had started supper, all beautifully weary and dirty and longing for that first bath which, after you've been out in the bush for a few weeks, feels so luxurious, when the telephone rang and an unfamiliar but young voice said, "You don't know me, but you went to school with my mother in Baltimore and she told me to call you." The memory of his mother was a good one so I asked him what he was doing in Kenya. Well, he and his brother had traveled from West Africa to East Africa and were going to climb Mt. Kilimanjaro, among other things. Could we give them any advice? So I said, sure come on out, and two adorable boys eighteen and twenty years old arrived with their guitars, and we had a fun evening. I remember how refreshed I was to hear the enthusiasm and openness of these two Americans, for we had been traveling with a young Englishman, one of our houseguests, of about their same age who was so sophisticated, so cool, and so terribly bored with everything and such a pain that these two boys with their joy and excitement delighted us all. Except, of course, the young Englishman. They left full of tips on how to get to Kilimanjaro on the cheap, where to stop on the way, how to cut across the game park instead of taking the long dull road around, and so on, and with promises of calling us immediately upon their return to let us know if they got to the top.

Just a few days later, Tom Mboya, Kenya's brilliant Minister of Economics, was tragically assassinated. I was walking to Jock's office to meet him so we could go to the funeral together, and as I passed the Thorn Tree, Nairobi's famous outdoor cafe and the watering hole for the tourists, I saw Jim, the elder brother sitting there at a table.

"Did you get to the top?" I shouted as I walked up to him. He looked up and for the first time I saw his eyes. I knew immediately something was unbearably wrong.

"My brother died on the mountain."

"What are you talking about?"

He told me that they had both climbed for three days when he got sick, and after an unsuccessful attempt to cover the final three miles he said he was going back down to the hotel. John, the younger and more fit of the two—and the more determined—insisted on continuing to the top even though he, too, was sick. I later learned that this was a very typical of him—that once before he had broken an ankle while playing lacrosse and played the game through, broken ankle and all. So Jim returned to the Marangu Hotel in Tanzania from where many start the climb, and John continued with his guide to try to reach the top. The next day a message came to the hotel from another climber returning that John was sick, too sick to walk back, and would they send a Land-Rover up to the first hut? They brought him down and called a doctor who examined him, gave him a shot, and said he would be all right. Jim found this hard to believe because never had he seen his brother look so ill. He sat on the bed with him until late at night and finally succeeded in giving him some soup. Then he turned off the lights and got into his own bed and they said good night to each other. Jim lay listening to the heavy uneven breathing and suddenly heard the silence he had dreaded. John had died.

It is bad enough to have such a thing happen anywhere, but imagine having to cope with your brother's body in a strange country where you know no one and which has health laws stating that if you don't get the body out of the country within twenty-four hours it can't leave for two years. It was difficult enough for poor Jim to get the body on a plane. There aren't that many flights in twenty-four hours. But worse than that was telling his mother and father back home what had happened.

Instead of going to the funeral, Jock and I went with Jim to the American Embassy to telephone his family. Tom Mboya was dead but Jim was alive and needed support—it would be presumptuous of us to think we could comfort him—but at least we could be there. We were waiting in the Embassy for the call to go through to the States when the riots broke out, the only riots I have ever seen in Nairobi, sparked by the tension surrounding Mboya's assassination. The tear gas used drifted up into the Embassy in clouds and choked us all, and when the call came through we were clutching our throats and coughing and tears were streaming down our faces. Imagine my old school friend hearing her son had died in faraway Africa, and then having the other one choking on the telephone. "What's wrong?" "It's just tear gas from the riots outside."

Well, it is unnecessary to report all the ugliness, but the point is that if anyone reading this is about to climb Kilimanjaro, or knows of anyone who is going to, please tell them to take oxygen. It seems that not infrequently people die on this mountain of pulmonary edema—a sort of instant pneumonia that happens at high altitudes, and this could be prevented if you had oxygen with you. Since then we have heard of three other similar deaths on Kilimanjaro. Jim and John's mother came here and went to see Kilimanjaro. Her husband said he could not have borne to come and she said she could not have borne not to come, and I understood both of their reasonings. John's mother donated portable oxygen cylinders to the hotels on Kilimanjaro (which had none) to prevent other deaths. But the trouble is most people just don't know about this sickness that can strike them dead at a high altitude, and many come here to climb the mountain as if they are going for a walk down a beach. I certainly didn't know it before this tragedy. It is said that the son of the Queen of Sheba, King Menelik, died on Mt. Kilimanjaro and was buried there in a cave with some regal possessions. Perhaps he died of the same thing.

The average visitor just riding around looking at the animals is not really exposed to the sort of dangers one might meet while mountaineering or hunting big game, and the danger on a typical photographic safari is negligible. Fortunately, we've never lost anyone on a Percival safari yet. Permanently, that is. We have lost people temporarily, and I'll never forget the two clients who came in eight hours earlier than planned and checked themselves into the Intercontinental Hotel, with the result that when Mary Atkin, our operations director who got strangled—I'll tell you about that later on—went to meet them at the airport at the right time, they weren't on the flight. The hotel goofed and left them checked in under the names of two people who had just checked out, so that every time we rang, which was once an hour for two days, Mr. and Mrs. Emerson had not yet arrived but were expected. In the end we had to telephone their travel agent in the States, whom they had just cabled, so we found them—and all the while they were only a few hundred yards away and could see our office from their bedroom window. You can imagine their fury at us—they missed part of their safari because of the mess—and our fury at the hotel.

But that's show biz . . . and how it goes in the travel business. It is an extraordinary business. Dealing with four thousand people each year is astonishing enough, but in Africa it can sometimes be disastrous.

In 1970 the largest airlift ever by light aircraft in Kenya was organized by Percival Tours who made arrangements for a group of eighty-six doctors and their wives, sponsored by the University of Southern California. One couple, an American black and his wife who were both doctors, had brought their twenty-year-old son along, and in West Africa on the way over they met a Ghanian the same age as their son who said he had never been to East Africa. Extremely generously they invited him to join them and offered to pay for his entire trip.

From Nairobi the whole group flew by light aircraft in a great squadron to Serengeti in northern Tanzania. Eleven mini-buses met them and took them to Seronera Lodge where there is an Immigration post. With eighty-six people and one Immigration Officer it was a slow tedious business, and people wandered around and chatted in little groups while they waited. Suddenly a horde of Africans flew out of some huts near the Lodge waving their pangas and throwing rocks at our safariers. No one knew what was wrong with them. Instant panic followed, but fortunately one of our best couriers was leading the group and he took immediate charge of the situation. He noticed the Africans were particularly incensed at the Ghanian boy—so much so in fact that they were about to kill him. Our escort grabbed him out of the turmoil, threw him into a nearby bus and instructed the driver, "Get him out of here! Just drive off into the bush—we'll find you later."

Soon the shouting and stone throwing stopped, everyone calmed down, and the police arrived and started arresting people—drivers, clients, the escort, anybody. No one knew what was happening or what all the trouble was about, but eventually the story became clear. It seems the Ghanian boy was the first to clear Immigration and he grew bored with the idea of having to wait for eighty-five others. He peered into a nearby hut which happened to contain the African assistant manager's wife resting on a bed. He decided to rape her. As he attempted it the assistant manager appeared, and this, understandably, is what caused the furor.

The Africans living and working at the Lodge knew only that the Ghanian was a member of the party that had just arrived in the buses and they were angry at the entire group—maybe they were all rape artists on a safari. After all, we run Doctors' Safaris, Teachers' Safaris, Garden Club Safaris, Baptists' Safaris—so why not a safari for The Rapists' Society? Everything was smoothed over in the end, but they were all very mad at the Ghanian.

Another time one of our safariers lost his passport in Nairobi, so instead of going on with the group to The Ark (an exciting game-viewing lodge deep in the forest) the next day, he had to go to the American Embassy to get a new passport. He would catch up with the group that night. Since it was he who lost his passport and missed his ride to The Ark, it was his responsibility financially to get himself the hundred miles north later on in the day. We asked him if he would like us to arrange a car and driver for him. He said yes, so we got one of our reliable drivers and a good car, but on leaving the hotel an African cab driver spotted the typical tourist and asked him if he was going anyplace that day. "Yes, Nyeri." "How are you going to get there?" "I have a car and driver." "How much are they charging you? I'll take you for half the price." And, of course—I would probably have done the same thing myself—he accepted the lesser offer because he did not know that some of the cars are totally unsafe and the drivers worse. So he canceled our good car and took the dilapidated taxi, and about ten miles out of Nairobi the driver ran over and killed an African child. Now, Africans in crowds will often beat up thieves or drivers who have injured or killed pedestrians, and they set to work on this taxi driver but ignored our client. The police arrived, and since the driver was unconscious in the bushes, they assumed our tourist had been driving and they arrested him. They could not understand his American English, nor could he understand their African-cum-British accents, so he went behind bars. We got the telephone call in the middle of the night and had to bail him out.

Once one of our sweet little old blue-haired ladies about seventy years old, traveling alone (no kin along) but with a group, stole a Colobus monkey skin rug—$500 worth—right off the wall at the fancy Mt. Kenya Safari Club. A warrant was immediately put out for her arrest. We spoke to our friend the Police Commissioner here, and he said if she gave it back, he would let it go. (Isn't it nice to know if you steal something in Kenya and get caught but give it back, you are not prosecuted?) We spent the next week trying to reach her in the bush in Tanzania to convince her to give the rug back before the police grabbed her at the border when she re-entered Kenya, where they were waiting for her. Finally we got to her, she gave the rug back, and her story was that the manageress of the Mt. Kenya Safari Club *gave* her the rug.

"Where can I get a beautiful Colobus monkey skin rug like that?" you can imagine her asking.

"Oh just take that rare, expensive one off the wall there, dearie."

Wow. A little old lady from the Bible Belt!

People just can't surprise us any longer. Jack Block, whose family owns Treetops and the New Stanley Hotel and Keekorok Lodge, among other things, is an intimate friend of ours here. He told us that he once invited a very prominent New York lawyer, a millionaire, to his house for lunch, and the man asked him if he would send a trunk of his belongings by sea because it was too large to take on the plane. Jack said he would be glad to ship the trunk, and told an assistant manager to attend to it. A few days later the assistant manager appeared saying the Customs were insisting upon a list of what the trunk contained prior to shipment, so Jack told him to open the trunk, which was not locked, and make a list. A few minutes later the manager was back again, eyes wide open in disbelief, and told Jack he had better come and have a look himself. There in the millionaire's trunk were silver coffeepots, cream jugs and sugar bowls, silver teapots and trays and blankets—all stolen from various hotels throughout the continent of Africa. There was quite a bit of loot from the New Stanley Hotel as well. Jack wrote a note which simply said, "I have returned the contents of your trunk to its rightful owners," and has never heard a word from him since.

A friend of ours in New York told us that his aunt and uncle went on a very luxurious Carribean cruise, and although they and most of their traveling companions were older, there was one delightful young couple whom they met and adored and with whom they became very friendly. When the cruise ended, they insisted they all must keep in touch and that the young couple must let them know when they came to New York, and come to their apartment for dinner.

A few weeks later the aunt and uncle received copies of pictures the younger couple had taken of them doing amusing things aboard ship and a note saying they were coming to New York on business the following week and would love to accept their kind invitation to dinner. After a happy reunion and excellent meal, the four friends went into the living room for coffee and brandy, and before the young guest had finished his last sip, he pulled out a gun and said, "This is a stick up" or some such gangsterish thing. The older couple laughed and said that was what had attracted them to him so much in the first place—his wit and humor. He then tied them up, and he and his wife took all their valuable paintings right off the walls, all their silver, some valuable antiques, figurines, chairs even, and asked the elevator man to help them load it all into a truck which was waiting for them downstairs. This was not unusual since many people move at night in New York to avoid the traffic, and the doorman had most likely assumed it was probably the couple's niece and nephew—they had been in the apartment for hours and certainly had been enthusiastically received by the older couple. They were never seen again.

I wonder when they will arrive on safari?

How did I ever get into this business? Let's see . . . I'll have to go back a few years to answer that question properly.

My father died when I was eleven years old and we had no money, my mother and I, so somehow my uncle, whom I resented ever after, talked my mother into the idea that I should sell eggs. Can you imagine a girl of eleven who was just getting interested in boys having to sell eggs? I had to go knock on doors in the neighborhood and get customers, and then each Tuesday afternoon—how I dreaded Tuesday afternoons—the farmer, Mr. Gruebecker, still the most hideous name in the whole wide world to me—Hitler and Gruebecker—brought eggs in crates, and I would sit on the kitchen floor and put the proper amount of eggs in paper bags (which I had bought cheap at the Food Fair). For each customer I would bag the correct amount of eggs—Miss Mooney, two dozen; Mrs. Schmenner wanted one dozen each week; Mrs. Meyerhoff only wanted six; and so on. Then I would put as many bags as I could fit into my basket attached to the front of my bike and go knock on doors or ring bells, and women would call, "Who is it?"—how I hated their voices singing, "Who is it?" because they sounded so happy and I was so miserable since I would have to answer, "It's the egg lady."

As they paid me their thirty-eight cents they would say, "Oh, someone new just moved in two doors up, maybe they'd take eggs from you too."

So I'd have to go two doors up and tell another dopey lady how good my eggs were—fresh and cheap and yes, ma'am buy from me. Then I'd go back and get the second and sometimes third load, deliver them, collect the money then figure out my order for the next week before Tuesday ended. All winter long I was blackmailed by my friend Ruth Baker, who threatened to tell everyone I sold eggs unless I did her homework, paid for her ice cream cone, traded my tuna fish sandwich for her peanut

butter one, etc., etc. The only reason she knew about my embarrassing profession—I wouldn't over my dead body have *told*
her—was the fact that she had to be my substitute for my egg
route for two weeks each summer so I could go away on vacation with my mother. For years I had to sell eggs. In fact, I was
almost *married* when my mother let me quit. I remember being
madly in love with a boy called Lloyd whom I finally married,
and one Tuesday afternoon I came home after my delivery and
my mother said, "Lloyd called but I told him you must have fallen
down on your bike or something—you usually weren't this late—
and that I certainly hoped you hadn't broken all of your eggs."

I can remember being wild with fury when she said this, but as
I looked at her I realized she was teasing me and we both
laughed. But I sold eggs a long time. And I loathed every minute
of it.

"Since then I must have had twenty-four other jobs . . . of
varied sorts. I got a job as a saleslady selling pocketbooks in a
downtown store in Baltimore but I was fired the first day because
I had lied about my age—said I was sixteen when I was only
fifteen—and got caught. I then learned how to work marionettes
and gave marionette shows, for money, until I was sixteen when I
got a part-time job selling lingerie in a department store. I also
joined the "Children's Service Bureau"—which was being the fuzz
at kids' birthday parties and making the parents think the children
were having fun when they only hired you in the first place to keep
the kids from ruining their houses. I learned never to say, "Do
you want to play ring around the rosy?" because some smart ass
kid always says, "no." You say, "We will play ring around the
rosy now, and I'll let *you* play too," to the kid who has no intention
of playing but is going to put a frog in the toilet instead. I had my
bag of tricks with me—marionettes and magic wands and other
revolting things—and it was psychological warfare between the
little dears and me for two hours.

Then I got a job as a research technician at Johns Hopkins
Hospital in the endocrine lab and put medical science back two
years. One of my tasks was to kill white mice used for experi-

ments. Dr. Schesinger showed me how to hold their necks back and quickly slit their throats. I said fine, fine, but I almost puked because I did not like that at all, so when he wasn't looking, I'd put chloroform in a jar, drop the mice in, shut the lid and when they were dead I would take them out then slit their throats so he wouldn't know I was squeamish. For months he couldn't understand why his experiments weren't working—something was interfering—another chemical? One day after hearing about it for so long I said, "Do you suppose it could be the chloroform?"

My next job was teaching nursery school—back in my own element.

Then I became co-owner of a new nursery school with my sister, which made me President of a Corporation but gave me little business couth. Then I was a professional model—people always think of modeling as a glamorous job, including me, until I became one, and found out just how unglamorous it is. I spent the next few years on an escalator—going up and down from the fashion department to the "tea room" in a large department store in Baltimore where fashion shows were held every lunch time. I do owe a lot to Zippy, a chimpanzee, though. In fact, Zippy made me what I am today—able to put film in a camera and get some sort of image on paper. I'll tell you why: I had a job once as a model for the Photographic Show in the Coliseum in New York City. The other employee for Nikon was Zippy, a chimpanzee who wore a gray flannel suit and roller-skated everywhere with nonchalant ease. He was as intelligent as any other model I ever worked with, and his job was to take pictures of people who came into this sort of prize-fighting ring where Zippy and I stood, with a Nikon camera on a tripod. My uplifting job as his subordinate was to write down the people's names so we could send them the picture. The gimmick was that if the camera was easy enough for a chimpanzee to operate, why not you? Well, it convinced me, and I have been taking pictures ever since. Then I got into TV commercials and was an American Indian doing a rain dance on a drum in my black wig and Injun costume for a beer commercial. After that I had my own interior decorating TV show sponsored by Firth Carpeting. I interviewed decorators and also did all the commercials, which no matter how they started, always ended up by my having to look into the camera and say in a soppy voice, "And remember, it's love at Firth sight." I almost threw up every time. I also organized and modeled in daily fashion shows in the clubhouse at Pimlico Race Track, I wrote a fashion column, raised money for a political campaign, helped form a local theater company and danced in *Pajama Game, Can-Can, Oklahoma,* etc. In between the lines I went to typing school and Johns Hopkins University night school, learned to develop and print film, had three children and three husbands.

So you can see, I have done many unrelated things and the worst one of all by far is being a safari leader. In fact, taking out safaris was something I had longed to do for such ages that for about three years I just refused to accept the fact that I actually loathed it. But I did learn something I'll never forget: My most adamant opinion is always tentative.

One of my early husbands once conned me into going with him while he cooked dinner and demonstrated pots and pans— Copperware or something—to about ten strange people. We had to buy all the food and to my horror, I was shoved into the kitchen and not allowed out except to serve and clear the table. I had to cook the dinner (I hate to cook) and then do all the dishes alone, while my husband gave the sales pitch. This disaster *cost* me five dollars, half the cost of the dinner, because we were going to split the profits—but there were none, ever. So I did that twice in one night—the first and the last time—but I'd do that again now before I'd lead a safari.

Yet I am the first to admit that 97.7 per cent of the people we take on safari are extremely nice, and I will also admit right off that some people we have met on safari are today our very good friends, and our life would be less bright without them. It is simply that I don't happen to like just "very nice people"—I want to be with my *friends*. And it has taken me a long time—my whole lifetime, in fact—to find people I really like, and I haven't enough time to be with them, let alone with new people. I really don't have room in my life for anyone new. In fact, there is standing room only now. Or perhaps I am just too selfish to have to spend twenty-four hours every day with anyone who is given to me—sight unseen. I like to be with people I have chosen to be with.

I suppose there is absolutely nothing wrong with men who are "in plastics" or copper wiring, or women who take Chinese exercise classes, but I am just not interested in those things, so I do not want to have to talk about them every day for twenty-two days. Saying the same thing over and over again about the animals of Africa is not much better, and I am not being paid to argue my political views—the people are on safari to have a good time and they are paying for it, paying *me* for it, so it is not fair for me to criticize or disagree with their views on religion or Ralph Nader. Yet I find it extremely difficult to remain silent, but I certainly don't have to agree with them. It is difficult also for me to communicate with people who talk about how many miles they get to a gallon or with those who say, "Nigras are all right as long as they stay in their place." I am in an inner rage, yet I must smile from 6 A.M. to midnight for twenty-two days. And sometimes I just hate a person because of the way he eats his soup.

Being a safari leader may sound very glamorous, but I assure you it is hard and tedious work. You not only have to take everyone who is given to you, you are then stuck with these strangers for sixty-six straight meals. You are everybody's servant, court jester, teacher, nursemaid, problem solver, porter, doctor, errand boy, bridge partner and psychiatrist. There are few other jobs where you must spend so much time with the same strangers. Shoe salesmen's customers come and go—I shouldn't imagine the salesman gets into their kidney and divorce problems. On top of all of this, the people on safari are boss, not you. A teacher has to accept any kid put in her class, but he has got to do what the teacher says—theoretically, at any rate—which is one up on the safari business. Normally one *chooses* the people one is going to eat sixty-six meals with. The other safariers on the trip have the choice of eating alone or with anyone they choose. You, as a courier, can't very well eat each meal alone—no, your job is to make everyone happy—lead the group in song. Everyone has paid and has the right to be happy, and it is *your* responsibility to make everyone in the group ecstatic—the old maid, the drunk, the homosexuals, the Methodist minister, the Jewish furrier from New York and his girl friend, the Arab from Cairo who just joined the group in Nairobi, the hippy, the John Bircher and the Left-Wing radical. Everyone—from eighteen to eighty—sits there as you go to greet them for the first time with that "Go ahead, you make me happy, I've paid for it and I'm waiting" expression on his face. I'd rather sell eggs.

I'll never forget one such group, all waiting for Jock, their safari leader, in the arrival lounge of Nairobi airport. This was Jock's first time at meeting a large group and he wanted really to make a good impression, so he went in sort of skipping and looking very cheerful and bouncy, but since he is shy he was slightly apprehensive and every eye was on him. What he didn't see, because he was feigning such a broad smile at the group, was a suitcase in the middle of the floor which he tripped right over and went sprawling out, spread-eagled, in front of everyone.

The above is not to say that I don't like certain aspects of the safari business—I do, very much indeed—I just don't like being a courier. Planning an imaginative and successful safari is very rewarding, and it is gratifying to know that where a safari just a few years ago used to be for only the very wealthy—at least $150 per person per day—it is now in reach of everyone's pocketbook—down to around $60 per person per day, which includes everything—tips as well as all accommodations and food and transportation in Africa, etc. Whereas before we had only a few wealthy people on safari, we now have masses of postmen and hairdressers as well. It is nice to know that almost anyone can make his dream of an African safari come true.

But, just by the law of averages, dealing with 4,000 human beings each year, we get some lulus. (Lulu means "pearl" in Swahili.) In a typical sample week in the safari business we have met a blind person, two honeymooners seventy-four and seventy-six years old, Peggy Cass, a man ninety-one years old traveling alone, two girls who were arrested in Uganda for wearing mini-skirts, two clients who were taking off in a small chartered plane at one of the game lodges and hit a zebra which ran into the plane —the zebra was chopped into little pieces, the plane demolished, but fortunately the people were not hurt at all—three Hollywood movie biggies, a Prince of Ethiopia, and one hundred eighteen others.

It was funny about the movie men. Doria Block, my good buddy in Nairobi, called and asked us please to come to dinner and bring our two American houseguests, Jane and Colleen, because three exciting male movie directors from the States, who were here hiring local people, were coming to dinner too. The three of us thought at last we'd be discovered and get Hollywood contracts. We spent ages rehearsing our auditions, practiced walking, took hours getting dressed, and swooped into the Blocks' living room fluttering our false eyelashes and performed our "casual conversation," which we had memorized.

Finally I got up the nerve, and still pretending to be casual asked, "What is your new movie about?"

We had been anticipating another *Clockwork Orange,* perhaps, because the set designer for that excellent movie was also at the Blocks. We held our breaths as we waited for the all-important answer. "Ants," they replied. And they were serious. Colleen managed to say she couldn't be in that because her ant costume was all worn out, but Jane and I could say absolutely nothing.

One of the best things about our life is that it is divided. We spend part of each year in Africa working on safaris, and part in the States, lecturing. We lead a dual life, which may help to explain why this book is schizophrenic.

Once, though, we went to the States when we didn't have to lecture because I had a $12.50 credit at Neiman-Marcus and had to use it. I told Lawrence Marcus at a dinner party in Houston that I had come to the States because I had a $12.50 credit at his store and had used it that very day. He was astounded, not that we had come all the way from Nairobi to use a $12.50 credit, but because he couldn't understand how anyone could go into his store and spend *only* $12.50.

It was a good thing I had that credit. It was the year we decided to go to the States the first of August since the weather is so delightful in Baltimore in August. Another reason was because Rick was already in Baltimore and Dancy and McDonnell were also going to the States the end of July to join *Up With People,* the musical group and traveling university, so Jock and I thought we would take our holiday in the States then. We wrote Rick and my sister, "Of," in Baltimore that we would arrive about the beginning of the month.

Then we were delayed because Mary, our tour operations director, was strangled. She was working in our office which is on the tenth floor of a large building in the busiest part of Nairobi. She was alone in the Percival office one evening when three Africans came in and asked if it was Japanese Airlines. She told them JAL was just across the hall. Without even closing the office door, one of them, sure now she was alone, pulled a gun.

"Oh you want the money," she said resigned. Indeed they did. It must have been an inside job because only once a week do we have cash in the office on the day when we have a large group of tourists coming in and the banks are not open before they go off early the next morning on safari, forcing us to draw the thousands of dollars from the bank the evening before and lock it in the office overnight. This was the night. With the gun pointed at her, she unlocked the money and gave it to them, which was the only sensible thing to do. Then they grabbed her own purse and took out $280 of her own cash which she had just drawn from the bank. Then they took her watch, and one of them said, "Shoot her." "No," said another, afraid of the sound of the shot, "let's strangle her." So one of them took knotted handkerchiefs (new from Woolworths just across the street) and stuffed them down her throat. The third tied her hands together and put her own silk scarf around her neck. They then dragged her from her office, through a reception area and into Jock's office, where they tossed her on the floor and began strangling her with the scarf. She said she was sure she was dying—everything went black and she felt as if she was sinking into a vast sea. The last words she heard were from the one with the gun, "Let's go—she's finished."

But in what turned out to be forty-five minutes later she came to, dragged herself to the switchboard and called 999, the emergency number. The police and ambulance arrived together in seconds, and the doctors told her that what had actually kept her from dying was her false teeth—evidently she has a couple of false bottom teeth, and as the burglar shoved the handkerchiefs down her throat, he knocked her teeth into her throat which kept an air hole open for her to breathe. Of course she was terribly bruised and could hardly speak for days, but that sure beats being dead. The thieves, near murderers, were never caught.

However, Jock and I had gone off at lunch time, before it happened, with Colleen of leopard coat fame and our New York friend Ed Keyes, and we had driven to the coast for a beautiful few days of rest and sun before our jaunt to the States. While the drama was going on in Nairobi, we were eating supper at Fat Ali's in Mombasa. You must go there some time; it is a marvelous place. You turn left at the African market and go down this narrow, twisted, evil-looking street. It is very old and dark, and wicked-looking balconies left over from Vasco da Gama hang over diabolic pavements. Suddenly, out of nowhere, a youth appeared running next to our car shouting, "Do you want rice? Do you want rice?" We later figured out that Fat Ali usually serves just plain curry, but Europeans like curry with rice, so when a car comes down that street it can only be that the people are going to eat at Fat Ali's—unless they just go to be mugged. So then the waiter runs out and buys some rice. We wondered if we were to order the rest of our meal while we were parking, but it was just the rice.

Then we entered a depraved-looking door—the whole block would have been condemned in the States. We climbed a narrow and crooked stairway which was painted institutional green a hundred years ago and has collected all the fingerprints and fly specks ever since. Fat Ali squatted at the top of the staircase on the floor, looking just like Buddha. He picked his toenails and didn't speak. We walked out on one of the balconies where there are only four bare tables and chairs and nothing else—no decorations, table-cloths, napkins—nothing. We ordered chicken curry. It arrived in a bowl that looked just like a dog pan, and with a spoon as the only utensil. We then gorged ourselves on the best curry in the whole wide world. Dinner costs fifty-six cents each. Of course they don't serve booze, being Muslims, but we had a bottle of wine in the car, and we asked if we could bring it up and drink it with dinner. No. So after a few bites, we'd run down to the car, take a swig of wine, run back upstairs, have a few more bites, down again, and so forth. The curry was so hot it hurt my ears terribly. In fact, my ears were so painful I had to leave and go across the street to a fruit stand and buy some bananas to make them feel better. No, you don't put the bananas in your ears, you eat them, but it makes your curry earache go away. I got back up with the bananas, ate some more, then ran downstairs for another gulp of wine. It was the busiest meal I have ever had. And you get so much exercise through dinner you never gain weight.

Anyway, after dinner we drove seventy-eight miles north to our house at Malindi, and early the next morning collapsed on the beach and fell apart in little pieces, relaxed, relaxed—and five minutes later someone came running in with the news of Mary's being strangled. We took the next plane back to Nairobi and left Colleen and Ed to do the relaxing for us.

So, we couldn't leave August first because we were minding the store while Mary recuperated. I wrote to Rick and to my sister and told them what our delay had been and that I would cable them when we knew exactly when we would arrive, but I forgot to mention that we had just decided to go to Rome for two or three days to visit my nun friend Sister Helen in the convent before we came on to the States. We had no time schedule, it didn't matter when we got to the States. There was no difference between our arriving August 1 or August 8—we thought. What we didn't know, but no one knew we didn't know, was that in the last week in July Rick had sent us a cable saying he was getting *married* August 6. We never got the cable. What a cable *not* to get! We had no idea he was even thinking of getting married; this was a big surprise, and he planned it for the sixth of August, thinking that would give us six days together in Baltimore before the wedding. But there we were in blissful ignorance at the convent in Rome.

Because some airlines were on strike, we telephoned Ken Beynon, the manager of Percival Tours' London office, for help with our Atlantic flight. I didn't know him well, so we had rather a formal conversation about timetables and the like. I was just about to ring off when he said, "Just a minute, Betty, I have something to tell you. Rick is getting married today." "Married!" I choked and burst into tears. "Why didn't he tell me? Who is he marrying? This is the first I've heard of it. He wouldn't do this to me." Ken, out of his depth with a hysterical mother, and probably wishing he didn't know me at all, tried to explain that he couldn't answer any of those questions—he was merely passing on a message.

Meanwhile, the nuns had heard the commotion and were gathering around. As I was trying to explain to them through my tears, the phone rang again, and this time it was my sister in Baltimore telling me of the wedding, how everyone had tried to reach us in Africa and in London, had finally learned we were at the convent, and that Rick, upon hearing we had never received the cable, had postponed the wedding until the next day. If we left immediately, we would make it. "Is she pregnant?" I asked, and then the nuns wished they didn't know me at all and tried to pretend to look as if they hadn't heard the question. She was not, which was a disappointment, but that was soon erased by the chaos of our trying to get out of Italy on airlines that were not flying. Somehow we did reach London and since Pan Am and all the others were solidly booked, we found a charter that would take us if we checked in five hours ahead of time. There were 945

other people also checking in for the same plane, into which 250
of us finally climbed—247 hippies and Jock, Colleen and me.

We found ourselves in the front of the line, and the ticket person
said, "Are you students from New York?" (This was a charter
flight for students, and only those who had flown over together
could return on it.)

"No," we answered.

"Did you fly over with this group?"

"No."

"O.K., board the bus for the airport."

We did and it left, and three hours later we were still riding on
the bus toward some remote airport. Colleen was ahead of us
about six seats, so she turned to us and called, "Do you think we
are on the right bus?"

Jock, the only non-American on the bus, called back to her in
his British accent, "Oh yes, this is the tour of Scotland."

You should have felt the momentary panic in that bus as
everyone turned to Jock, staring in horror, but then we all
laughed.

On the flight over we stopped in Gander, Newfoundland, for
refueling, and bought the wedding booze there, which I thought
was an exotic touch. We arrived in Baltimore just in time for an
instant wedding, and there is much to be said for that. Rick had
very thoughtfully invited all of our friends as well as his own
(then canceled them all and invited them for a day later). My
sister had very kindly agreed to have the reception—no huge planning for months, no tremendous expenses, and Dancy and McDonnell came down from college and made the sandwiches. Colleen
stopped off in Philadelphia from New York and got her mother-
of-the-bride dress left over from her daughter's wedding two
months earlier, and brought it to me in Baltimore because all I
had were blue jeans. So they propped me up against the altar and
I watched, through falling eyelids, a charming, easy and delightful
wedding.

And if I hadn't had that $12.50 credit at Neiman-Marcus, we
might have missed the whole thing.

Garbage Soup

MAINLY BY BETTY

The title of this chapter was originally to have been, "There's a Rhino in the Rose Bed, Mother," but then when that became the book title we had to think of another chapter heading.

Robert Ruark, whom Jock knew, once gave him a formula for writing books. He said to pick a paragraph that sets the tone of the book for an opener, then give a few anecdotes, follow this for quite a while with "nose-picking material," then get down to the body of the story. We thought of calling this "The Nose-Picking Chapter" but feeling that it would offend some people—all people, probably—we decided on "Garbage Soup" because that is what I often make at home with all the left over everything I don't know what to do with. I throw a lot of ingredients together—a plate of spinach, lamb gravy, a tossed salad, three mushrooms, a ham bone—all unrelated originally—and I just hope that this chapter turns out half as well as the garbage soup.

Though this book is called THERE'S A RHINO IN THE ROSE BED, MOTHER we haven't even mentioned a rhino yet, and come to think of it, I'm not sure we ever will. No, this chapter isn't about a rhino, it's about some of the small but nevertheless astonishing things one encounters here in everyday life. Many years ago I do indeed remember our daughter, Dancy, yelling to me one day, "There's a rhino in the rose bed, Mother!" We were at a lodge in Uganda in a little *banda* (hut) which had a rose garden outside, and sure enough there was a rhino in it. A perfectly normal situation for the setting, but I bet most American mothers don't hear those words often. I mean you hardly ever see rhinos in rose beds in Maryland any more.

It was in the same *banda* one evening that we were sitting about reading when I happened to glance up and saw an elephant staring in the window at us. It is just that you feel so *silly* saying, "There's an elephant looking at us through the window."

Later on that evening the children were on the front porch playing cards, and from around the side of the house an elephant, perhaps the same one, came running as fast as he could. Rick picked up Dancy under one arm and yanked McDonnell with the other back into the house. The elephant, a very young playful thing, that was acting like a bad boy playing hookey from school, took Rick's shoe from the front porch. When the children had recovered from the shock of an elephant's joining their card game and saw it was such a little elephant just being frisky and playful, they went outside to see if they could get the shoe. Have you ever played hide and seek with an elephant? The boys crept around one side of the house, and the elephant crept around the other, and at the corner they met—face to face! I don't know who was more surprised or frightened, the boys or the elephant, but I do know that many arms and a trunk were all flung up in the air and everyone scattered in different directions. Much to the boys' disgust, I made them come inside the house, so they went into the bathroom and hollered at their elephant friend and soon he had his trunk in the bathroom window looking for his playmates who were standing on the bathtub backed against the wall and squealing with delight. In another few minutes the mother elephant arrived and took her delinquent child away.

On that particular trip we were in Uganda on our way to Zaire, which was called the Congo in those days, because we particularly wanted to see the African elephant the Belgians had trained and used for work—the first experiment of its kind to succeed with the volatile tempered African elephant. On our way to the border we ran into a flooded road, and with the water practically up to our windshield at times we caught glimpses of fish swimming alongside the car.

Trying to find a deviation around the swollen river we got lost and traveled sixty miles on what turned out to be a "camel track" on the map. We paused at a place that looked like the surface of the moon with boulders strewn all over the road, and after our picnic lunch Rick said, "Well, let's get this show back on the rocks."

Then we heard that the border to the Congo had just been closed so we never managed to see the working elephant, and later we learned that the Congolese rebels killed and ate them all and so far as I know, no one has tried the training since.

But on with some of the wacky things that affect one's daily life here.

In case you ever wonder why I shave my legs sitting on the kitchen stove and beat whipped cream sitting on the bathtub, it is because of the most senseless system in East Africa of having five different-sized electrical plugs and sockets. In other words, the wall sockets, instead of having two holes into which you just plug everything as is the case in the "civilized" world, sometimes have three round holes, sometimes two small and one medium, sometimes three large square holes, sometimes two medium round and one large round hole, and sometimes just two medium round holes. The plug on your electric razor may have three large square prongs, for example, but the wall socket in the bathroom, bedroom and guest room may have one of the other four types, so you spend your life running around with electrical equipment to every plug in the house, realizing six times each day that round pegs won't go into square holes. Or you learn how to take plugs off the cords and put other plugs back on. Why it is not standardized, I simply do not know. As if that isn't bad enough, each socket has its own switch too, for heaven's sake, which means if you go to a lamp or iron and turn it on but it doesn't go on, it doesn't mean necessarily that it is broken—it may mean that the switch on the wall socket is "off," and then you get

the ridiculous performance of running back and forth trying to
synchronize the two.

When I moved to Africa in 1960 I brought a kitchen clock
with me from the States. I switched plugs, stuck it in the socket
(three large square) hung it on the wall, and switched on. The
clock melted. It just ran down the wall in a gooey mess. I
discovered later that in the States the current is 180 volts, but in
Britain and Africa they have 240 volts, which simply burns up
American appliances unless you use a transformer, which is a
cumbersome and ugly device weighing about eleven pounds that
acts as an intermediary between the high-voltage current and the
puny 180-volt blender or vacuum cleaner. (If writing books or
lecturing or tourism should fail, I can always write manuals on
electrical engineering, I suppose.) I had also brought my record-
player with me from the States, and even though it had an AC/DC
adaptation switch, and even though the kitchen clock episode
had taught me about transformers, the record of the Stones
nevertheless sounded as if they were certainly stoned. It dragged,
not horribly, but certainly perceptibly, and the reason was that
American electric motors run at so many cycles, whereas the
wretched Limeys build theirs to operate at a different number.
For an electric mixer or can-opener, who cares if it runs a small
percentage slower? But the effect on a record is to throw it out
by about 5/7ths of a tone, which is excruciating, even to my
not very musical ear.

(*However,* there is a handy little gadget weighing about twenty-
three and a half pounds and costing $389 that will correct the
cycle deficiencies. I decided right then that I already knew far
more than I wanted to about matters electrical, and I started again
from scratch—bought a new record-player and a wind-up kitchen
clock.)

Another thing here is that there is a safety law that electrical
switches for bathroom lights must be *outside* the bathroom. The
temptations are obvious. No kids, or adults for that matter, can
resist plunging their brother or sister or friend who is enjoying
the serene tranquility found only in bathrooms, into sudden and

distressing darkness. American guests, on the other hand, enter our bathroom, close the door, then search for fifteen fruitless minutes in the dark for the light switch.

And if you wonder why I dance when making a dentist appointment or ordering groceries by telephone, it is because our telephone picks up the radio programs. One of our two stations usually has good music— ". . . and a head of lettuce, cha-cha-cha . . . two bars of soap . . . dum-da-dum . . ."

So if you want to hear the news broadcast or anything on the radio, just go to the telephone and dial a number, any number, and you will get the radio program through the telephone. One day a friend of mine visiting from the States, dialed the airport and got a Philip Sousa march, and the airport too, of course. She asked if we had "Dial a Song" here. Although it is very nice to be able to get radio programs without a radio, and a lot cheaper too since everyone else has to pay for a license as well as the radio, the problem is that from our phone you cannot make a telephone call *without* getting a radio program even if you wanted to, and sometimes it is very disconcerting to hear the Salvation Army's interpretation of God's word at the same time as you are talking to your girl friend about her current extra-marital love affair. But often the program is better than the conversation, particularly if your friend is telling you how she is taking her child to town to buy tennis shoes and simultaneously there is the latest bulletin on Watergate. The only thing to do is to keep absolutely quiet and concentrate on the radio announcer and ignore your friend. You see, the snag is that the person you're talking to cannot hear the radio—only you can. (The radio towers are very near us and only our telephone picks it up.) But if you start to explain it all, you'll miss the news. You have to fake your way through the conversation with your friend muttering things like, "Sorry, I dropped the phone and missed what you said—for the last ten minutes."

There is only one TV station in Nairobi, and this does not go on the air until 6 P.M. Sometimes it doesn't go on then because the cameraman hasn't arrived—"a technical difficulty." (East

African Airways announced their flight from Nairobi to Malindi would be delayed due to "technical difficulties," and an inquisitive friend of ours on the flight checked into the matter and learned the "technical difficulty" was that the pilot was home asleep in bed.) When the television does start, if there is an interesting talk show, for example, they just keep on going over the allotted hour for however long everyone wishes. Time is not terribly important in TV here—on the lone station the commercials are played only at the beginning and the end of the program, and I must admit it was a true joy to watch "Elizabeth R" and "Search for the Nile" uninterrupted. Sometimes the programs go on as scheduled and sometimes not, and sometimes they are not even scheduled. Then you must stay up just waiting to be surprised and to be told as the station signs off what *may* be shown the next day.

When television was introduced to Kenya just before independence, one of the first things to be done was to build a tall television mast. The Ministry of Communications was responsible and the minister was an Indian (more about Indians, often referred to as Asians, in East Africa, later). English is the second language for Indians as well as Africans and, naturally, idiomatic mistakes creep in now and then even among the highly educated. Heads of government departments the world over are inclined to be possessive about their projects and boast of "my irrigation project . . ." or "my housing project . . ." and this minister was no exception when it came to his television mast. In a speech to mark the first transmission, having explained the excellent technical aspects of the station and congratulated the contractors for speedy completion, he had one final boast about the fact that no building or structure of any kind in East Africa was as tall. At this formal ceremony, addressing dignitaries and parliamentarians he concluded his speech ". . . and I am proud to tell you today that I have the highest erection in Eastern Africa."

Just doing a simple thing can become very elaborate here. For example, when you have been invited to someone's house for the first time and you ask, "Where do you live?" that would seem to be a very simple question which might be settled in a maximum of one minute by merely writing down 1025 Main Street, or 732 Fifth Avenue, Apartment 3A. But not here. There are no street numbers and some streets don't even have names, so you must make a map to get where you want to go. Many people have maps printed and send them to their guests to save about fifteen minutes of explanation over and over again. Since Jock and I are not map-printing types, we just keep on explaining over and over again. Suppose we want to go to someone's house, the person describing where he lives starts very optimistically with something nearby, hoping the visitor will know it and he will not have to start three miles back.

"Do you know where the Veterinary Research Lab is?"

"No."

"O.K." Backing up a mile. "Do you know where the Banda School is?"

"No." Farther back.

"Do you know the railroad station or the post office?"

"Yes."

"Aha. Well, you turn left at the post office and go straight for about five or six miles. You'll see a sign on the right that says 'Westwood Park,' so you'll know you're on the right road. Do you know the Ding Dong Club? No? Well, you'll see it on the right set back off the road, and there is a sign out front that says 'Tusker Beer.' There you turn right and a few yards on that road you'll see a large cactus plant on the left, which divides the road. Take the right fork and continue around the circle until you see a name board that says 'Farrant.' Turn in here, go past the big house, bearing to the left all the way, and just past the chickens and the ducks, turn right and you'll see our house." I can remember once trying to follow these actual directions, and I worried how I would ever find where I was going if someone had eaten the chickens and the ducks.

Sometimes when you go to the movies at Malindi, a little village on the Indian Ocean, they show the first reel first, then the sec-

ond, then the fourth reel and finally the third. One such time the
hero died three quarters of the way through the film and was walking around alive again at the end. This often improves many of the
films. At least trying to fit all the pieces together keeps one from
being bored.

Once we went to the movies and were given free samples of
skin-lightening cream.

In East Africa you see many cultures and many customs
functioning fully and you see things in which you never had the
least bit of faith—such as witchcraft—actually working. I still certainly don't have any faith in witchcraft, but I cannot say it
doesn't work. It does work for those who do believe in it. I dis-
miss witchcraft by explaining it as applied psychiatry plus a dash
of herbalism, and I sincerely hope I am right. However, you do
begin to wonder sometimes about medicine and religion—especially when you see a good Muslim become a bad Christian—
but let's not get into that, let's get into medicine instead. A European here had a slipped disc or one of those awful back ail-
ments. He had been to chiropractors in the States, osteopaths
here, had had surgery on his back in London, had been in trac-
tion for three months in France—everything. Finally, an old
Indian man with a long white beard and a turban, who sat cross-
legged on the floor of a shoe shop and mended shoes, told him that
there was an Indian "doctor" on River Road (the shady part of
town) who *walked* on people's backs, and this was a sure cure.
The European thought, what the hell, he had tried everything
else, why not try this too? So he went to River Road, found the
grotty house, and explained to the "doctor" all about his ailment.
He then lay on the floor and the man walked all about on his
back. And do you know, he was unable to get up off the floor.
They had to get an ambulance to get him out of the house, and he
was in bed for two weeks before it was back to where it had
been.

When you live in a city as international as Nairobi, with so
many different nationalities and religions—therefore, many different accents, cultures and customs—you are bound to have oc-

casional senseless conversations. A Russian said to me one day
at a luncheon in Nairobi, "I have a cousin in Yova."

"How nice," I muttered.

"You hev been to Yova?"

"No," I confessed.

"No? I hear you hev visit every state. Why you don't know
Yova?"

I thought and puzzled, Yova? Yova? "Where's Yova?" I asked.

"Where's Yova? YOVA!" he said, louder and louder, "is in the
United States." He spelled it out, "I-O-W-A." But of course Yova
would be the Russian pronunciation. And many times I've heard
Pennsylvania pronounced, "Penn-*sláv*-ia" and I won't even try to
tell you what happens to Connecticut and Sioux City, and what
Jock, who considers himself perfect in pronunciation ("The Queen
and I say it this way"), did to La Jolla and Cheyenne.

When I first met Hapte Selassie, now a good friend of ours,
who is Minister of Tourism in Ethiopia, there were many people
chatting in a living room in Addis Ababa, and I noticed he was
speaking in perfect English, and I mean perfect. To someone
sitting on one side of me he spoke Spanish, and to the person
on my other side he rattled away in Greek. I asked him how
many languages he spoke and he said, "Seven fluently and one
fairly well."

"Which one fairly well?" I enquired.

"My own," he answered, "Amharic."

Hapte was born in Ethiopia just at the time of the Italian
invasion, and since it was so dangerous then for ruling-class
Ethiopians his parents gave their small baby to a Greek who was
leaving Ethiopia and returning to Greece. Hapte was raised
from a two-month-old baby in Greece and, naturally, grew up
speaking Greek. His foster parents were poor, and Hapte sold
newspapers as a young boy to earn a little money. From a Russian friend also selling newspapers he learned his second language. He said he wondered once or twice why he was black and
his parents were white, but it didn't bother him in any way and
he forgot to ask why. One day when he was a young teen-ager a

strange black man appeared and said something to Hapte which he couldn't understand. The man came back with an interpreter who said to Hapte, "This man is your father."

Since an interpreter was a nuisance, his father offered Hapte what is equivalent to our nickel for every word Hapte could learn in Italian, his father's second language. So Hapte, who thought this was a marvelous offer—much more money than he earned selling newspapers—learned Italian quickly. His father then took him to Ethiopia where Hapte was introduced to his mother and sister at the age of thirteen. He saw two women standing at the front door of a house as they drove up to it and his father said, "There is your mother and your sister."

Hapte went up to one and said, in Italian, "How do you do, Mother," and she said, "I am your sister. This is your mother," pointing to the other lady.

He was not entirely happy in Ethiopia, or perhaps he was just homesick for Greece, but at any rate he ran away and went to Paris where he got a job as a dancer in a night club, and there he learned French. Then when he had saved enough money he went to the States, and the first thing he did was to buy a gray flannel suit and a few second-hand books and started hitchhiking out West—he said if he wore the suit and carried the books everyone would think he was an American black student and give him a ride. He was right. He wanted to become a student, but he had to earn the money to go to college, so he got two jobs at once. The first was painting houses, but he made sure he was paid by the job, not the hour, and he painted with two brushes in order to finish quickly so he could move on to the next job. At night he got a job breaking Coca-Cola bottles in a Pepsi-Cola factory—or was it breaking Pepsi-Cola bottles in a Coca-Cola factory? (It seems that when bottles come back in to be cleaned and reused, the best thing to do is just to break the ones that don't belong.) Eventually he had earned and saved enough money and he went to college in the States. Somewhere along the way he learned Spanish and German and spent time in the countries themselves. Finally, in his twenties he decided to return to Ethiopia. Amharic was the last language he learned, and with not too much enthusiasm, since most Amharas, the ruling class, speak English. He still refuses to eat Ethiopian food—*injera* and *wat*—his wife must cook that for herself and something for Hapte like peanut butter and *moussaka* sandwiches. Although he looks like an Ethiopian, he really is a Greek-American with that special charm of the Frenchman thrown in too. Everyone Hapte speaks to in his own language says he speaks without an accent and grammatically perfectly. I have heard him say only two things that would make anyone suspect he may not be American: One was in the States when he had been calling everywhere looking for me, and when he finally found me he hollered over the phone, "I have been looking for you all over the place. What are you doing, playing seek and hide with me?" And the other time he said he wanted to go to Tennessee to see the "Hilly Billies."

Speaking of Greeks, a Greek ship captain thought Malindi, the coastal village where we have a house, would be a good place to wreck his ship and get the insurance, so he steered it onto the reef, saying he thought it was the Mombasa port, and there sat the ship and crew for nine months while the insurance companies investigated and fought. During this time one of the Greek sailors from the ship arrived in Malindi with some beautiful Omega watches. He said he had to sell them because he needed some cash, and was letting them go at an outrageously low price, and so Jock and a friend each bought one with great glee at getting such a good bargain. Omega watches are usually $150 and they got these for $35 each. In Nairobi, they took them to be appraised, and they were worth $6.95 together. When you looked closely you could see the Omega insignia had been newly pasted on the watch's face. Those things always make me laugh—why is it so funny to be taken, even when it is yourself who has been cheated?

The Africans cope with English far better than I do with Swahili. Our cook, Bowoto, barely reads or writes, yet he speaks five languages, and our other servants all speak three. That is 200 per cent more than I do. In fact, I have never even tried to speak Kikuyu or Wakamba or any tribal language, and if I did, I doubt very much if I would learn one quarter as quickly. The average African is intelligent enough, he is just not familiar with Western contrivances and methods. It is this, and the fact that we tend to judge people by our standards and not theirs, that results in delightfully comic happenings.

An African gun bearer on safari claimed he got food poisoning the night before from a tin of butter he had eaten. (Canned butter is always used on safari.) The hunter, worried that perhaps the butter had gone rusty or rancid or something in its tins and that everyone would get sick, investigated immediately. He asked for the old can from which the gun bearer had eaten and was handed an empty tin of clear shoe polish. The gun bearer couldn't read. Now you and I might easily open a can of shoe polish for butter if it were written in Chinese, but I just can't imagine *eating* it all. But maybe that, too, is judging someone by one's own standards—maybe he likes bread and shoe polish.

I once brought back some tuberous begonia bulbs given to me by a horticulturist friend in the States who insisted I grow them in Nairobi, but my mother-in-law ate them. (My friend had put them in an empty box of chocolates . . . she didn't actually devour them, but she bit into one thinking it was a chocolate-covered something, but I like telling everyone my mother-in-law ate my begonias.)

Grocery lists are a source of great puzzlement. They are made for me by the cook and written in English and Swahili. The English is spelled "fonetikally." Sometimes it takes a very long time to read them. "Bekoni" is easy—bacon, in the way that "basakili" is bicycle. (The only time they say "bacon" is for my friend Mrs. Peyton: "Mrs. Bacon is on the phone.") "Sitiwo" (pronounced "see-teé-woo," with the accent on the "tee") had us stumped. It turned out to be steel wool.

Our good friend Esther Burton's cook will copy, very sensibly, from the empty can or package, and she ends up with the entire commercial. For example, a brand name for toilet paper here is "Andrex," so he prints on the grocery list, "Andrex, in four soft colours, blue, green, yellow or white," or for canned milk, "Nestlé Ideal Milk, 9% Butterfat, Net Weight 14½ oz. (410 grams). Prepared in Kenya under agreement with Nestlé's Products Ltd., Nassau, Bahamas, Trademark Owners."

My African hairdresser told me, seriously, that she was "fragrant" (it was a boy), and we have "foached eggs" and "fuffery fie"—strawberry pie. "Fudding" is pudding. Some things are said so prettily: *"Lala"* is the Swahili word for sleep, which sounds just like sleep, I think, and once I mentioned to Bowoto that we needed rain and he answered. *"Mvua na lala,"* (The rain sleeps), which is certainly more poetic than, "No, hon, it's not raining out."

I taught him how to make iced tea, a revolting way to ruin tea, so Jock tells me. However, I love it, especially at the coast, but I never seem to drink it in Nairobi. One day though, two English friends stopped in to see us at about four o'clock, and I asked, as I was supposed to, "Would you like some tea?"

Of course they would. It was a terribly hot day and the thought of hot tea any day always makes me feel as if I should be sick— my mother used to say to me when I was little and had been in bed throwing up for two days, "Would you like a little hot tea and toast?" and that was all I ever knew about hot tea. I suggested they try some iced tea, and yes, indeed, they would—very adventurous friends we have. So I told Bowoto to bring some iced tea "as you do at the coast." But it had been two weeks since we had been at the coast, and there he makes it in the morning and puts it in a pitcher which disappears into the dining room where we add the ice and lemon, so he didn't really know how to make the finished product, and here I had asked for some immediately. In about five minutes, he arrived carrying a tray with a pot of steaming hot tea and four cups, each containing one ice cube and a sprig of rosemary (we grow mint only at the coast and this was the closest thing to it in appearance in our Nairobi herb garden). All of this and the chocolate cake was placed on the tray on top of an American flag. I was astonished, I admit, and was glad it was two British friends who would not be offended at the American flag being used for a doily. It seems that McDonnell had a flag hanging in his bedroom and somehow it got washed . . . perhaps it fell off the wall or they took it down because it didn't look clean. Anyway, from the ironing board it was placed in the drawer with the napkins and place mats, and Bowoto thought the flag a very pretty doily indeed. I must admit the entire tray looked as if it belonged in the Museum of Modern Art.

Another time I gave Bowoto some tea bags I had been given in the States and asked him to make Jock some hot tea. He stood there, and right before my eyes tore open the tea bags, dumped the tea in a teapot and proceeded to make it from scratch. He had never seen a tea bag—why should he know what they are? What would you do if an African handed you a piece of bark from a tree —eat it? Probably not, but maybe you should—it might be cinnamon.

Again we get back to judging people by our standards and not theirs. In Kenya many people have "hatches" between their dining room and kitchen. A hatch is a small sliding door in the wall behind the dining room buffet table that opens onto a counter in the kitchen. A couple here were having one put into their house, and they told their cook how much easier life was going to be for him—he wouldn't have to walk around with the food any more, just put it through the hatch, etc. Finally, the hatch was ready, and the first night they planned to use it they had a dinner party. When everyone was seated at the table waiting for food, the hatch opened and two huge *feet* appeared— their servant was climbing through with the food.

An American friend here had a cook who made the best apple pie she had ever eaten. She told him so, and added, "Next time, we'll put vanilla ice cream on top because that is what Americans really love—it is called 'pie à la mode.'"

"Oh fine," he answered enthusiastically. A few days later he made the pie again, this time for a party, and she reminded him, "Don't forget the ice cream on top."

"À la mode," he answered, remembering well. The pie came to the guests already sliced and placed on separate plates just as she had requested, and balanced on top of each piece of pie was a round glass dish with vanilla ice cream in it.

Soup comes in dehydrated packages here, to which you just add water or milk. A bachelor was entertaining, and a friend's wife was helping him buy the groceries. She handed him a few envelopes of dehydrated soups and said, "If you have soup first, this is certainly easy." He thought it was a splendid idea and showing the envelopes to his cook, who could not read, he asked, "Do you know what these are?"

"Oh yes," his cook assured him.

The bachelor explained, "We'll start with soup—all you have to do is add hot water in the soup bowls."

Dinner time came and the first course served was hot water in the bowls. The man went into the kitchen and asked his cook where the packets of soup were.

"Soup?" asked the bewildered cook, "What soup?"

"In the envelopes."

He had planted them. He thought they were seeds—same sort of package—and sure enough, outside in the garden was freshly planted soup with sticks stuck through little paper envelopes like flags at the end of each row identifying what would grow: Beef noodle. Cream of chicken. Consommé.

A good friend, Sherri Hunt, owns and runs a beautiful shop in Nairobi called Studio Arts. Almost three hundred Africans come to her market place to sell their wares. Sherri has a cook named Christopher Columbus (an odd name for an African), whose mother lives miles from Nairobi in the middle of the bush in a pretty mud hut and makes beautiful pottery by hand so that each piece is slightly different and crooked. I think it is lovely and have bought lots of it from Sherri for our dinnerware. I asked her if she could have a teapot made to go with the plates and cups and saucers, and she said she would write to her cook's mother, but that it would take months because she lives so far away and has to wait for her young son's school holi-

days so he can read the letter to her. Then she has to make it and
then it has to get all the way back to Nairobi. Anyway, Sherri
wrote the letter and drew a picture of a teapot for her to copy.
Three months later it arrived—in a package about the size of a
dice. She had made the teapot the exact size of the drawing—
which must have been extremely hard to do. We had to start all
over again, and I still don't have a teapot, but once again I realized
how we are inclined to assume that because we know what a teapot is, everyone else in the world does too.

One time Sherri was invited to the theater, and because she
lives eleven miles from Nairobi and did not want to drive home
late at night alone, she asked Christopher Columbus to come to
town with her, wait for her, then drive home with her. She got all
dressed up in evening clothes and on the way in to town she
asked him if he knew what the theater was. Of course he knew—
it was where sick people went and got cut up by doctors. (The
British call the operating room the "operating theatre.") No wonder some Africans think the *Wazungu* (white people) are nuts—
they get all dressed up in evening clothes and go off for two hours
of watching operations.

Friends of ours bought a house with a lot of ground, and one
of the many beautiful trees on it was a large baobab. Soon after
they moved in an African arrived and informed them that a
ghost was living in the baobab, and for five shillings he would
bring his dead chicken head and other necessary exorcising
equipment and get rid of it. He did and claimed later that it had
worked because flowers now were growing at the base of the
tree—which they had never done before. How will you ever
know? It is like people asking, "Did the pimple cream work?"
How do you know?—they might have gone away anyway even if
you hadn't used it.

Anyway, I suppose hiring the African to get rid of the ghost
is the same thing as getting the exterminators to get rid of the
cockroaches in the States, but there you can at least see the
cockroaches and feel certain you are getting your money's worth
when they are gone.

I wish someone would come to us and apply for a job as an instant exterminator. About six times a year we have the flying-ants appear as in some horror movie. Once Jock and I were driving along when suddenly we were completely encompassed in a cloud so thick we could see nothing in front of us. Flying ants. At home they suddenly just start flying into the house and everyone runs about shutting doors and windows and stuffing towels beneath the doors to keep them from pouring in—of course we never wholly succeed, and sometimes there are literally as many as a few thousand ants flying around inside our house. Their bodies are about an inch and a half long and look like a sort of hairless caterpillar, and their wings are also each about an inch or so long and translucent beige. But they don't fly very long. They come out of the ground right after heavy rain usually, but they fly for only a half hour or so and then their wings drop off and they die. They are harmless and never bite, but there are so many of them it is hard to see where you put your drink on the coffee table—or even the coffee table. When they have died, we shovel them out of the house and empty the basins in the bathroom and kitchen for that is where they all go to drink —or die together—the basins are filled to the brim and you just scoop them out. Or you can eat them. To some remote African tribes and to McDonnell, the flying ants are considered a great delicacy—to eat alive. This is done by merely tweaking off the wings and popping the wiggling caterpillar part in your mouth. McDonnell says they taste like butter, but then when he was about three years old he used to eat Baltimore bugs and insist they tasted like bacon, so we have long since ignored all of his culinary advice.

We have other ants too, and one day we had our Percival group of safariers out to our house for tea, as is our wont. All twenty-five of them and Jock and I were standing on our front lawn admiring the poinsettia and marijuana, and we were talking about our next door neighbor's dog being taken by a leopard and how we have buffalo and other game on our lawn too. Suddenly every single person began jumping around, stomping, slapping his legs and hollering. Unbeknown to us we had all been standing in *siafu,* the marching ants which bite like hell, usually waiting until they have climbed far up your legs. There is no mere brushing off the *siafu*—they cling with their pincers and the only way you can get rid of them is to pick them off one by one. To do this, you have to take off your slacks. Everyone started running for some secluded corner or behind a tree and pulling his clothes off—it must have been a curious sight to passers-by.

A friend of ours here, an older man who has hunted for years, was out duck shooting with some friends. He is an excellent shot and fearless as well. When duck shooting he will stand in very cold water up to his waist for hours. On their way home after this particular shoot, the hunter started wiggling around and hollering, "Stop the car, stop the car."

"What's wrong?" his two companions asked.

"Something is moving about in my underpants."

"At *your* age?" teased the friends. Anyway, they stopped the car, and the hunter jumped out, unzipped his fly, and a large frog jumped out.

So many things are odd here that you almost get used to the crazies—like, "The Drug Store" in Nairobi which sells only shoes and playing hide and seek with elephant—that soon they don't strike you as crazy any more. (That is when you need to watch out—you need a change of scene.)

For instance, all plans for building projects must be officially approved, and it is a requirement that roofs must be able to hold the weight of a five inch *snow load.* The building by-laws were lifted straight from the British safety laws governing such things, but they forgot to delete the clause about the snow load even though Kenya is on the equator. I just thought you should know that.

It seems normal here, but how many stone masons working on a construction site in the States, for example, won't even take a drink of water all day in the hot sun, much less eat? Here, many good Muslims won't even swallow their saliva during the fasting month of Ramadhan until the hours of darkness.

And how many of you in America have someone working for you who won't put Mercurochrome on a bad cut or take anti-malaria pills because of his religion? And how many times have you sent or received "Heartiest Gurpburb Greetings"—a standard Indian telegram? And have you had *gekko poop* on your dining room table recently?

In a little Arab fishing village I once went into a *duka* (store) and saw some purplish crystals. I asked, "What is this?"

"Potassium permanganate."

"What do you use it for?"

"Staining furniture, washing vegetables, and snake bites. Many other things too."

I bought a lot to give for Christmas presents; I figured no one should be without it.

"Can I get a drink out of the bed?" was a strange question my daughter asked one Christmas at Malindi when all the water supply stopped and we had no water for weeks. Everyone was standing in the ocean washing his hair and shaving, and you couldn't even pour the sea water down the back of your loo to flush it because the salt would corrode the pipes. We had cranberry sauce stuck between our toes because we had a buffet for seventeen people and somebody had spilled the sauce on the floor and we had all walked in it. The whole thing was an awfulness that we survived only by having two water beds, which went down day by day.

Not that crazies don't happen in the States—I remember once we had fried turkey for Thanksgiving because I forgot to take the turkey out of the freezer and so we had to hack it up and fry it. Another time the dog ate the entire cooked turkey which was sitting beautifully on the kitchen counter waiting to be carved and eaten, and so we just had mashed potatoes and cranberry sauce that Thanksgiving.

But here things seem to be even crazier. For example, how often have you sat looking out of your coast house and seen two camels walking up the beach, followed a few minutes later by a man in a kilt playing bagpipes?

So much is bizarre here that if nothing odd happens one day you begin to worry that something is wrong. I wonder whether or not the children will ever be able to adjust to normal life.

At the school McDonnell went to here, there had been the same headmaster for about a thousand years—he was there when Jock was, and Jock says he was old enough then to shoot. However, he finally retired, and the school acquired a new headmaster. Now remember, this was a fancy British school that sends boys on to Eton and such places—not "a school for emotionally disturbed teachers" as Woody Allen described his school in the Bronx. The new headmaster turned out to be a homosexual and was trying to seduce all the boys. O.K., so everyone can make a mistake. The board of directors got him out of the country and hired another man. Now, this second new headmaster turned out to be a homosexual too. It must be extremely difficult to find two homosexual headmasters right in a row. I wrote to John and Nora Reddy, our dear friends in the States, and mentioned that although the last two headmasters at McDonnell's school had tried to seduce many boys and had succeeded in seducing quite a few, McDonnell had never even been approached, which was rather insulting. John, who is a senior editor of *The Reader's Digest* and has a wonderful wry sense of humor, replied that he hoped McDonnell's being rejected wouldn't adversely affect his personality in the future.

McDonnell was always a little peculiar right from the start, anyway. I remember his coming home from school one day and saying he had studied Jean Dark in history that day and wasn't she great? I confessed I didn't know who that was and he got so disgusted with me and said, "You *do* know her. She was burned at the stake."

I asked if his teacher had called her Jean Dark, and he said no, he had read ahead in the book all by himself and found her, Jeanne d'Arc. Shortly after this he announced that were he still in the States it would be a holiday on Monday because it was George Lincoln's birthday.

When he was about four he got an ear infection, and I took him to the doctor who looked in his ear, saw something in it, and probed around way down in his eardrum and finally said, "It's a crayon.

McDonnell was delighted. "A blue one?" he asked with great enthusiasm—he had been looking for that one for so long. Whenever he lost anything after that he always got Dancy to look in his ear first.

When they were four and five years old, Dancy, McDonnell and I were standing in line waiting to see Santa Claus, and after Dancy had told him about all the dolls and doctor sets she wanted, Santa lifted McDonnell onto his lap and said, "And ho-ho-ho what do you want, little boy, for your Christmas present?"

McDonnell looked him straight in the eyes and answered, "A thubscription to *Playboy* magazine."

Santa Claus looked at him and me with distaste, shoved a balloon into his hand and went immediately on to the next child in line. Astonished, I asked McDonnell how he knew about *Playboy*. Well, his friend's big brother had lots in his room and told him they came in the mail through a thubscription. I asked McDonnell why he liked *Playboy* so much and he said, "Well, I like looking at those naked ladies. I don't know why I like it so much, but I do. Their tops aren't as empty as yours."

His school here looked like a summer camp in Maine or a school which Abraham Lincoln might have gone to. When he was twelve years old McDonnell was "Victor Laudorum," which means he won the cup for being the best athlete in the school, and he was indeed very pleased. (In fact, it had gone to his head and he was as obnoxious as hell about it.) Sports Day was a big occasion on which all the boys did their various athletic tricks and the parents went to clap. Came time for the high jump and McDonnell, trying to break the school record, had the bar raised higher than it had ever been before. He jumped. He fell. He didn't get up. I thought

he must have the wind knocked out of him, and trying to be a
good mother and not embarrass him by running out to him as I felt
driven to, I stayed in my seat. Three doctors who also had children
at the school were at Sports Day too, fortunately, and they all went
up to him. Then one of them turned and came toward me. Needless to say I was no longer in my seat but rushing toward the doctor
who said, "I'm afraid he has broken his arm."

He won the competition when he jumped, but he landed beyond the sand-filled pit and fell on hard ground. McDonnell, having fallen, looked at his arm and saw something "sticking out of it,"
and thought a piece of wood had gone *into* his arm, so he called to
the referee who was nearest to the jump to "pull it out." The
referee tried to, but to his horror he found he was actually
pulling on McDonnell's arm bone—it wasn't something stuck into
his arm, it was his bone coming out. The arm was literally hanging by skin only, but one of the doctors splinted it as well as he
could and we had to drive eighty miles back to Nairobi. Neither
the school nor the doctors had anything to give him but a few
aspirin, and he was very brave indeed—much braver than I
was. The school had telephoned the orthopedic surgeon in Nairobi who was waiting at the hospital. He operated but for some
technical reason could not set the bone—he only cleaned the
wound and stitched his arm. A few days later McDonnell's temperature soared—gas gangrene had set in. They had to operate
again to clean it up and to set the break as well as they could.
Finally he was cured and came home from the hospital, but he
had missed many weeks of school, and since all his friends
were away at boarding school he needed a friend, so we bought
him one—Shirley Brown, our black Labrador.

Eventually the cast came off, but his arm was crooked and
puny—really useless—as limbs always are when they first come
out of a cast ("plaster," as the British would say). However, a
weak arm did not stop him climbing Mt. Kilimanjaro within a day
of the cast's coming off. Today his arm is fine but still slightly
crooked, although not enough to notice unless he points it out. He

has a beautiful scar, though, which he can wriggle revoltingly and make sixteen-year-old girls scream.

Most of the time I seem to have my three children on three different continents which I don't like at all. When Rick finished school in Africa, he went to Georgetown University. Then Dancy finished school here and she went to Switzerland. McDonnell was still here—one in the States, one in Switzerland, one in Africa—awful. I have many mental funerals. However, finally McDonnell joined Dancy in Switzerland and when they finished their schooling there it was March—dopey Swiss schools—but they didn't have to be at their university in the States until September. I had to think of something to keep them off the streets, so I made them take French and typing lessons. Every afternoon, they went to a Frenchwoman's house for French conversation, but finding a typing school was more difficult. Finally I tracked down an Asian secretarial school in a fourth-floor walk-up in the slums where the hours fitted in with theirs, and I enrolled them. It was extremely expensive—$11 per month. They were the only two "European" children in the whole school (token whites) and McDonnell was the only boy. All the girls sat forward facing the blackboard, but the teacher made McDonnell sit sideways facing the wall—Asian segregation of sexes, based on tradition and custom.

In Kenya, generally speaking, there is little segregation, though. If you are going to marry someone of a different race, this is certainly the place to do it. It isn't that no one minds, it's that no one seems to notice, though some African parents resent their children marrying outside the tribe. Perhaps because we Europeans are such a tiny minority group—less than a half per cent of the population are white—and so used to living in a country which belongs to Africans, that blacks don't remain "blacks" but just people who are conservative and radical and good and bad and smart and stupid and handsome and ugly and rich and poor and bigoted and liberal, and soon you are color blind. There aren't as many "professional blacks" among the

Africans as among the American blacks. It must be much easier for the Africans than it is for the American black because the African *is* boss, he does govern and run his own country, and on that premise hangs a lot of difference. So it is not with lack of understanding of the difference in the situation that I report the following event:

One of those altruistic groups—Vista, Crossroads or something, I don't remember which—had a group of Americans here for two years' teaching. The Minister of Education, an African, Taita. Towett, was scheduled to give them a farewell speech and the American blacks in the group contacted him and asked him if he would speak to them separately, not with the whites. Mr. Towett refused, and at the integrated meeting he said, "None of us choose the pigmentation of our skin, and what matters is not pride in our color but pride in our ability to work with peoples of other colors for the good of everybody. There is no place here for color prejudices. The American black is welcome in Africa but Africa cannot afford to import American politics."

Amen.

It is unimaginable to me that this next story happened, yet it is true. A Roman Catholic Cardinal from Tanzania was going to the opening ceremonies of the Cathedral in Washington, D.C., when it was first built. He landed at Kennedy Airport and had a car and chauffeur waiting for him. He needed a haircut so he asked the driver if he would stop at a barber shop he saw as they were driving through New Jersey. The driver waited in the car while the Cardinal went in, but in two seconds he was back in the car again.

"Drive on," he said, "they don't cut niggers' hair in there."

I've been thrown out of two places; once in Gulu, a village in northwest Uganda. We were on safari with Texan friends, Rita and Watson Bettis, and we arrived at our hotel in this tiny little dumpy town just as it got dark. We decided to eat at once and to have a bath and go to bed immediately afterward in preparation for an early start next morning. The spotless dining room was almost full and we were the only white people. Everyone eating was neatly dressed and all the men wore ties and coats. We were in safari kit—bush jackets and so on. The African headwaiter gave a courteous smile, welcomed us to Gulu and told us that we would not be permitted to enter his dining room until we chose to dress properly. He was very decent about it, though, and said that we could eat, if we liked, at a serving table in a corridor between the kitchens and the dining room. We had a delicious dinner, interrupted only by the flapping of the swing doors and the constant stream of passing waiters. The only other time I have been thrown out was from the Athletic Club in New York in 1970 when I arrived for lunch in an extremely elegant pants suit. But there they didn't have the *savoir faire* to offer an alternative table in the passage.

I mentioned marijuana a few pages back. Cannabis is a wild plant in many parts of East Africa and has the reputation of being very good grass. McDonnell and Rick have recently gone into the student safari business together, setting up inexpensive but properly organized tours since it is absolutely impractical for kids to hitchhike through the game areas—it is not like traveling around in Europe or India. McDonnell made a short film of the safari, which he shows at universities in the States to drum up business, and Rick takes care of ground arrangements in Africa. (Dancy was offered the job of secretary to her two brothers, quit after the first afternoon, and went to London to study music.)

McDonnell and Rick feel sure that if they advertise the tours as "Safaris Through the Grasslands of Africa" they will be swamped by student clients.

I would caution anyone trying to take pot out of East Africa because although until recently Kenya has been relatively lax on the enforcement of marijuana laws, they have suddenly become concerned about drugs being brought into the country. And they are quite right, too, since we have negligible use of hard drugs, and the clampdown on marijuana (a non-drug, really) is part of the general awareness to keep the bad stuff out. Many visitors have been fined—perhaps $35 for the possession of two pounds of cannabis—and it may be worth the fine at that price. But if the Government really wanted to get tough, a jail sentence, or even a lashing which can still be part of a sentence here, would not be so pleasant. The authorities know all the tricks about putting the grass inside drums and other curios and shipping it back into the States, so beware, you have been warned.

A friend of mine in Maryland has a dog named Lucy, a Doberman, whom she adores. She shows, breeds and worships her. One afternoon she came in from shopping and her nineteen-year-old son came running out to her car and said, "Come quickly, it's Lucy."

It seems that her son had hidden his grass in a plastic bag in his music speakers and Lucy had sniffed it and had eaten three ounces. She was stoned out of her mind, completely unconscious, eyes rolled back in her head—zonked on the floor. My friend and her son had no idea of what to do with a stoned dog. She told me she was afraid to call the vet because he didn't like her—they had had many arguments in the past—and she thought he might report her to the police for possession of marijuana. I asked her what made her think the vet would know what to do with a stoned dog anyway. They carried Lucy outside, laid her on the ground, fanned her, called her, and did everything they could think of, which wasn't very much. Finally, because the dog was still completely zonked, my friend decided to go get another dog-lover friend who might be able to think of something. By the time she got back with her helper, Lucy was running around chasing balls and feeling fine once more.

Rick told me that a friend of his was at a party in Washington, D.C., and one youth who had been smoking announced that he had to drive to New York right then. Everyone told him he couldn't drive to New York—he was too stoned—but the boy simply insisted that he had a job he had to get to, and promised everyone over and over again that he would drive slowly. He got in the car alone, promised for the hundredth time not to speed, and drove off. On the New Jersey Turnpike right after the Delaware Bridge, he noticed police lights turning around and around in his mirror. "Oh-oh," he thought, and the policeman pulled him over to the side of the road.

"How fast do you think you were going, buddy?"

The boy cringed and softly guessed, "Seventy-five?"

"Guess again, Mac."

Horrified, the boy whispered, "Eighty-five?"

And the policeman said, "You were going *four* miles an hour"—he had the traffic backed up to the bridge.

A friend visiting us from the States once said she would like to try some grass brownies since she had never had any. Some eighteen-year-olds down the beach very enthusiastically offered to oblige and when they had baked the brownies they put them in a tin box with a lid on and left them on the kitchen table, waiting to give them to our guest. The youths then went out themselves. Two little girls aged eight, daughters of good friends of ours also down the beach, wandered into the empty house. They snooped around as little girls do, found the brownies and each ate two of them. Half an hour later their mother saw the two tots staggering down the beach stoned out of their minds, but she couldn't imagine what was wrong with them since she knew nothing about the brownies. They stared at light bulbs, asked her whether they were dreaming, giggled, and acted very strangely indeed. She thought perhaps they had been bitten by a snake, but reasoned that a snake wouldn't bite both of them. She asked if they had eaten anything—poison berries perhaps?

"Only little chocolate cakes down the beach."

"Aah"—the dawning.

Fortunately, her eldest son had been in on the brownie baking and had mentioned to her previously that he was going down the beach to "make cookies"—a statement which she thought most unusual at the time—and so it clicked. The girls had eaten marijuana, and way too much of it, but all that happened was that they went peacefully to sleep about 6 P.M. and were fine the next morning.

Although I do not disapprove of marijuana as much as I do of booze, because marijuana is far less dangerous, I personally prefer a drink or two to a joint or two. Alcohol accentuates personality traits and makes me even happier, and I love everyone even more than I usually do, which is a lot, and of course I tell everyone so. Grass makes me withdraw and feel so passive I can't even think of anything to say, and that makes me nervous, which, in turn, makes me paranoid. "They're after me, all of them are after me," I think—something I never think at any other time in any other circumstances. So at worst I am miserable and at best I find it boring and dull. Jock and I went to a party recently where everyone was smoking instead of drinking. We seldom smoke or drink, so we did neither and after leaving the "party," which had about as much life to it as going to an insurance brokerage meeting, I said to Jock that I certainly preferred drunks. At least they are funny or obnoxious or fight or wear lamp shades or something—but these people just sat around in silence looking dopey—it was like being in the recovery ward in a hospital.

Grass wards off reality, makes life fuzzy, and to annihilate oneself seems to me such an affront to life itself. This goes for booze too, of course. Many people annihilate themselves with liquor which is worse because it is habit forming, which grass is not, and alcohol is also very harmful to you physically—to your liver and brain—which grass is not. Many people fear marijuana because they know so little about it, and ignorance breeds fear. No one could have been more ignorant than me. The only people I had ever heard of who smoked marijuana were sordid drummers in New Orleans, certainly no one I knew. Marijuana was evil. It was not that I was prejudiced, I was just unenlightened—which, come to think of it, often produces as bad results as prejudice. But now I have learned about marijuana, I no longer fear it—I just do not like it. I find life—straight day-to-day living—provides me with a greater high than booze or marijuana.

Of course everyone is prejudiced about something and has experienced prejudice directed against himself, too. When Dancy was in *Up With People* and they traveled from town to town in the States, an advance team would go ahead to arrange for the kids to stay with families for a few days. Since the cast of *Up With People* contained students from all over the world in addition to the Americans, the advance team had to be tactful over the question of non-whites staying in white homes—even though 99 per cent of the time no problems or objections were encountered. (It is interesting to note that the question was euphemistically phrased, "Do you have any racial preferences?"—but it really meant, "Are you a racial bigot?") Just after Dancy had joined, an advance-team girl, who had not yet met her, asked a family in Frederick, Maryland, if they had any objections to offering a bed to a girl from Africa. The household in question consisted of a young married couple living with the son's parents, and at the time they were approached the parents were away and the newlyweds happily agreed to have the "African visitor." They did ask, though, whether she was very dark, and the advance girl, guessing, replied, "No, not very."

Dancy duly arrived and the reason why the young couple had asked the question about her color quickly became apparent. The father, who in the meanwhile had returned, was a racist. He was appalled to learn that someone from Africa would be staying under his roof and although he did not succeed in throwing her out, he refused to acknowledge her existence in his house for the three or four days that she stayed. He slammed doors in her face and never spoke a word to her. The fact that Dancy has unusually white skin, blue eyes and long straight hair in no way served to lessen the intense hostility he exuded toward her—if you're from Africa you've got to be black—and to his son and daughter-in-law who had brought this awful thing upon him. Dancy, who is the essence of the easy-going, cheerful modern youth, did her best, but she came away understanding for the first time in her WASP life what it feels like to suffer racial discrimination.

When McDonnell first went to the States to go to the university, he knew nothing about America, its crime rate, how unsafe New York was supposed to be, or anything. (Stupid foreigner.) Upon his arrival he immediately lost his wallet with all his money in it and had to hitchhike from Washington, D.C., to Hartford, Connecticut, to school. He slept by the side of the road on the New Jersey Turnpike one night, and later got a ride into New York City where he started hitchhiking again. A cab with an American black driver stopped, and McDonnell said, "I wasn't waving you down, I don't have any money. I was just hitchhiking."

"Yeah, I know—get in—I'll take you, but don't sit on the seat —crouch down on the floor."

"Don't you want anyone to see me?" asked McDonnell from the floor.

"No, that isn't it—the meters are wired to the seats. We've been giving too many people free rides—so now the minute you sit down the meter starts."

So McDonnell thanked him and told him he had lost his money two days ago and had not one cent, and the driver asked if he had eaten. McDonnell said no and that he was starved. The driver asked McDonnell if he wanted to come up to "Hurlam" (as McDonnell pronounced it, since he had never heard of Harlem before) and get a bite to eat at his house. McDonnell said sure. I began at this point in the story to get nervous. So McDonnell and the cab driver went to "Hurlam," stopped at an apartment building, went to a fourth-floor apartment and into the kitchen, where McDonnell was handed some chicken and a cold beer.

"Want to eat it up on the roof? I'll show you the view." McDonnell again said sure. I got more nervous. Up on the roof McDonnell had the Empire State Building, the United Nations and all the other interesting sights pointed out to him and described. Then McDonnell said he finished his food and announced he thought he had better get on to school, and the driver said O.K., but first he would like to introduce McDonnell to his father—his father had never met anyone from Africa. So they found his father visiting in someone else's apartment in the building, and then the driver told McDonnell that he would take him to the George Washington Bridge, but not over it because of the toll. McDonnell said no, he would hitchhike from there, but the driver insisted he would take him that far. So, at the George Washington Bridge McDonnell got out, thanked him, they shook hands and parted.

I tell this story because I still believe many good things happen most of the world over—I know they do to me and mine—for which I give many thanks. As people have often said, if only some nice stories could be printed—one nice story every day in each newspaper—just to give more joy and a little hope. And so, among all the terrible things in newspapers about everyone's getting knifed or shot or killed in Harlem, I would like to see McDonnell's story printed too.

Before McDonnell was born, his father, Dan Bruce, and I discussed for ages if he were a boy whether his name should be McDonnell Marshall Bruce or Marshall McDonnell Bruce. We had decided we were going to call him McDonnell (my maiden name) and I felt that even if Marshall McDonnell sounded better, his name should be McDonnell Marshall, because if you part a name on the side, like M. McDonnell Bruce, someday he would end up being called Marshall—in the army or by immigration officials or some such body—but if it read McDonnell Marshall on his birth certificate, he would *always* be called McDonnell. Dan did not agree, and so we were still arguing when McDonnell was born early.

I filled out the birth certificate the next fuzzy morning, and when Dan asked, "Did you fill it out McDonnell Marshall or Marshall McDonnell?" I truly couldn't remember. Dan's mother had put the birth certificate in her safe deposit box, but no, she hadn't looked at it, she had just folded it and put it in her bank. She thought it was Marshall McDonnell. Three years later we had to fill out a form for McDonnell to enter a school. It said, "NAME." We didn't know. So Dan went to his mother's safe deposit box and looked at McDonnell's birth certificate, but he was busy and hurried, and on his way home he *forgot* if it was McDonnell Marshall or Marshall McDonnell. So we laughed and just put Marshall McDonnell on the form and let it go. Another form later, I said I actually thought it was McDonnell Marshall I had put on the birth certificate, though I couldn't be sure, so we put McDonnell Marshall.

This vacillating went on for seventeen years. From time to time someone would say, "We *must* find out what your name is, McDonnell." McDonnell didn't care at all.

Then came the university in the States, and since McDonnell had spent all but the first three grades of school in Africa under the British system, he knew nothing about American universities, and of course neither did Jock nor I, so we three stooges trooped into the dean's office at the University of Hartford to ask a lot of very stupid questions about "Marshall's" future, as the dean called him after a glance at one of his enrollment forms.

"Do you want to matriculate, Marshall?" the dean asked McDonnell.

"I don't know," answered McDonnell and explained that he didn't know what matriculate meant. Jock and I couldn't imagine what it meant either.

"What courses do you want to take?" asked the dean logically.

"I don't know," McDonnell answered, again not knowing what courses American universities offered. We were all embarrassed because we didn't know anything—not how many credits one had to have each term, nor what average one needed to pass.

The dean was very patient and explained everything to us very carefully and finally said, "Oh, by the way, one of these forms has Marshall as your first name and the other says McDonnell. What is your first name?"

With that Jock got up and left the room, and McDonnell and I glanced at each other and started to giggle as we sometimes do when we don't want to. It was terrible. The dean didn't look convinced when we tried to explain why we didn't know what his name was either. We *must* look it up one day . . .

No one could have more trouble over names than our entire family.

Jock's grandfather was the Earl of Leven and Melville, and the title went to the eldest son, who was Jock's uncle. Jock's father, became The Honourable David Leslie-Melville, then following procedure Jock has everything erased from his name but the "Esq." afterward. All this is very confusing, and many people think Jock's correct title is "Lord," or at least "The Honourable J. D. Leslie-Melville," and frequently address mail to him in these incorrect ways. They also abbreviate it to "The Hon. J. D. Leslie-Melville"—Dancy picked up a letter addressed this way and said, "The HON J. D. Leslie-Melville?" as if someone was calling him "Honey" shortened. You can imagine the confusion of having a double name in the States. It will not fit into a computer for airline tickets and you always have to ask people behind hotel desks who say, "No, nothing for Melville," "Would you look under L?" and they get mad—especially if it *is* there. Once Jock had a letter addressed to Mr. J. Lousy Melville, and "Mr. Mezvivto" was how Leslie-Melville came on a bill recently. He is frequently called Chuck because Americans are not familiar with the name Jock but think it is Chuck or Jacques pronounced funny.

Rick called me "Miss Betty" until he was six years old. When he was just one and a half years old I took him with me while I taught nursery school, and since all the other children called me "Miss Betty" he did too.

Names have always intrigued me. I wish Jock and I had a child so we could name it—girl or boy—Leslie. Leslie Leslie-Melville. Runyonesque. Rhino Fosdick is the name of a man here—great name—sounds like Dick Tracy. Rick knew a girl named Lulu Devine, and she wasn't even a stripper. We met a Diamond Economy once, a real name of a Greek, and Jock had a friend in England named Bluebell Green, known, obviously, as Blue Green. But best of all are the names my sister comes across in her job as a social worker. Her job is to interview people to see if they qualify for medical assistance from the State. She was asking one woman her daughter's name and she replied what sounded like, "Pis Alm Civ."

"I beg your pardon?"

"Pis Alm Civ. Right from the Bible."

"The Bible?"

"Yep—written right there."

"Would you spell that please?"

"P-s-a-l-m C-I-V."

Psalm CIV. My sister also learned of twins who are named "Chocolate and Vanilla Smith." It was their mother who also told my sister she suffered from "Iwo Jima" (emphysema).

Bitten By a Chicken

I have said many times that my favorite species of animal is man—I am a people lover not an animal lover—and if I had to choose between people or animals I'd choose people every time. Discussions of whether poodles are more intelligent than dachshunds have always seemed absurd to me, for I have never known any dog, no matter how smart, to afford intellectual companionship.

However, this does not mean I do not like animals. I do. They have many endearing qualities—and one of the nicest things about animals is the lack of responsibility one has to assume for them in a moral sense. I am not responsible for anything an animal does, nor for its behavior toward another animal, nor do I have to teach them to read or write or vote or keep their city clean.

Animals are also authentic. In a world where we spend so much time wondering what is artificial behavior, the authenticity of the animals is refreshing, and in the same way that I do not like children for their mentality, I nevertheless love their authenticity.

Animals also afford me an expression for one of my two talents. Since I am retarded and cannot sing, sew or play the piano, I take pride in the only two things I can do well: tap dancing and game spotting. That is why I am always doing the time step and asking people if they can read that street sign three blocks away. I have incredible eyesight at a distance and it

is extremely useful on safari. Of course, I can't read a newspaper or a book unless it is held by the person sitting in the row
in front of me—but that has to do only with my arms being too
short.

If you have the gift of distinguishing things at a distance, then
it is easy to train yourself to look for game. You don't specifically look *for* a rhino or a lion, you sweep your eyes over the
countryside and search for something that doesn't fit in the land-
scape, that doesn't quite belong. It is, in a sense, a negative search.

Texans are better at this than most other Americans, I guess
because they have had practice looking at their cattle in the
distance. New Yorkers are impossible.

"Look at that elephant," you say.

"Where?" asks the New Yorker.

"Right there—standing on your foot."

At any rate, modesty does not prevent me from telling you that
I spot game extraordinarily well and display this ability very ob-
noxiously whenever I can. Once in Ngorongoro we had a Maasai
guide with us, to whom the good Lord had not only given terrific
eyesight but also six fingers on each hand and six toes on each foot.
Standing up barefooted in the safari vehicle through the hatch he
pointed and said, "Two rhino standing, one lying down."

I looked, but couldn't see them. "Where?" I asked.

He pointed, "Over there."

I got the binoculars and much to my irritation I still couldn't
find them. Finally, after much embarrassing coaching, I found
three sizable rocks about four miles away.

"Two rhino standing. One lying down," he repeated.

We drove over to settle it, which was a big mistake. There were
two rhino standing and one lying down. Wouldn't you think one
of them would have lain down on the way over, just so as not to
have made quite such a fool of me? It happens all the time—the
Africans are just incredible at game spotting.

Although my favorite of all animals by far is man, this certainly
doesn't mean I like all men. Not that I have any enemies. I'm sure
there must be many people who don't like me, but I dislike no one

I can think of because if I do meet somebody hateful I merely walk away—life is too short to have to bicker and fight. Similarly, I can treat animals on an individual basis too. I am absolutely crazy about our Labrador, Shirley Brown. She was in the hospital overnight once, and I would rather have gone in myself. She had an ear operation because, just like every other kid on the block, she gets coral ear at the coast—a fungus from the coral, which causes an infection—and this time her ear had abscessed. We asked the vet if she could be in intensive care and have nurses around the clock, and he was very glad to see her go because we telephoned him every five minutes to see how she was. If you don't tell anyone, I'll confess we even have birthday parties for Shirley Brown every June 4, with chocolate cake and candles and presents and much praying that no one will drop in and catch all of us at the table, including Shirley Brown sitting in a chair with a silly hat glued on her head, opening her own presents, which are wrapped with pretty paper and tied with bright ribbons, and eating the entire cake all by herself.

Nor does preferring man to the rest of animals mean I am not interested in preserving the game in Africa, but as I confessed before in *Elephant Have Right of Way,* my efforts are to preserve the animals for the enjoyment of man primarily and for the sake of the animals secondarily.

Nature is not sentimental at all. I am—embarrassingly so—but seeing a kill does not bother me in the slightest. At first I was really surprised that I wasn't upset at seeing a pride of lion eating a zebra because I do not like gore, and I will drive ten miles to avoid seeing an automobile accident, and I know when I die and go to hell I will find myself in an emergency room in a hospital for eternity. And to see a dead dog in the road really upsets me. Perhaps it is the waste, because to watch a vulture eating the eyes out of a dead buffalo and the hyenas pulling its guts out and devouring them while the jackals eat the tail, doesn't bother me at all. A dog's being killed by a car is an accident—a needless thing —but to see a lion kill a buffalo is the law of nature and purposeful—the lion gets fed. Man is the greatest and the most wasteful predator—animals kill only for food. Vultures and other scavengers clean up and also keep disease down—while we pollute our environment. I like vultures—why do so many people hate these garbage cans of Africa? Everyone is always so rude about them—the British even have an attractive expression to describe how they feel with a hangover: "My mouth tastes like a vulture's crotch." Isn't that lovely?

The lioness is a very sophisticated killer—she suffocates an antelope by holding its nose in her mouth, and death comes in less than three minutes. There is little brutality in a lioness's kill. Can we say that of man? But then can we ever say we knew a lion that was a pacifist? So, seeing kills and seeing the animals feed off each other is the law of nature, and it is almost a pretty sight to me because of the order of it all, the logic and the lack of mess. The lioness kills and then roars to let the male know she has food. He eats first, the lioness and the cubs wait for him to finish (chauvinist pig), but if the lioness has killed a small animal and the male eats it all, the lioness and the cubs simply do not feed. However, if the kill is a zebra, say, after the male has gorged himself the lioness and cubs can eat, and while they are guzzling, the vultures and the hyenas and the marabou storks and the jackals all wait their turn, and when they are through the zebra has disappeared—all but his bones. Sometimes the vultures eat so much they are unable to take off in flight (just like me at Thanksgiving), and their favorite tid-bits are the dead animal's eyes. Did you flinch? How about the Arabs who eat sheep's eyes, and Esther Burton, our friend originally from Detroit, who pops the eyes of a baked fish into her mouth and chews them and swallows them with glee.

Lion are fascinating people. They always look so docile—as if they would love you to get out of your car to roll with them and scratch their bellies and then they would lick your face. You can go to within a yard of them in a car without their seeming to mind. They look into your eyes with what appears to be as much affection as you are feeling for them. Experts say lion do not associate cars with people and the gas fumes mask our scent, but the minute they see head and feet they know it is man. We were talking about this one time when Jock and I were taking two elderly women on safari and we had been watching a pride of lion for almost an hour. "What would happen if you got out?" asked one of our clients. We said we didn't really know, but we weren't about to risk finding out. Famous last words, for just then as Jock put our car into gear, we realized we had a flat tire. He bumped off a little way on the flat, but still within easy sight of the lion he opened the door of the car, broke the never-get-out-of-your car rule, and stepped out to change the wheel. An astonishing thing happened. Those lioness who had looked so peaceful and friendly changed instantly to the most vicious and mean-looking animals I had ever seen. They tensed and bared their teeth and the most fascinating thing was that they somehow communicated to their cubs to run off, for within seconds every cub was trotting away in the opposite direction. (Lion do have a language, but though we never heard a sound from them it was obvious the cubs had been told exactly what to do and were obeying. Joy Adamson of *Born Free* fame and who has had so much experience with lion has stated that she is convinced that they have a telepathic form of communicating and they may be able to use it over many miles.) Lion crouch to spring and attack, so Jock knew the two angry lioness were not going to come after him just then, and he calculated he had time to get back into the car if they moved. He had his eyes on them and was changing the tire by Braille. Just then a Land-Rover appeared with some people standing up in the hatch hollering, "Get back into the car—quick, HURRY."

Jock scrambled in and the people in the Land-Rover drove up and said there was a male lion crouched behind a bush seemingly about ready to spring on Jock. We had not seen the male the whole time we had been watching the pride, nor had we seen him approach, but somehow he had been summoned by the lioness and was there ready to defend his family. The Land-Rover parked between us and the lion so he would not be able to see that Jock was out of the car. Jock said he set the world record for the fastest changing of a flat tire. When he finished and got back into the car everyone heaved a sigh of relief, and one of our clients spoke for the first time. All she said was, "This isn't in the brochure."

Lion dislike children, and some theorize that it is because they hate baboons and cannot tell the difference between them and children. I am inclined to accept this theory because I frequently have difficulty in telling the difference between baboons and some children I know.

There have been a number of tragic accidents here involving children, and two game wardens we know have had their children attacked, though mercifully not killed, by "tame" lion.

One day Jock and I and the children were with some game people who were trying to tranquilize three lion in a large wire enclosure before crating them for shipping. They would not come close enough to be given the shots until suddenly we remembered the children trick. We drafted a couple of kids of a friend who were hanging around in the background watching, dangled them in front of the wire, and as the lion rushed up we threw the live bait into the car and slammed the door. It worked like a charm.

George Adamson's famous Boy, one of the lion stars of *Born Free,* attacked and killed an African he had known for years and George had to shoot his beloved pet.

Although many people have been killed by lion it is only the man-eaters that devour people. Even today we sometimes read in the paper that a man-eating lion is in a certain area and the game department sends someone out to shoot it. Invariably they are old or sick animals, too weak to catch anything other than a human. (Stupid foreigners?) In Ethiopia a man-eater had eaten thirty-two people, and the Emperor asked a friend of mine, an American hunter living there, to go kill the beast. He did, and when he got up to the dead lion and examined it he saw that it had a very badly abscessed tooth which he reasoned had caused its madness. He drew the tooth, had it set in gold and gave it to me as a present which I wear around my neck today. "Man-eaters" frighten every-one, but I just don't see what difference it makes if a lion is going to kill you, whether he eats you himself or leaves you for the hyenas to eat after he has killed you. Either way you are dead.

A case of man-eating lion was recently reported in Tanzania, where two men had fallen victim. The game scouts were quickly on the scene and arrived at the second kill in time to find the dead man eaten halfway through. They shot one lion, but others got away. A few days later the Park warden of that area had left his office door open as he was working. He looked up from his desk to find himself staring into the eyes of two large male lion who stood in the doorway. The official report read, "Surprise and fear made him forget all about the pressing office work and the danger in which he found himself—and in turn he gazed back at the lion." (Does it mean because of "pressing office work" he should have said, "I'll be with you as soon as I finish this account?") The warden claims they stared at each other for ten minutes, none moving an inch, and finally after looking him over, they decided against eating him, gave a flick of their tails and made off. The report continued, "Greatly relieved, the warden dashed to the door and shut it—just as three lioness made their appearance near the office, apparently on their way to join the males." The report then congratulates the warden for his "calm and brave behavior in a very tight spot." The "tight spot" thing sounds to me as if the Africans are going to be just like the British about understatements. I thought the report would at least have said he ran to the door and puked or fainted or messed himself—but all he did was shut it.

The identity of individual animals can lead to funny situations. When the film *The Lion* was being made a large, cozy, tame old male called Zamba was flown in from California for the starring role. Our friend Monty Ruben who has been involved with many films here and has produced a couple of pictures himself—the latest being *The African Elephant*—was driving Zamba from one location to another and it was sitting happily in the back seat of his car. Passing the entrance to Nairobi Game Park he thought

he would have some fun at the expense of the African Game
Rangers who control the gate and patrol the Park. Monty parked
his car and walked up to a Ranger.

"I found this lion in Nairobi," he said (the Park is fenced on
the city side to stop the animals from wandering into the traffic).
"You shouldn't be so careless."

The ranger, looking anxious and puzzled, walked up to the car
and peered inside cautiously. With superb and quite unconscious
African aplomb he pricked the balloon of Monty's joke. "That's
not one of our lions," he stated flatly, and walked back to the little
office. No amazement at seeing a huge male lion in a car—no
questioning of Monty's story that he found it in the city—no
curiosity about the spectacular beast—just indifference having established that the responsibility was not his.

I love practical jokes like that. Nobody is physically assaulted
(pushed in swimming pool), caused real fear (putting a harmless
snake in the bed) or publicly humiliated (tripped up at gradua-
tion).

A close friend of Jock's at school was David Cockburn, whose
uncle was one of the all-time, world-series, superstar practical
jokers—and his era was just after the First World War. He played
many elaborate jokes such as the occasion when he and a friend
tricked the British Navy into sailing past them while one of them
took the salute, posing as a fictitious Indian Maharajah. But it was
a small, exquisite gem of a practical joke he undertook on a Satur-
day morning in Bembridge in the Isle of Wight which has always
enchanted me.

He bought a cow's udder from a butcher and carefully cut off
one teat. Selecting a composed looking policeman on a bustling
street corner he protruded the teat from the fly of his trousers and
just stood there looking in a shop window. Almost at once the
policeman approached him and with an embarrassed cough and
super British cool said, "Would you mind adjusting your dress,
sir?"

Glancing down in surprise he exclaimed, "Oh, I'm terribly

sorry, officer," and taking a large pair of scissors from his pocket he snipped off the teat and tossed it into a nearby rubbish basket.

To get back to wild animals again, I have a whole collection of notes I took at the museum here when we have attended wildlife lectures and films from time to time. One list reads:

1. There are one thousand lion in Serengeti and they are needed for wildebeeste control.

2. There are five hundred thousand wildebeeste.

3. Wildebeeste migrate but maintain their territory in a relative short breeding time. (I don't understand that, do you?)

Then there are some facts that are interesting because they have a purpose, or if not interesting they are at least purposeful—such as game ranching, which is the treating of wild animals like cattle in order to eat them, which I suppose is basically a good idea in such a protein-starved nation as this. Animals' digestive systems vary, and approximately thirty different species eat different foods and can live in the same territory without competing with each other. Therefore, you can farm perhaps a hundred mixed wild animals on the amount of land which could support only about thirty cows and have better land utilization.

The most interesting of all my notes was one on progress. With progress as the excuse, the government goes into Maasai country and immediately wants to improve things. For hundreds of years the Maasai and the animals have lived in a marvelous juxtaposition. They share the plains, and the animals never bug the Maasai, except for the lion taking cattle, and the Maasai never bug the animals other than spearing male lion for sport. Then along comes the government—the former British Government in the first instance—and decides that the Maasai herds are not only too small numerically but are composed of scrawny animals that are barely fit to be slaughtered by the Meat Commission. A decade of inoculations, dips, breeding programs and the rest are foist upon the Maasai cattle and the herds become larger and the cattle fat and sleek and the Meat Commission licks its corporate lips.

The trouble is that there are now more cattle and they are more voracious and are competing with the wild animals for the same amount of grazing that existed before. Man is more purposeful and forceful than wild animals, and it is the latter who will be pushed back and will dwindle. Well, you may say, man must advance, we are in the twentieth century and it is too bad. But is it? Perhaps in the nick of time—let us pray that it is so—the light has clicked on. Ecologists and economists are taking a careful look to see if there would not be better land utilization in a national sense by leaving the wide plains to the animals. Their existence in great herds in their natural setting draws thousands of tourists, and it is possible—indeed probable—that more cash benefit, if that is all progressing man can think about, will be derived from certain acreage by leaving the animals alone and raising beef elsewhere.

In a way I suppose it could be said that medicine has had a negative effect on the human race. We now have "death control" which results in people living twice as long and there are too many people. The answer is, of course, birth control, but it will be years before the concept of the quality of life rather than the quantity of life seeps through to the vast majority of Africans. Many children, for the unenlightened African, denotes riches, status, and security in old age, and for many of the semi-enlightened, represents all these things *plus* a blow against "the white man's master plot to limit the black man's numbers and eliminate the non-whites from the face of the earth by the diabolical use of birth control." Poor human beings—we are our own worst enemies so much of the time.

Poor animals, too. These days they are being so studied and scrutinized and enumerated. One unfortunate wildebeeste got tranquilized and woke up with an ecologist on his back.

I think it is very nice to know that a wildebeeste produces one calf a year and that a lion makes a dozen unsuccessful attempts at a kill for every one that succeeds, and if that is what interests you, I think you should throw yourself into it—I support any passion—but I really cannot see the point of studying animals—even chimpanzees—as a comparison to man. To me, the two are just so far apart—I mean has an animal ever studied man? And do you think one ever will? I clap if the zoologists study animals because they want to study animals, but to "help understand man" to me is just not an argument. For a better understanding of man, I think *man* should be studied more—we have exhausted the how-we-are-like-animals routine. Man, because of his brain, can break down the territorial imperative. I know it is very fashionable to say we are only animal and of course we are, but we are so much more as well. As Ayn Rand said in *The New Intellectual,* "An animal can learn to hunt and hide, but an animal has no choice in the knowledge or skills it acquires. An animal has no choice to be good or evil—it instinctively knows what is good or evil for itself and automatically acts in accordance with it to ensure its survival. It cannot act consciously for its own destruction. Man is the only animal which can do that. An animal has no power to extend or evade its knowledge or to ignore its own good, choosing evil and acting as its own destroyer."

An animal always adjusts to its background. Man alone has the power to adjust his background to himself. Man is the only animal who can suffer someone else's pain or share someone else's joy. And besides, the only animal that laughs is man.

A few years ago it was reported on European TV that two hunters were on their way to Kenya to bag Ahamed, the famous eleven-foot-tall elephant with the biggest tusks in existence—estimated at 160 pounds each. More than five thousand postcards urging special protection were sent to Kenya, and Jomo Kenyatta declared Ahamed a living monument of Kenya, totally protected from man. Now this giant elephant, who has to sleep standing up because he would never be able to get up again if he lay down, gives joy to many who travel to see him in his enchanted forest of Marsabit. Animal survival depends on man, or rather on the awakening of the conscience of man. Since 1900 an average of one animal species a year has become extinct—I read there are no more dodos, great auks (whatever they were) or Caribbean monk seals to name just three. For this we can blame man. Here perhaps we should follow the example set by the elephant—they are pacifists, they have no enemies at all, except for man, and then only as a defensive reaction. They are kind—they will feed a fellow elephant who has lost his trunk, will lead blind elephants, and will raise fallen companions with their tusks.

The spectacle of animals in general need not involve one emotionally. In fact, by marveling at the laws of nature in maintaining her balance, you erase the "ugliness." But it is strange how even a transitory association with an individual wild animal can emotionally involve one. Just a brief personal contact with an animal can get you in up to your heart. Jock and I once found a baby zebra stuck up to its neck in a muddy swamp with only its head showing. The entire herd was standing around aware of its plight but unable to help. How long the baby had been stuck or how long the hundred or so others had been waiting there, we didn't know—it could have been an hour or two, or it could have been a day or more. The Maasai tribesman who was with us tied a rope to the front of the car and looped the other end around the zebra's neck, then gently we backed the car away. The poor baby's neck stretched so that we worried the strain would break it, but instead the rope broke, and still the zebra had not budged an inch. After many tries the rope did begin to inch the baby from the mud a little at a time. Then it would be sucked back, we would pull it out, but the mud would gulp it back once more. All this time the other zebras looked on with hope, and I was sure the most hopeful looking one was the baby's mother. Finally, we won our battle with the mud and dragged the zebra clear. It lay there unable to stand or even open its eyes which were caked over with mud. We washed its face with water and tried to give it some to drink. The Maasai warned us to be careful because he had once seen another man trying to help a zebra in this same way have his finger bitten off. We hauled it to its feet, but the baby was so weak it could stand only a few moments, then would fall back again onto the ground. Finally, after many tries, it was able to stand by itself, and by then we were so encouraged, we left it, hoping that the warm sun would dry it out and revive it, and it would rejoin the herd. Later that afternoon Jock and I returned to the spot hoping to see it next to its mother running with the herd. But instead we saw our baby zebra dead, half eaten by hyenas, with the vultures finishing the rest. The herd was still there watching. Both of us were very upset and felt a great personal loss—for this had become "our zebra."

And therein lies a trap. For some, the wish to own an animal, especially a glamorous one, is so strong that in the outpouring of affection and love, the well-being of the animal is overlooked.

The whole question of exotic pets is something we have spoken and written about before. With a small handful of exceptions, our advice is to get a cat or a dog. Individuals who own lion, for instance, are usually doing it for some kind of ego trip. Possession of a lion *cub* is quite different, they are adorable and affectionate, but there comes a point when cub and owner should be parted in the interests of both—the lion gets too big and rough for the owner to have around and should in kindness be allowed to flex his muscles with animals of his own size.

Jack Paar and his family, with whom we have had so many warm and wonderful weeks in Africa, and who are our dear friends in the States as well, had an adorable lion cub named Amani. Fond as he was of the cub, and in spite of the anguish of parting, Jack recognized the need for Amani to leave Bronxville's winter and a small yard in order to join other young lion in five hundred open acres of Florida sunshine. The result was that the cub pined for him, grew weak, and died of a virus infection. Jack, who had steeled himself to act in Amani's best interests by letting him go, was not only heartbroken at the parting but was desolated by his death, wondering if he had done the right thing after all. No animals are as satisfactory as dogs if the measure is to be the kind of mutual affection and communication possible between an owner and his dog while it is alive—from puppyhood to old age.

Otters are great, of course, but again there are practical problems of much water, fishing and freedom.

Bushbabies—adorable squirrel-sized animals with huge round eyes and hands and feet like a monkey—are popular but are hard to house-train and are strictly nocturnal, only really coming into their own when you are ready for bed.

Our friend Gaby Sheikh decided to smuggle a bushbaby to a girl friend in the States. His trip entailed a night stop in Frankfurt and he checked into the hotel with the bushbaby asleep in his pocket and to save a lot of hassle he didn't tell the management, since no animals were allowed. When he went out for dinner he shut it in the bathroom so that it could bounce around and have some exercise instead of being cooped up in its little box.

Returning late at night he was puzzled to find the bathroom quite empty—no sign of the bushbaby. A more detailed inspection revealed that the single removable tile used by plumbers to get at the drain connection of the bath had been left out and the bushbaby had crept into the dark space between the tiles and tub itself. It would not come out, and there was no way of reaching it. Gaby's flight to New York was due to leave in three hours. He decided to confess to the hotel manager who was, as expected, very annoyed, and absolutely adamant that he would not instruct the hotel maintenance man to break tiles along the side of the bath—the only apparent means of solving the problem.

So Gaby had to arrange for a man from the zoo to come the next day and to hide with a kind of butterfly net at the ready, waiting to pounce on the bushbaby when it decided to come out—for no kind of food or coaxing or poking had persuaded it to leave the hole. He had to pay for the room for a further twenty-four hours, he had to pay a fee to the man from the zoo, he had to pay someone to deliver the bushbaby to the airport, (it was finally netted late the following day) and he had to take a taxi out to Kennedy to meet it. In the end it was a very costly present.

Although we haven't had any really harrowing adventures with animals other than Jock's being chased by a buffalo, and a couple of narrow escapes from lioness, and our almost being stabbed to death by a rhino's horn, we may have something truly harrowing to report in a few months. We are going to see the gorillas. (Note that I use the popular singular for the plural in all other cases—ten lion, a herd of elephant, five hundred buffalo, two rhino and so on, but because gorillas are my favorite of all animals—next to man —I want to set them aside and talk about twenty-five gorillas instead of twenty-five gorilla.)

The gorillas live in Ruanda with Diane Fossy. Others say Diane Fossy lives in Ruanda with the gorillas—it all depends how you look at it. In any case, they all live up there together. We've heard rumors that after her National Geographic grant runs out, she is going to open a small guest house and take people to see the gorillas so she won't have to abandon her studies. We will be the first in line. I have a beautiful hang-up about gorillas—I am just crazy about them. I have no idea why—I just adore watching them and to see them in the wild is my idea of ecstasy. In fact, if someone offered me a trip any place in the world—to Japan, South America, Australia, anywhere—I would say no thank you, but please can I go to Ruanda to see the gorillas? And, just think, it is about to come true, because if we don't go with Diane Fossy, there is a Greek who lives up there and his cook knows the gorillas and will take us to see them.

The main thing you need is leather gloves. You must climb in the rain forest for about five hours at an altitude of twelve thousand feet in slippery mud and wet. To keep from falling you grab for the bushes and branches, and in that area the bushes and branches have thorns—hence the gloves. Finally you reach "gorilla territory" (as Clark Gable said to Ava Gardner in *Mogambo*) and when the gorillas see you, they start to scream and beat their chests and charge. Yes, charge at you. Now you must not run, you must just stand there, for if you retreat the gorillas wring your neck off. (Isn't that adorable?) But if you stand your ground, they will stop, we are told, and prefer to believe. After this, it is rude to stare at them, so you stand there and break twigs and sneak looks at them and they stand there and break twigs and sneak looks at you.

We have invited the children to join us on our gorilla jaunt. But Dancy absolutely refuses to go, and McDonnell will consider it only for a huge sum of money and if someone will tie him to a tree because he says he knows he could never just stand there with a gorilla beating his chest, screaming and charging at him. Rick said politely that the trip sounded "fantastic, but what if the gorillas don't go away? Do you just have to stay there *still*, *breaking twigs* and sneaking looks at them?" I must find the answer to that question.

Anyway, I got to wondering what would happen if someone went up there in a gorilla costume? How would the gorillas react? I don't imagine they've ever seen a gorilla costume before. We had a vote as to who would wear it and Rick won, but he doesn't know it yet. He already has the costume though. One of his friends got married and at his bachelor's party they had the great huge cake in the middle of the floor, but instead of a naked lady popping out of it, Rick popped out in his gorilla costume, which he and I both thought was very funny, but the boys at the bachelor party and the groom didn't. People are so strange. Anyway, after his visit to the gorillas in his costume, Rick might be able to make a lot of money from the *Reader's Digest* for his "The Most Unforgettable Character I've Ever Slept With" article. Or I could have a lot of fun with the costume by wearing it into Dancy's bedroom. Or sending someone in it up into the mountains just an hour or so away from when we started to climb, and have them just sit there with crossed legs holding a martini glass and smoking a cigarette, and watch Diane Fossy's face. All kinds of possibilities.

So, my favorite animal next to man is the gorilla, then ants and then nudebrancts. Or maybe I just like using that word so everyone will think I'm smart, because people suppose you are intelligent if you know something they don't. (A nudebranct is one of those dopey things that undulate under the sea, swooping along in the Indian Ocean looking like a demented pancake.)

I often wonder if I would mind shooting a bird. I think I would. I even put flies and spiders and bees out of the window, and I don't like flies or spiders—though bees are intelligent and interest me slightly. I dislike birds, especially pet birds. I ignore the others but can admire some for their beauty—at a distance. One friend has this parrot that just walks up to me every time I go there and bites my ankle—damned bird. Someone else told me they have a parrot that is 135 years old and sings "Over There," that First World War song, all the time. An acquaintance walks her ducks every evening. Wasn't there a story about a New Yorker who tied a string on his cockroach and took it for walks? People do have strange things about animals. One American lady tracked us down when we were lecturing in the States and telephoned us to obtain a guarantee that she wouldn't see any caterpillars on safari—or she couldn't possibly come to Africa. Neither of us remembered seeing caterpillars in Serengeti, but we couldn't absolutely guarantee that she wouldn't.

As you may see, it is difficult to guarantee that anything will or will not happen in Africa. After one of our lectures an elderly lady came up to us and said she had been on safari in East Africa a few months earlier. I asked if she liked it, and she said yes she loved it, but it had been an embarrassment to her because it ruined her reputation. I asked why, and she said she was at a lodge in Kenya that had a pet zebra walking around the grounds with an African attendant. The attendant walked away for a few minutes, and the zebra started up the outside stairway to the second floor of the lodge just as she was walking around the bottom of the stairway. The zebra slipped and unintentionally kicked her in the eye, and although there was no serious injury, she did have a black eye. When she got back to the States the mailman rang her bell with a package and asked, "How did you get your black eye?" and she answered, "Well, I was in this hotel and a zebra kicked me," and he told everyone on the block that she was "drinking."

Because we come from Africa many people ask, "What do you think about zoos?"

The true answer is that I never really thought about zoos and when I first did—not thought, but felt, anything about them—my feelings were very unbeautiful. Jock's reactions to zoos were hardly enthusiastic—how could they be after seeing so many free wild animals. Ashamed that we really knew little about the subject, we rushed out and got some views on zoos.

A friend of ours, John Seago, catches animals for zoos all over the world. We always look forward to going to John's, not only to listen to his adventures, but to see the animals he had captured as well. There I have seen buffalo in boxes, cheetah in crates—all kinds of animals going all over the world. After capturing the animals in harmless traps, he takes them to his base in Nairobi and puts them in outdoor open pens where they can roam. They are then carefully conditioned for their forthcoming journey and their new life in captivity. Situated at the end of each pen, like a little house, is the crate in which the animals will eventually travel, and every day they are fed in the crates and petted there by the attendants—but the door is always left open so that they are free to go back into the pen. Quite soon the crate becomes their favorite place, and they will run in there for security if alarmed. After the animals have become happy and secure in their crates, the doors are closed, first for a short while, then for increasingly longer periods, and finally for good. At this point the crates are loaded onto a truck and shipped to their final destination. From the moment of capture to the moment of shipping may take three to four months, and most people are not aware of how much careful preparation is given to the animals during this conditioning period to ensure they do not suffer. Sadly, not all game trappers are as meticulous in this respect as John Seago, whose care and gentleness with the animals has made him so popular with zoo people all over the world.

Before knowing John, my only knowledge of animals being captured for zoos was from the movie *Hatari* in which John Wayne was portrayed as the game trapper. He lassoed rhino and other game from a chair attached to the outside of a Land-Rover —both he and the Land-Rover were flying around dramatically, and the rhino were dangerously charging, presenting the "action packed thrilling spilling spectacle" as advertised. Then John Seago, the real John Wayne, told me that the way they actually catch rhino, indeed almost all large animals, is usually by shooting them with tranquilizing arrows. Almost immediately the beasts start to stagger around as if drunk, finally falling down and going peacefully to sleep, after which they are gently loaded into a truck—and everyone is safe and happy.

Before meeting John, I used to worry about the horrors of the capturing of animals. One day in Nairobi I saw two giraffe, which I had met and actually fed at John's, being transported in crates on trucks to the port at Mombasa. They were looking around Nairobi with great curiosity. I wondered in which part of the world they would spend the rest of their lives, but soon I forgot about them. Three months later we were at a friend's for dinner in Philadelphia, and the hostess was peeved because her brother had not yet arrived. Eventually he came running in apologizing and saying,

"You'll never believe why I was late, but I swear it's true. On the turnpike the traffic was held up for over a mile because there were two *giraffes* on an open truck with their heads sticking out of these boxes—honest to God—and they were too tall to pass under the bridge. Men climbed to the top of the bridge and dangled carrots on strings below the level of the giraffes' heads trying to make them bend their heads low enough to pass under the bridge. It was unbelievable!" I was thrilled—*my* giraffe right in Philadelphia. Later I asked if the carrot trick worked, and he said no—that the last he had seen of them they had turned around and were going back in the direction from which they had come. I often wondered how they did get to the Philadelphia Zoo, and how could they like it there?

Years ago I stood once before a single giraffe in the Washington Zoo with tears streaming down my face because not only was the giraffe caged, but alone. How would he even know he was a giraffe if he could never see another like himself?

Everyone is always collecting money to have new animals sent

to zoos, and I really wanted to collect money to send this lone
giraffe in Washington back to Africa.

I thought of Isak Dinesen's words in *Out of Africa:*

In the harbour of Mombasa lay a rusty German cargo steamer,
homeward bound . . . Upon the deck there stood a tall wooden case,
and above the edge of the case rose the heads of two giraffes. They
were going to Hamburg, to a travelling Menagerie.

The giraffes turned their delicate heads from the one side to the
other, as if they were surprised, which they might well be. They
had not seen the sea before. They could only just have room to stand
in the narrow case. The world had suddenly shrunk, changed and
closed around them.

They could not know or imagine the degradation to which they
were sailing. For they were proud and innocent creatures, gentle
amblers of the great plains; they had not the least knowledge of captivity, cold, stench, smoke, and mange, nor of the terrible boredom
in a world in which nothing is ever happening.

Crowds, in dark smelly clothes, will be coming in from the wind
and sleet of the streets to gaze on the giraffes, and to realize man's
superiority over the dumb world. They will point and laugh at the
long slim necks when the graceful, patient, smoky-eyed heads are
raised over the railings of the menagerie; they look much too long in
there. The children will be frightened at the sight and cry, or they
will fall in love with the giraffes, and hand them bread. Then the
fathers and mothers will think the giraffes nice beasts, and believe
that they are giving them a good time.

In the long years before them, will the giraffes sometimes dream
of their lost country? Where are they now, where have they gone to,
the grass and the thorn-trees, the rivers and water-holes and the
blue mountains? The high sweet air over the plains has lifted and
withdrawn. Where have the other giraffes gone to, that were side
by side with them when they set going, and cantered over the un-
dulating land? They have left them, they have all gone, and it seems
that they are never coming back.

In the night where is the full moon?

The giraffes stir, and wake up in the caravan of the menagerie,
in their narrow box that smells of rotten straw and beer.

Good-bye, good-bye, I wish for you that you may die on the

journey, both of you, so that not one of the little noble heads, that
are now raised, surprised, over the edge of the case, against the blue
sky of Mombasa, shall be left to turn from one side to the other, all
alone, in Hamburg, where no one knows of Africa.

As to us, we shall have to find someone badly transgressing
against us, before we can in decency ask the giraffes to forgive
us our transgressions against them.

After becoming acquainted with the humane methods by which
animals are captured and the enlightened administration of the
modern zoo with its moats, spacious aviaries and occupational
therapy for animals, it is no longer necessary to be so depressed.
It is said by some that certain animals may be better off in a zoo
where no predators can reach them, where plentiful food is provided daily, and where they are not subjected to terrible droughts
and privations brought upon them by nature. However, I, personally, would rather have the good *and* the bad, the ups and the
downs of freedom, than just to remain bored the rest of my life,
and I like to think animals would too.

Zoos do enable millions of people who might otherwise never
see the animals to become aware of their existence. One can
hardly hope that people will contribute to conservation projects
at home and abroad if their imaginations have not at some time
been fired by the sight of a strange animal from distant lands.
One giraffe in a zoo could save multitudes of his cousins in
Africa.

It is also possible that certain rare species could be saved from
extinction by zoos which might keep them alive, pending the day
when they could cautiously be repatriated, always supposing that
man, the cause of all extinction, would mend his ways.

The film star, Jimmy Stewart, and his wife, Gloria, are great
conservationists, and one night at dinner here they told us that at
a zoo in the States there are three cages with the usual plaques
stating the proper name of the species, where it comes from and
so forth. But all three of these cages are empty—except for a
sign standing inside which reads: EXTINCT—ELIMINATED BY MAN.

It is easy to get very depressed if one broods about things like

that. The problems for man and animals are so monumental
that if you just sat and thought about them you'd go bananas—
and then you wouldn't be any good to yourself or to anyone else
for that matter. But living in Africa—possibly living anywhere
if you have the right frame of mind—there is always some nutty
thing that happens or that you hear about that cheers you up
again before long.

The British have a great sense of humor and particularly a
love of the ridiculous, and if the circumstances don't offer light
relief—why, they go right ahead and contrive their own. Wajir is
a tiny Somali village built round some wells in the middle of
Kenya's northern frontier district. For hundreds of miles in every
direction a sandy desert stretches, covered with stunted patches
of bush and an occasional small acacia tree. The British built a
small Beau Geste type fort there which they used as an administrative center. In the evenings the various officials, the
policeman, the veterinary officer, the administrator and the doctor
would gather on the flat roof of the building for drinks in the
cooling evening breeze. Only single men were posted to Wajir because it was thought to be too tough and isolated a place to send
the wives of married officials.

Years ago some "wag" (which means humorist—Jock just told
me that word) decided that a club should be formed and that
those who drank and chatted on the roof in the evenings should
become members. A Constitution and Rules were drafted and
the half dozen men voted one another in, elected a chairman
and secretary and established blackballing procedures—in fact
the whole works. They named this roof-top meeting place the
Wajir Yacht Club.

When the Prince of Wales visited Kenya just before he became King, the then chairman of the club wrote to him inviting
him to join as an honorary member and seeking that he bestow
the magic "Royal" upon the club. The Prince was so impressed
with the humor—that the men hundreds of miles from a spot of
water should have a yacht club—that he readily accepted, granted
the title, and it became officially The Royal Wajir Yacht Club.

Anyhow, years later an official from the Government Audit Department was due to visit Wajir for a couple of days on government business. The secretary of the club wrote to him in advance asking him to dine with the members at the club (all six of them) and informed him that it would be a "black tie" occasion. He was surprised, but dutifully packed his dinner jacket. Arriving at dusk he was shown to his quarters and informed that the party would start in an hour. He changed, made his way up onto the roof, and found the others wearing kikois, (loin-cloths,) sandals, no shirts and neat black bow ties around bare necks.

On the way up the auditor had stopped at Isiolo where he had eaten something which upset his stomach. Feeling the need, therefore, but having first enjoyed several good drinks and much laughter, he asked the whereabouts of the bathroom. Someone explained that although there was a little shack with an Elsan bucket around the back, most of them preferred just to walk out into the desert with a shovel. Besides, a cobra had been seen several times lurking around the shack and perhaps the desert was best in the circumstances.

The auditor was a fastidious man and had always been stationed in the city. The whole scene at Wajir was pretty outrageous by his standards, and the idea of a shovel and the desert was too much. He opted for the privacy of the hut despite the snake factor, and they gave him a small kerosene lantern.

A minute later there was a terrified yell from the shack and the poor man burst out, his pants around his ankles, clutching his rear end. The doctor was away, having ridden by camel to a village fifty miles to the north the day before, but a brave veterinary officer knew roughly what should be done. They bent him face down over a table and examined him by the flickering light. Sure enough, there were two red punctures from the fangs, about half an inch apart. With a razor blade the vet made four deep incisions, crisscrossing the area of the bite. Taking a mammoth swig of gin to give himself courage for what had to be done next, he applied his mouth to the exposed backside and sucked at the wound, spitting out the blood and hopefully the poison

with it. (Actually, there is no danger involved unless you have a
cut lip where the venom can enter the bloodstream. If you ac-
cidently swallow snake venom it is immediately rendered harmless by stomach juices—in case you're about to suck somebody's
snake-bitten bottom.)

They then patched up the shaking auditor with Band-Aids
and repaired to the roof once more to have several more drinks
and to see what would happen. He seemed to be all right, and
after a while someone suggested that it was ridiculous to have a
cobra in the loo and that they should dispatch it at once. A shot
gun was produced, they all had another drink, and strode in a
procession to the shack. The Game Warden reasoned that snake
shooting came under the aegis of his department, but the District
Commissioner argued that as the senior officer present the responsibility was his. The Agricultural Officer, who was the chairman of the Yacht Club, declared that club premises and related
problems were for him to resolve, and the Veterinary Officer
announced that since he was the one who had already exposed
himself to danger and unpleasantness as a result of the snake, he
wanted the satisfaction of killing it. Nobody felt that the matter
was any concern of the auditor—least of all him.

In the end the Game Warden, whom they all conceded was the
fastest and most accurate shot, tiptoed up to the shack while the
policeman held a flashlight for him. There was no door on the
little building since the entrance faced away from the club onto
empty desert. The bucket, with its seat and lid attached, sat
squarely in the center and they shone the flashlight into each corner. Nothing. Edging up, the intrepid Game Warden reached out
with his foot to flip open the lid which had fallen shut as the terrified auditor leaped up. Peeping inside over the barrel of the gun he
saw a large and angry chicken sitting on her eggs in the bottom of
the disused bucket. Her sharp pointed beak was open about half
an inch and she took a fierce peck at his shoe.

Rowlands and Livingstone

MAINLY BY JOCK

The first time I ever left the States I went to Ujiji. No one had ever heard of Ujiji, let alone me, so I was very surprised when I got to Paris to meet someone who had. The flight to Nairobi had been canceled and the manager of Air France, trying to placate me, was enquiring about my trip, and when I mentioned I was going on from Nairobi to Ujiji he answered gravely, "Ujiji is not a very funny place."

He knew his geography, but I think that every American must have had chicken pox when he studied African geography in school, and measles when he studied African history. I certainly must have. How many of us know it was Rowlands who said to Livingstone, "Dr. Livingstone, I presume?" when he finally found him in Ujiji? Stanley's real name was John Rowlands. He was illegitimate, and his Welsh mother refused to acknowledge him, so he was brought up in a workhouse. At fifteen he went to the States and was "adopted" by a wealthy American businessman called Henry Morton Stanley, whose name he bore for the rest of his life.

I had always assumed that East Africa sort of started with Stanley and Livingstone, but it actually all started millions of years ago with Australopithecus and Zinjanthropus. Who? Original man—man himself originated right here in Africa. But written history as we Westerners understand it started here about a hundred years ago. Isn't that a relief? I always figure I can cope with a hundred years of history, but when someone starts, "In the eleventh century . . ." I do not mean there wasn't a lot going on here in the eleventh century, but we know little about it. One of the earliest recorded things in this part of the world is the fact that in 1414 a giraffe was sent from Malindi to a Chinese Emperor. Giraffe were sacred in those days in China (as all animals are sacred in the States today). Then Vasco da Gama "discovered" Mombasa in 1498. The Arabs were hostile and attempted to sink his ships, so he sailed to Malindi, an Arab Sultanate, which was then a walled town of 6,000 people headed by the Sheik of Malindi who sat on a mother-of-pearl throne and listened to bugles and trumpets carved of ivory. He was an Arab of the ruling class, very rich, and the Africans were all his slaves. In 1589 a Turkish pirate tried to capture Malindi, but he was defeated by a Portuguese captain who was bright enough to move his single cannon around, firing it at the ship from different points, so that it looked as if he had a battery of artillery. Then 15,000 Zimba cannibals from the Zambezi ate their way northward devouring everyone in sight, and when they reached the outskirts of Malindi there were only thirty Portuguese to defend the town—but they were smart cookies. Half of them hid while the rest faced a Zimba charge. Those who had hidden then popped out at the rear of the Zimba hordes and decimated them with gunfire from behind.

After all that, a fine port was built at Mombasa, and this started the decay of Malindi which remained unheard of, historically, until 1903 when it officially became a town. There were eight Europeans living there then. In 1931 the first hotel, the Palm Beach, now called the Blue Marlin, was opened and two of the first tourists to stay there were Ernest Hemingway and Alfred Vanderbilt. Malindi has the distinction of being one of two towns in East Africa bombed in World War II by the Italians. (Today there is an Italian rocket site just a few miles north of Malindi. In the States we read in the papers that a rocket is going up at Cape Kennedy at 01:58 hours—and it does. When the Italians launched their rockets into space, the newspaper announcement states ". . . tomorrow some time between 9 A.M. and 3 P.M." So Italian.) Malindi only got electricity in 1957. It produces cashew nuts, kapok (which grows on big trees and frequently the white cotton bursts out of its pod and trims the tree like Christmas), whale throw-up, which is also called "ambergris"—but I bet you'll remember whale throw-up—and is used in perfumes (I'll never feel the same about perfume again), and sesame, which is not only the magic password to open doors but an oil-yielding seed.

I like romantic history like this—Arab Sultanates, sacred giraffe to China, Vasco da Gama, a fort called Fort Jesus—who could ever forget that name?—cannibals, Hemingway, whale throw-up, sesame—everything but a chariot race. And the names are fun to say, like "Tipoo Tip," the famous slave trader; or familiar like Stanley and Livingstone, who must be as well known as Laurel and Hardy; or exotic like Zanzibar; and the thoughts are awe-inspiring like "the origins of man."

But we, the Western World, became interested when everyone started running around looking for the Nile, and we became involved in this part of Africa for two reasons—evangelism-cum-guilt and curiosity. European countries had only abandoned slaving in the 1830s themselves, but with the fervor of the converted they immediately became sanctimonious and filled with righteous indignation that the Arabs should still be hard at it.

It is not easy to sustain moral outrage at a high pitch for very long, and luckily a sort of competition started (in our age it was who would get to the moon first, Russia or the U.S.A.) about who could find the source of the Nile.

Thus, with Speke and Burton and Stanley & Co. staggering around looking for the Nile—dramatizing the area, you might say—attention was simultaneously drawn to the efforts of the early missionaries—especially Livingstone—and the continuing slave trade for which Zanzibar was the headquarters, where fifty thousand slaves a year were being sold by Arabs to the Arab world. It was a dead easy and very profitable business because the slaving caravans would shoot elephant by the hundred and make the slaves carry the ivory to the coast where both the man and his burden were sold.

Some of the early Scottish missionaries who managed to establish tiny outposts in the interior were shrewd enough to deduce two things which they reported home with speed. First, they reckoned that martyrdom and evangelism were all very well, but that proper lines of communication and established centers for trade were really the only means of controlling the grisly business of unchecked, wide open, first-come-first-served slavery. Secondly, they could see that the lands that early maps haughtily described as "Sterile Regions" in actual fact looked pretty good in parts. Thus, to evangelism and curiosity, greed was now added. As the word got around in Europe, trading companies were established and then governments started to show direct interest.

It was mainly to thwart Germany's attempt to grab most of Central Africa that Britain decided to do something big and spectacular—and, as it turned out, difficult and dangerous—like building a railway from the port of Mombasa to Lake Victoria. By now they knew that Lake Victoria was the source of the Nile, but they figured, so what, we'll cash in on that too, even if it is an old gimmick.

What a grind! It took from 1896 to 1901 to complete, it cost the British taxpayers ten thousand pounds a mile—three times more than the bloke who had worked it out on the back of an envelope had figured—and everybody was as mad as hell. During the construction the British Government nearly fell over the voting of further funds, and snide remarks were bandied about in Parliament about the "Lunatic Line, leading nowhere, from nowhere, with no known purpose." In the end, of course, it all worked out, the slave trade was stopped for good and from the single-track beginning, a rail and inland waterway system was developed to serve the 700,000 square miles of present day Kenya, Uganda and Tanzania, carrying people, ivory in the early days, hides and skins, coffee, grain, cotton and, from time to time, Jock and me—we love traveling by train here and chugging round Lake Victoria on a steamer.

There is a great book called *The Iron Snake* by Ronald Hardy, which gives a thrilling and often hilarious account about building the railway. There were unending problems. For a start, Indian coolies had to be imported to do all the work because the various African tribes wouldn't—at that time couldn't—do the semi-skilled labor. In fact, one of the tribes, the Nandi, through whose territory the line passed for fifty miles before reaching Lake Victoria, very much resented the unseemly intrusion and would swoop down at night and swipe the rails as fast as they were laid by day, carrying them off into the forests where they would melt them down and make spears out of them, which they then threw at the workers laying more rails, and so on.

Unnerving as this may have been, it was nothing compared to the terror caused by man-eating lion in the Tsavo area. They created almost unbelievable panic among the coolies, 119 of whom were eaten, and the cunning the lion exhibited by snatching their victims from "secure" hiding places in the night, coupled with the inability of hunters to shoot them, had the effect of endowing them with magical and awesome powers. The work came to a complete standstill, and there was even a mutiny at Tsavo because of the lion. Colonel Patterson, a military martinet who was an engineer on the project, finally shot most of the lion, and it turned out that no more than half a dozen animals were responsible.

Patterson, according to Ronald Hardy, took himself very seriously and was inclined to be pompous, which made a number of things that happened to him at the Tsavo camp seem especially funny.

It seems he loved, above everything, the ritual of a hot bath each day and traveled with a stout portable rubber tub. Water had to be heated in cauldrons over an open fire and poured into the bath. One morning his Indian servant, seeking a short cut in order to save time, filled the tub with water and lit a fire underneath it. Patterson was awakened by the smell of burning rubber and arose to find the soggy charred remnants of the only bath tub in Eastern Africa.

That put him in a bad mood for what was to follow. An African sergeant named Abdullah was the next victim for the man-eaters. Patterson and a tracker followed the marks made by his body being dragged into the bush to the point where the lion had devoured him. Nothing at all remained except one boot—with Abdullah's foot still in it. The Colonel, responsible for burials, among other annoying duties, was confronted with a problem. Should he return the corpse—the foot, that is, to Sergeant Abdullah's wives at Kilifi—or should he bury him (it) then and there at Tsavo? And if the latter, was he justified in laying on a full military funeral for just a foot? After much heart searching and thumbing through the manual he chose the correct military funeral and Sergeant Abdullah, in an appropriately reduced casket, was interred with honors and a salvo from his smartly uniformed squad.

Shortly after this Patterson was confronted with another irritating burial problem—as if he didn't have enough to do trying to build a bridge over the Tsavo River with a gang of hysterically nervous coolies that was diminishing nightly as the lion grew fatter. To try to keep out of the reach of lion at night, the poor men were sleeping high up in trees, on top of a tall steel water tower which only held a few, in trenches barricaded with dense thorn bushes; indeed anywhere offering a degree of safety. There were a number of tremendously strong steel water tanks for use further up the line, which would easily accommodate one man and which had a hole in the top through which a person could squeeze, but not a lion. One luckless Hindu climbing into his refuge found that it was already occupied by a spitting cobra—and that was the end of him. His pals didn't find out about this until the morning, by which time rigor mortis had set in and it was impossible to get him out of the small opening. There being no equipment sophisticated enough to cut the tank open, and the ground being so hard that it would have taken too long to dig a hole big enough to bury the whole tank, Patterson demonstrated his flair for improvization. He proposed to roll the thing along the track to the half-completed bridge over the river and to push it in. The burial party—perhaps "sinking party" would be more apt—were dubious and had reservations about a ceremony that seemed to diverge more widely than they cared to consider from the Hindu practice of open cremation. However, in the absence of any better suggestion, they glumly agreed and the weird funeral procession was under way. Pausing at the extremity of the bridge, the grim but impeccable Patterson uttered a few words fitted to the occasion, gave a shove, and with a big splash the deed was done. But instead of a burial, albeit an odd one from a Hindu standpoint, the mourners found that they had participated instead in a launching. By ill luck the weight of the body in the tank was so arranged that the hole remained uppermost, well clear of the waterline, so that there was no hope that it would fill up and sink even if it floated all the way to the Indian Ocean a hundred miles away.

This is where Patterson truly showed himself to be a man of action and initiative. Seizing his rifle, he set off down the river bank in pursuit of the bobbing coffin and emptied an entire magazine into it as low as he could. It sank with loud gurgles and some large bubbles.

Despite such difficulties and the unforseen expense of it all, the railway line finally reached the shores of Lake Victoria at what is now Kisumu.

In the years after its completion, the British taxpayers were still irked by having put up the cash and having seen little in the way of immediate returns. So the Government started to encourage settlement in Kenya by farmers and planters from England. The idea was that they would grow crops that would be carried by the railway to Mombasa, and in the end the line would pay for itself.

Meanwhile, there were a number of interesting decisions to be made. Though there were vast tracts of totally uninhabited land, there were also very definite tribal areas belonging to each of the forty-two tribes living in Kenya. To give due credit, the

British decided that they should not just grab everything, pushing back the Africans or shooting them, but that the tribal boundaries then in existence should be frozen. The white man could settle on land that didn't seem to belong to anybody. There was an exception in that they negotiated a somewhat dubious treaty with the Maasai, whereby the settlers could farm a carefully defined area of their land (for practically zero rent or services in return). Even in later years the Maasai were not too upset by the deal because they could afford to be generous since they were a numerically small nomadic tribe who reigned over much more land than they could ever possibly utilize.

It was decided that the British would administer Uganda, could initiate government schemes with the object of profit, but that there would be no settlement as in Kenya. Tanganyika was a German possession and was to remain such until the First World War. (After the war the then League of Nations gave Britain a mandate to administer the territory, but again there was to be little settlement as compared with Kenya.)

The African tribes that inhabited these countries received the white man with varying degrees of disinterest, depending upon the immediacy of the impact on any given tribe. Those in remote areas hardly noticed anything—life was not to change suddenly for them, and in really isolated corners life has not changed that much for the people even today. One notable exception is that whereas in the past famines reduced their numbers every few years, now trucks, the train—even planes—carry food to them in lean times.

Probably the most advanced social structure the early missionaries and colonialists found belonged to the Baganda people of Uganda, whose king had his palaces where Kampala stands today.

In the northeastern part of Kenya, the Somalis were advancing, extending their borders south a little further each year. Tall, refined and highly intelligent Hamitic people who embraced Islam, they were slowly pushing south and the relatively backward Bantu tribes they encountered were no match for them.

Colonialism halted their advance, but it is interesting to speculate how far they would have reached by now had they not been checked.

The missionaries of different denominations competed with one another (to the confusion of the Africans) for converts and souls. Perhaps their most important contributions were schools and hospitals. The written word was introduced, and with the arrival of vaccines the death rate, especially of babies, declined sharply. Expressed the other way around, the birth rate or survival rate rose dramatically. Even so, life expectancy is still only thirty-eight years in Tanzania today.

The Colonial Service planted its officers throughout the vast area of East Africa—the administrators, the doctors, the veterinarians, the soil conservationists, the schoolmasters, the agricultural officers and, we must not forget, the police. Tribal conflict and cattle rustling, traditionally highly diverting pastimes enjoyed by everybody, were forbidden. Soccer was no real substitute for a good skirmish with the neighbors across the valley, and tiresome restrictions were introduced. Things were no fun any more. The British, while individually benevolent and well motivated for the most part, made life dull and they certainly succeeded in making the Africans feel inferior.

Much nonsense has been spoken and written about the altruism of British Colonialism. It was done for reasons of profit, for gaining new trading areas and markets, commodities, and hoped-for riches. It was done for spheres of influence, for the warm feeling of possession and control, and to stop others from having it instead. If the end results were often "good," it was because of the enlightened methods of going about it and the extraordinarily high standards of the officers in the Colonial Service. But Britain only relinquished her colonies when she could no longer hold them—not when she was magnanimous enough to grant them sovereignty, as she would sometimes have the world believe.

Much nonsense has been written, too, about the brutality of British rule. True, there were rough and shameful incidents from time to time—the police or army clashing with tribesmen; individual settlers beating or even shooting an employee—but these incidents were isolated and exceptional, not the facts of everyday life. On the contrary, the improvement of health (witness the fantastic population explosion), agriculture, communications, and the establishment of the rule of law were the matters preoccupying the administrators. No, harm to the people was not physical—they could have borne that—it was the aloof, arrogant and generally patronizing attitude of the white man that caused much longerlasting psychological wounds.

The early settlers were quite something. There were real pioneers among them who opened up the country—my father introduced the first Jersey cattle, and others brought fruits and seeds and trees and methods and transformed the diets of many tribes. Potatoes and maize (corn) became staples almost overnight. Men like Lord Delamere went through vast fortunes importing cattle to upgrade the puny native stock, but losing them all again and again to strange local diseases and deficiencies. He persevered until the problems were licked and he was nearly broke.

But there were others, too, in search not of challenges but of an easy life of sundowners (cocktails) and servants. Labor was cheap, land was cheap, and with little effort it was possible to maintain a life that was vanishing in Europe for all but the very rich. There was polo and racing and big-game hunting and elegant country-house living, and much fornication with other people's wives and are-you-married-or-do-you-live-in-Kenya? and weekend parties lasting seven days, and the Muthaiga Club where half the members were titled British and the other half were retired colonels and captains and majors from India. There were drop-outs from Europe, and remittance men—paid to stay away from England by their prominent families for such breaches of good taste as cheating at cards at Brooke's or getting the maid pregnant and being found out—and even some scandals uncomfortably close to Buckingham Palace.

Meanwhile some of the Africans became educated, visited

Europe, fought in World War II abroad, and returned home and could not set foot inside Torr's Hotel—except as a waiter.

The Indians who had stayed after the railroad was finished bred as if it had been ordained from above that they should outnumber all men, and they became traders, big and small, and no matter how far you got from Nairobi or Kampala or Dar es Salaam there was an Indian store where you could buy a tin of plums or a fan belt for the Ford or caviar or a blanket or a bar of yellow soap.

And more Africans became educated and visited America and became doctors and could not set foot inside the Stag's Head Hotel in Nakuru—except as a waiter.

And still more white men arrived from Britain who were mechanics and had not been to London University and had no degree and who had two servants within twenty-four hours of stepping off the plane and became instant Bwanas and loved the taste of the beer in Torr's Hotel and the Stag's Head.

You see, what was happening was that the white man had said, in effect, for half a century, "You are not like me. You are not yet educated and cultured and we believe that you do not wash as often as we do and you had better go and sit over there."

For some funny reason (it was hard for an African to grasp) he said the same thing to the Asians, and yet many of them already owned factories and chain stores and two Ford Mercurys and a Mercedes and in two known cases had sons at Harrow; and furthermore, these kinds of Indians washed very frequently.

It began to dawn on the Africans that even when they became like the white man, exactly like him so that you could not tell talking in the dark who was black and who was brown or white, that they would still not be allowed to participate, or own land at Naivasha, or be a police officer rather than a sergeant, or grow coffee on their tribal land in the reserve (it had something to do with restricting the quantity grown, thus keeping the price up for the white man), or go with their friend the professor from the University of Wisconsin, who was here on a visit, to Torr's Hotel for a beer.

Anyhow, it was all very demoralizing and degrading—particularly so when the European history books which the white man waved in the schoolroom with such pride spoke of "free elections," "majority rule," "universal franchise," "equality of man" and "escaping from oppression."

The Kikuyu tribe in Kenya is the largest single tribe in the country—about two million at present. They are unlike most other Africans throughout the continent in that almost at once they grasped the Western man's belief that individual achievement and excellence is considered laudable. Perhaps Tanzania's Chagga and Nigeria's Ibos should be classed with them, but for the most part Africa's peoples still traditionally submerge their own individual identities and conform to community requirements, functioning as part of that community first and only secondarily pursuing individual goals.

The Kikuyu, by geographical accident—the southern tip of their small but densely populated tribal area touches Nairobi—and by temperament, were thus the right people to grapple with the twentieth century. Intelligent, aggressive, acquisitive and not frightened of hard work, they plunged into the new life, soaking up both ideas and techniques. It was the Kikuyu who worked the farms and learned to drive the tractors for the settlers. It was largely the Kikuyu who served the carefully chilled champagne in Muthaiga Club and who mastered the use of lathes in the industrial area. And, finally, it was the Kikuyu who grasped the possibilities of what might be accomplished by concerted political action. It took about twenty-five years from the arrival of the first Europeans till the moment when a handful of Africans, mostly Kikuyu, and egged on by a few Indians, realized the possibilities.

It took another twenty-five years before anything of real significance happened. True, an African member or two ("nominated" by the Colonial Office, not elected by popular vote) sat in the legislature which was otherwise comprised of settlers elected by other settlers and Colonial officials. True, African District Councils had a limited say in local affairs (carefully watched over by the British District Commissioner), but there was still no real African political force.

Then came Mau Mau. The aims and objectives of the movement were an end to Colonial power and a redistribution of land occupied by white settlers. Jomo Kenyatta had nurtured the movement from the start, and the British thought they could halt it by detaining him and half a dozen henchmen. But the impetus was already there, the framework existed, and it was after his detention and isolation in a desert far to the north that the action really began.

In point of fact, and despite dramatic world coverage, only thirty-two European civilians were killed by the "terrorists" or "Freedom Fighters" (it depended which side you were on), but thousands of British troops and police were engaged in trying to restore order.

Mau Mau, as a political force, had weaknesses. It drew its support largely from one tribe, the Kikuyu, and a couple of cousin tribes but did not attract much active nationwide support from other tribes, who, in aggregate, made a large majority. Also, following the detention of Kenyatta, it took a turn toward extreme violence, oath-taking, and intimidation, directed largely against those members of the tribe who, while supporting the general objectives, had reservations about some of the extreme means. This allowed the British, past masters of "divide and rule," to drive a wedge down the center of the tribe by enlisting support from disaffected Kikuyu.

While all this was going on, far away on the west coast of Africa, in Malaya and the Far East, and throughout the British Empire one-time colonies were being granted independence. Ghana was already a sovereign state. It was apparent to many in Kenya, black and white alike, that although Mau Mau was under control and Britain was firmly back in the saddle, ultimate independence was not far away. British Prime Ministers spoke of "winds of change blowing through Africa" and it was obvious to

Cabinet Ministers in London that their own electorates in Britain would not stand for the shooting and detention of thousands of black men in order to maintain a way of life for a handful of whites.

All that remained was to decide the method of transition and a timetable. Britain, already experienced in empire liquidation, understood the necessity of handing over power slowly and to a population that agreed among themselves, but not so slowly as to cause frustration, and on December 12, 1963, the Kenya flag flew over a country ruled by Jomo Kenyatta. Tanzania and Uganda were already newly free.

The reality of independence and the assumption of responsibility is a sobering thing—for whoever may wind up in the hot seats. Even before the final date the African leaders, a surprisingly conservative bunch considering the fiery demagoguery of pre-independence politics, realized that to throw out all the Europeans and Indians and to distribute settler land (a relatively small area when compared with the lands which the Africans had held all along) would accomplish nothing but a death blow to the economy, and they needed an economy to provide the means of filling election promises—more schools, better hospitals, new roads. They also needed technical know-how and a world image of "reasonableness" to attract foreign capital and investment.

From among the Europeans, those who could not stomach the thought of being ruled by black people packed up and went to South Africa, Rhodesia and Australia. The Africans and the remaining Europeans (there had been vitriolic differences among the Europeans prior to independence about the course of events) were glad to see them go. It is a curious thing, that even though the Africans hurled insults and abuse—often justified—at the white colonialists as a monolithic entity, the relations between individual Africans and Europeans who worked for or with each other and came into contact in many ways was really quite good, man to man.

It was exciting for an African at a political rally to envisage himself oppressed, beaten by a red-eyed settler and having his blood sucked mercilessly as he toiled at back-breaking labor under the lash of a rhino-hide whip. But when he truthfully considered his own case he had to admit that the Bwana seldom scolded him, paid something over the going wage for the job, had taught him many useful tasks over the years—increasing his pay as he learned—and was contributing out of his own pocket to the education of his eldest son.

The European, though he didn't see why those politicians should say so many unfair things at rallies, really liked the Africans who worked on the place. He found them, by and large, cheerful, philosophical in attitude and very nice people, always ready to laugh and prepared to put in a tremendous effort if you worked with them on an important task. And recently he had met Africans other than workers. Take the new secondary school headmaster and his wife down at the village. Really bright chap with a good sense of humor who had spent two years at that teacher training college near Bournemouth on the south coast of England not far from where grandmother still lives. Asked him to the house for a drink a couple of times and Barbara gives his wife a ride to Nairobi for a day's shopping now and then. Next year our Tommy will be at Nairobi School with their young Njuguna. He can collect the kids at half term and I'll take them back—save a lot of mileage for both of us. Tommy speaks Kikuyu with Njuguna sometimes and is becoming quite an expert on tribal customs.

And so the blending proceeds. Cultures and customs run deep and most Africans still prefer to relax with other Africans; Europeans with other Europeans. Friendships between black and white are formed round the catalyst of work for the most part— sometimes mutual interest. There is economic interdependence in that the African may need European capital and know-how and the European may need African political approval for his scheme. But the friendships thus formed are not sterile or cynical because of it and trust and affection can easily creep into such a relationship parallel with the recognition and quiet acceptance of different origins and backgrounds. The children at school stand a chance of real relationships—if their parents on either side will leave them alone and allow it to happen.

And so life ticks along in a number of independent African states. The ordinary African may wonder why the Europeans still have big houses and two cars—but at the same time they do provide a lot of jobs and on the whole behave reasonably. The European has fits of frustration at the incompetence and inefficiency and corruption, and he cannot conceive how it can take six months to get a decision out of the Government Ministry for such a simple project which can only result in benefit to Africans and the country—but meanwhile it is a nice place to live.

But in Kenya what are we talking about?—40,000 white people and about twice that number of Asians among eleven million Africans. The majority of European kids leave when they must start to look for a job, and those Asians who can manage it go to England or India. Those of minority groups who already have a job may retain it and may well retire here. Few new people from overseas will come. Kenya, and all the other independent African states are just that—African states. They want to get what they can from the white man and the West, but they want to do their own thing in their own way, as they should.

There are signs of hope and a wish to advance, but there are also annoying and unsettling aspects for those who care to see.

For instance, there is too much development of the cities, where only 5 per cent of the population live, and too little effort to make the rural areas prosperous.

Incredibly, there is a "brains drain." Many of the super-bracket African students, the really bright kids returning from Europe or the States or Russia, get depressed at the slowness of things and at "old guard" political leadership and nepotism. Let's face it, not everyone is a potential missionary, dedicated to helping his less-fortunate brethren, and these ambitious young men and women may give it a go for a year and then decide that they would be happier and more prosperous continuing their work as professors in physics at a superbly equipped university in Manchester, where they can pursue fascinating research proj-

ects amid sophisticated equipment. Maybe they have become
theater buffs or are deeply into Yoga or Thelonius Monk. I
mean, really, there is not a hell of a lot to do in Kakamega
after the day is done. So they return to the bigger brighter scene
of stimulation and challenge and awareness. They fly back to
Sweden or Canada or Frankfurt.

One of the troubles for the intellectual African is that there are
not enough of him—yet. In Africa such a man finds himself being drained all the time by those around him seeking information,
picking at his brains. But who fills *him* up? Who recharges his
batteries or causes the electricity to crackle by asking him a
penetrating question or challenging a theory he has just posited?
It has been estimated that nearly half of the "super brights"
from independent Africa do not live and work in Africa. The
mass of the people of any country never get off their butts and
make themselves or their country great—they have to be led or
kicked or coaxed or shoved by a tiny handful of visionaries. With
half of the true brains expending their energies elsewhere, the
chances of meaningful progress are correspondingly reduced.

Then there is the inability of a nation to leapfrog—to leave a
whole slice of unnecessary tediousness out of its development by
observing others. It would be like asking a child to skip adoles-
cence—often a tiresome phase for child and parent alike—but
impossible to miss out.

Nationalism is a good example. When the more advanced
countries of the world are just lowering barriers and advancing on
joint ventures, when there is increasing recognition that nationalism is a menace likely to lead to war and to hamper progress,
what do you see in Africa? Impassioned nationalism, puerile
posturing vis-à-vis the country next door, and incitement to war.
But it is not hard to see why. Most African countries contain
many different tribes, and if the country is going to work, the
tribes must all feel a loyalty toward it, so feelings of national
identity must be encouraged. Individual African leaders, Haile
Selassie and Kenyatta to cite two, have proved themselves to be
master defusers of incendiary situations between neighbors, but

mostly the tub-thumping of "nation" rings out daily through the continent—and it is so *boring*.

Now, more than at any other time in history, there is developing an "international set," not of socialites or jet-setters but of ordinary Americans or Africans or Danes who have lived and worked and come to know India or the Argentine or Iran. They work for large companies with widespread interests or the World Health Organization or airlines. These people see the stupidity, the outmodedness of nationalism, and understand it more each day. But nationalism is something to be consciously dismantled when you have enjoyed it and gotten over it—it is not, unfortunately, a phase you can simply leave out.

Another example of a phase that could well be missed out in Africa is what Charles Reich described in his *Greening of America* as "Consciousness II." Briefly, this states that material possessions plus job status equals success. The swimming pools, the fancy cars, the superior house, the vice-presidency of the company all add up to, "Look at me, I am a success." And of course the unstated, "I am only a schoolteacher or not too senior a social worker or a librarian, and I am a failure."

Just when the kids in the Western World are questioning the artificial values of gross materialism and are concentrating instead on proper attitudes toward other human beings, many Africans are moving right into the gray-suit, shiny-car, cocktail-lounge syndrome. If only they could miss all that.

But, of course, as Albert Camus said, "Exclusion is only gratifying when self-imposed." To reject that which you have had, and experienced—maybe even enjoyed—is one thing. Never to have sampled it and to be expected to by-pass it loftily is quite another. The American kids disdain the affluence which they have experienced all their lives, but the Africans have never known affluence and are dying to try it on for size.

In actual fact, one of the best things about most African societies is the attitude toward other human beings. They tend to be easygoing, they do not interfere, they are dignified and hospitable to strangers, sharing that which they have, and they have a strong sense of family and community. Ironically, many of them are already the desired "Consciousness III" people, whom Reich would have us be, without knowing it, and are taking a step *back* by going overboard for symbols and jobs that shout "status" in a sense that is on the way out in the West.

An African student who arrived in the States recently, in a neat blazer, gray flannel pants and closely trimmed hair to start on a law course was utterly bewildered to find his peers at the college rejecting those very things he had come all that way to acquire.

To go to a party given by a typical successful Nairobi African—a top civil servant, maybe, or a businessman—is a pretty distressing experience. The "worst from the West" might describe it. For a start, everybody will be ultra well-dressed in impeccable business suits—self-consciously so. Next, there will be much too much heavy and deliberate drinking of Western booze—gin, scotch, brandy and so on—producing the same banal inanities that you would encounter in the States at a convention of hosiery manufacturers in Omaha. Somebody will turn on music—early Elvis or Jim Reeves. The lighting will be far too bright and a machinery manufacturer from Germany will be making offensive and embarrassing advances to some pretty little African girl who giggles because she doesn't want to be rude. Alitalia ash trays will be found on plastic-topped 1946-style tables, and the whole scene is unnatural, un-African and undignified.

Let's fantasize how it might be instead. Africans are basically relaxed people. Some form of Kaunda suit (a collarless tunic with matching trousers) instead of pin stripes and neat ties might be more comfortable, or for the daring, a robe of some kind and sandals. Instead of standing around a la cocktail party, why couldn't they sit in a circle or a number of smaller circles on low stools or cushions, with a token candle to symbolize a fire in the middle and coconut shells or bambo sections for ash trays. The lighting could be low—more like an African hut—and drinks could be served in cow-horn cups—an African pombe, or scotch for the visitors and those who like it. Tribal music, and lots of it is available on records, might be played quietly in the background. A ritual of *Hodi* and *Karibu,* African requests for entry and welcome respectively might be required in the interests of good manners, together with equivalent farewells. Well, maybe I got a bit carried away and maybe, too, you can't just invent or contrive a way of doing things, but at least what I have suggested would contain some elements of the African's own courtesy and customs, albeit diluted and updated. And it has to be better than a cocktail party, for God's sake.

But I fear it is wishful thinking to suppose that phases through which England and America have passed and which are unattractive can be left out completely by developing countries.

Occasionally there are encouraging signs. The African shows indications of not wanting to be a carbon copy of the white man, but of devising his own blend of "African-Modern." To zero in on an "African culture" and to retain it is not practical, if only for the reason that there are so many very different African cultures dotted around the place, even within the boundaries of most African states—such as the forty-two tribes in Kenya, for example. True, some are cousin tribes to each other, but fifty miles away are utterly different people who eat fish and do not circumcise. Whose culture will be the model?

For the present generation of middle-aged Africans through much of the Continent who have had enough education to place them in "top" positions, there exists a set of circumstances that can cause them grave psychological difficulties. While older and less-emancipated men still tend to be steeped in tribal ways, and while younger men stand a chance of being able to understand and to adjust to the twentieth century, the middle "emerged" bracket find themselves belonging neither to the old African order nor to the new Western world of the twentieth century.

These men marched out of the village, leaving behind traditional ways and a belief in spirits, and bravely donned the white man's gray suit and his scientific mode of thought. They abandoned the tribal way, but not quite. They adopted the way of strangers, but not quite. There is still a yearning for the familiar, for the feeling of background and belonging and identity.

And in the new camp they just fell short as well. Dealing in a strange tongue, in an entirely new currency of thought processes, they were at a disadvantage, and for racial reasons the white men did not adopt them socially to an extent that would have made it more bearable. Academic education alone, they found, was insufficient and a degree, while very handy, did not necessarily bolster the recipient with sufficient self-assurance and that infuriating confidence which seemed to carry the European through so many difficulties. Inevitably, feelings of inferiority crept in and with them the attendant neuroses. Many Africans in this bracket tend to posture unreasonably, lash out in bursts of frustrated rage, mouth clichés and never admit that they or their colleagues could be wrong.

Self-awareness, the spirit of fierce competition, introspection, with its attendant self-doubt—these are all unfamiliar to the tribal African who is inclined simply to accept things as they are and to enjoy the security of his role and automatic progression within the framework of tribe.

In the bewildering world of the white man one is expected to stand or fall by one's own efforts. For the first cadre of Africans to enter the tough new order of things, not only were the rules unfamiliar—the entire premise was alien, and nothing in African life for a thousand years had prepared them for what they were to encounter.

The present generation of African teen-agers who are the sons and daughters of those who made the initial plunge may very well stand a better chance. Many of them have grown up in cities, have spoken English or French from early childhood, are orientated to cars and Western music and television, and have been raised all their lives within an educational system introduced by the Europeans. They have not had to abandon the tribal spirits— they never really knew them intimately—nor have they suffered the guilt pangs of those who turned their backs on deeply inculcated ways. Their lives have not been subject to the interruption

—that lack of continuity—experienced by the man who abruptly stopped being African in the true sense, and became instead a not quite white man. Not that being a "white man" in this sense is necessarily any kind of a target or standard to which an African should aspire; indeed many of the younger white men in the West are at this very moment questioning and rejecting much that the white man has become. Perhaps a better description would be something along the lines of "twentieth-century man" or "modern man."

In any event, these young Africans raised in cities by well-to-do parents must face a different set of problems. As yet there are too few of them and they may suffer the loneliness of "odd man out." And they can be subject to a different guilt that arises from feelings verging on scorn they may have for their less sophisticated brethren or a twinge of embarrassment experienced when a truly country cousin comes to town. We know young Africans who really feel more "at home" in London or San Francisco than in the village where their grandparents live.

There is so much to drag down the would-be modern African. As if the demands of grappling with a sophisticated job were not enough, there is a whole range of distractions and responsibilities visited upon him by his large, extended family. To say nothing of his wife and children, sick aunts need money, second cousins want financial assistance to continue studies, grandparents need corrugated iron sheets for the roof of their house, a nephew wants a word dropped to the personnel manager of a factory (possibly bribe money, too,) so that he can get a job—it is endless. By tribal custom he is obliged to help them, and very possibly he is the only member of his family who is in a position to do so. Instead of going to a golf course or the movies after work, like his Western counterparts, the poor man leaves one set of problems in the office and returns home to another set. Sometimes it is just too much, and instead of going straight home, he joins friends for a drink or three—and then that becomes yet another problem.

I sometimes think that the whole thing has become cockeyed,

and I end up feeling more sorry for the diligent capable African who has just made it into the executive ranks of an insurance company than I do for his brother who lives on seven acres of rich soil a hundred miles from the city. One could argue convincingly that the latter enjoys a better quality of life even though he lives a subsistence existence and his brother draws a decent salary.

But what really impresses me over and over again is the two-phase battle fought with alien ground rules that a number of Africans nevertheless succeed in winning. First there is the escape from village and tribe and the arduous climb up a strange academic and technical ladder, which must then be followed by survival in a new jungle where tortuous trails wind through the undergrowth of bureaucracy and the tangled forests of technology and legality. The African who can find his way and who emerges smiling with his perspective and integrity still intact, is, by my measure, quite somebody.

There is no turning back now. Progress has come to Africa along with all the dire pitfalls and the ecstasies of fulfillment that accompany it. But this is a long and complicated subject, and in this book we are only trying to give a glimpse, not a post-graduate course, for heaven's sake, of some of the factors that influence the outlook of Africans vis-à-vis the modern world.

It seems fair to say that Christianity, as a substitute anchor in the place of tribal custom and belief, has failed. Not only have the diverse denominations available confused everybody, but the fact that most of the white men whose religion it is supposed to be neither believe in it nor practice it is hardly a convincing advertisement.

As Africa opens up to the world, friendships spring up between her people and others of different races and cultures, but I have a feeling that it is easier for two people to come close when both are subconsciously confident in their own cultural or national backgrounds than when one of them is not. By this I mean that a relationship between a Muslim and a Christian or a Swedish agnostic and an Ethiopian—between widely diverse people who

nevertheless feel secure at their home base of nationality or
culture—stands a much better chance of true depth and reality
than between such a person and a modernized Achole tribesman
from Uganda, for example. This is a subject which I have discussed with not a few ambassadors from around the world who
have lived in Nairobi. One hears the same thing from them again
and again.

In Ceylon, they will tell you, they made friends with this delightful Ceylonese family. They write to one another three or four
times a year and the daughter is coming over to spend next summer with them. Then they know this wonderful man from Iran,
and of course their dearest friend in all the world is Thanny from
Burma. But after five years in Africa they have to honestly confess
that all they have established here is a few pleasant enough but
largely superficial relationships . . .

Why? In attempting to answer I must send some purely fictitious characters skating over ice which I know to be thin.

Let's imagine a highly educated Ugandan Achole working for
a United Nations agency in New York and let's surround him
with a Swede, an Ethiopian and a Hindu from India. The Achole
has, of course, stopped being a full-fledged Achole. He has left the
hut and the river and the cattle and but for a fleeting visit home
from time to time (when he stays in his brother's new stone house,
anyway) none of his early life is a part of his present self.

The Indian, the Ethiopian and the Swede have stopped being
typical representative figures as well, but after work the Indian
can find a temple, the Ethiopian a Coptic church, and the Swede
can go out for a smorgasbord—though in practice none of them
will do any such thing. They will go to a movie on Forty-second
Street with their Achole friend to see *Naked on Roller Skates*.

After the movie the Swede and the Ethiopian peel off to go
home on the subway, change their minds, and head for a small
but excellent restaurant on Third Avenue. The Swede is having
bad marital problems and his ulcer is becoming serious. So, all
through dinner he unburdens to the Ethiopian, who as a friend
of the family, knows all the background anyway.

Meanwhile, between Fifth Avenue and Sixth Avenue on Fifty-sixth Street the Achole and the Indian are enjoying a superb Italian meal. The Achole is secretly worried because his nephew, who has recently arrived at Michigan State University on a scholarship, has fallen in with the wrong crowd and must face drug charges which could mean prison or being asked to leave the States. Either way, there will be great shame and disappointment for all the family at home if the boy fails them.

The Hindu is privately terrified he may have lung cancer—he has always smoked too much. He will know the results of the tests the day after tomorrow, but in the meanwhile he is really scared.

The Indian and the Achole have known one another for more than ten years and they first met at a conference in Geneva. They have sat on many of the same committees, and for two weeks they once shared a hotel room during an international trade seminar in Algiers when the city was so crowded that some of the delegates had to double up. As they eat they chat at first about the devaluation of the dollar. Then, because the Achole is to open an African art exhibit in the morning, the conversation turns to that. They laugh about a bizarre sequence in *Naked on Roller Skates,* they have a nightcap and share a taxi home since they live within a block of one another. They have a relaxed and easy relationship, they are comfortable, they work well together on an important committee. But neither man speaks what is on his mind. The Achole never mentions his nephew or the Indian his cancer. They remain at all times superficial.

Now you are going to holler at me about my facile fictitious example, and you'll tell me about this Argentinian you know who is married to an Achole, and about how it all depends on the individual, and I agree with you; I agree.

What I said at the beginning is that it is *easier* for people from established, living, time-tested, recognized backgrounds to cross the borders, to slough off their vulnerability, to give of themselves and to receive in return. It is harder in some indefinable way for those whose obscure, although probably excellent roots, are shriveling away under the impact of the twentieth century, who have not yet had time for full absorption elsewhere and who, consequently, lack that element of unconscious confidence that allows the Ethiopian to glance over his shoulder at 2,000 years of Christianity, the Swede to recall his Viking ancestors and the Hindu to feel even more smug than either. Not that any of them consciously look back much—but the Achole doesn't know that.

The situation is as old as history, and our forebears in Britain must have felt odd for a generation or two when those smart Romans arrived with a lot of fancy notions and found them running around in skins and blue paint.

In five years time the Achole will go home and there will be no witch doctor at all. A small canning factory will stand on the old market site, piped water will mean that nobody goes to the river any more, and the younger kids will have never witnessed the ceremony following the placing of the last thatch on the roof of a new hut. No lasting remnants of the old life will exist in twenty more years, since thatch and mud are not durable, and few written legends will survive—though a young Achole anthropologist has put out a small booklet of collected folk tales. Some of the parents will try to keep traditional ways alive in modified forms, but the boys are preoccupied with making the soccer team and the girls listen to soul music on the radio.

All this will have happened in the life of our Achole before he is sixty, and it may be the basis of a submerged neurosis that is little understood by those afflicted or by casual people watchers like me.

Actually, our Achole has become so far removed from tribal ways that he has found compensations. He is crazy about Italian cooking and is very good at it himself, and, of all things, he is an avid collector of English horse brasses following three years in London. But his parents never tasted pasta or saw a horse or knew that such an animal existed. He has almost no inherited continuity in his present life.

The truly sad part is that the Hindu, the Swede, and the Ethiopian all think the Achole is a terrific person. They like him because he is amusing and quick and professionally competent, but none of them have got through to the real inner him. Is it that he won't let them because he is not sure what or who he is on the inside? He is not ashamed of anything, he is proud of his nice tribe as he knew it as a boy, and he is proud of telling how he came from a tiny African village to an important post at the U.N. He is proud of being an African and is free of chip-on-the-shoulder racialism. Why did he hold back, then? Why didn't he and the kind Hindu talk about the errant nephew or the lung cancer? Maybe he just doesn't know why.

Paradoxically, the crossing-the-border business between races and cultures can be easier on a different level between a completely educated person and someone without any formal education at all. A white Harvard graduate who has turned professional hunter (more fictitious characters, I'm afraid, but their counterparts do exist, I assure you) can develop a fine relationship with a primitive African tribesman. They can have great respect for each other and affection and over the years can become really close without either becoming the least bit like the other. The hunter's relationship with the Samburu elder, near whose village he often camps, is worth thinking about for a minute. The Harvard hunter is, despite his occupation, a pure product of his background. The Samburu chief is equally a pure product of his, having never been to school or learned a word of English and whose only concession to the modern world is to wear a fine red blanket instead of a skin and occasionally to indulge his passion for canned butter.

The two men have known each other for twenty years, are approximately the same age and treat each other as equals. There is no area where they compete, neither is a threat to the other and each is 100 per cent confident in himself and his role in life. The hunter once took the Samburu for his only visit to Nairobi and had him stay at his house for two nights. The bedroom was so strange he opted to curl up in an extra blanket on the verandah at night.

Once when the hunter arrived late at the village and it was raining heavily, the Samburu lent him a hut—but only for one night. He found his nice clean tent under a tree, a quarter of a mile from the village was infinitely preferable. Their common ground if analyzed is approximately zero, but each will go to his grave with the memory of a lifelong friendship and the highest possible esteem for the other.

It is their absolute differences, parallel with an intuitive recognition in each other of nearly identical human standards and values, if you follow me, that makes the relationship honest and valid and real.

The African may be unhappy that the African way is being progressively swamped by the white man's way—but he finds himself unable to be selective about the ideas and methods he adopts. Once you own a car you have a vested interest in the oil industry, the national highways, parking lots, the behavior of other road users, and before you know it you are committed to the whole deal. And so it is with everything modern you touch— its direct and side effects dictate a whole related range of additional but limited options. In its simplest form, how do you make an "African bicycle" and an "African radio" when the concepts of bicycle and radio are not African in the first place?

In the last fifteen years throughout much of Africa another disquieting and confidence-dissolving thing has taken place. The attainment of political independence. But surely, you will ask, is that not cause for immense African pride? The answer is a big yes but with a little no tacked on. The positive part has to do with the actual acquisition of sovereignty; the negative part relates to what you do with it when you have it. In colonial days it was easy to blame others for deficiencies, but after a decade of doing their own thing African leaders and those who elect them must start to take credit, and worse, the blame, for what has or has not been done. Nobody likes to goof (I absolutely cannot stand it), but inevitably from time to time we all do. When the modern African goofs, the fact of it is so hard for him to take that I really believe he blocks it out mentally and subconsciously adopts a defense: The wicked, wicked world has conspired to undermine him and his failure has nothing to do with his own shortcomings because it is unthinkable (out loud) that he could have short-comings. He is not psychologically equipped, after all the up-rooting that has happened since the turn of the century, to cope with the possibility of failure now, and as a matter of fact, I am not sure that I am either.

I have probably exaggerated, generalized, dabbled in half-truths, and succumbed to the temptation of playing homespun psychologist. I shall probably get a lot of flak from African and European friends, who may even turn to enemies, and in fact I am not at all sure I should have written about this. But, on the other hand, I do feel there are truths lurking around in there somewhere, albeit feebly expressed.

The Cruel Paradise

MAINLY BY BETTY

On August 7, 1972, I picked up a paper and read a small column captioned COLOR BAR PREVENTS DOCTOR'S BID TO SAVE GIRL—"A girl in labor waited two hours for a desperately needed emergency operation while the qualified doctor at her side could do nothing because he was not white," the Johannesburg *Sunday Times* reported. "The girl, eighteen-year-old Caroline Amas, colored, was having her baby delivered by twenty-nine-year-old, colored, Dr. Carl Abrahamse, when she suffered a fit. But the hospital regulations prevented Dr. Abrahamse from entering the white operating theater [the only operating room available] or from using the services of the skilled white staff. He called a white doctor who performed the caesarian operation after a delay of two hours, but the girl died three days later. Dr. Roux Cloete, white, Medical Superintendent of the Ousthoorn Hospital where this happened would not comment on the case, but confirmed that "non-White doctors are not permitted to work with White Staff. This would create all sorts of problems."

I reread the article, for certainly I must have misunderstood something. I hadn't.

This is South Africa.

At almost every one of our lectures we are questioned about South Africa, so we are taking this opportunity to tell you something about that cruel paradise.

If you were on a quiz program and were asked which is the

seventh largest city on the continent of Africa, what would you answer? First you'd probably leaf through the fiftyish countries on the vast continent and decide that Cairo, Johannesburg, Lagos, Kinshasa in Zaire (which used to be Elizabethville in the Congo) were among the biggest, so you'd take a guess—Casablanca? Wrong. But even if you had guessed Nairobi (half a million people) or Addis Ababa or any other familiar-sounding name, you would still have been wrong. The correct answer is Soweto. I bet you've never even heard of Soweto. I certainly hadn't until we went there. Soweto is the abbreviation for the "Southwest Township" fifteen miles southwest of Johannesburg, and the Africans who work in Johannesburg are kept there— 700,000 of them.

Yes, kept, like animals in a zoo in that they are forced to live there if they want to work for the whites in Johannesburg. There is only one water line and one power line from "Joburg" to Soweto, so at any time the government deems it "necessary," both could be cut off. If he works in Joburg, the African may not, by law, live in the white man's area, nor in the Indian's, nor the colored's area, but only in Soweto. In all of South Africa everything is separate for blacks, whites, and coloreds (any mixture of races). A white may not have a Coke in an Indian hotel for example, or as a woman, I cannot get into a cab alone with a black male driver. There are separate buses and taxis, separate post office counters, places of entertainment, beaches, hotels, toilets, washrooms, hospitals, libraries and of course dwellings. The word "apartheid" (pronounced "apar-tate" to rhyme with "hate") means "separateness" but the Afrikaners prefer the euphemism "separate development."

The famous child's horse book, *Black Beauty,* was banned for awhile in South Africa, because the Government thought it was about a sexy two-legged black beauty. Much of Hemingway, Tennessee Williams, most famous Russian authors, as well as United Nations publications are still forbidden. *The French Connection,* the award-winning film, was shown in South Africa to "white audiences only." A friend of mine bought the paperback edition of *The Godfather* at the airport in Nairobi and carried it in her hand. When she got off the plane in Johannesburg she was interrogated by three immigration officials who demanded her name and address and an explanation of why she wanted to read *The Godfather*. They would not believe her when she said she "just *wanted* to read it," which would seem a perfectly good answer to me. They confiscated the book and kept her name and address on record for the book is banned in South Africa.

An Asian friend of mine in Nairobi told me her family has always lived in South Africa, and although she had moved to Kenya when she was married, from time to time she went to visit her family. Once, when she was eight months' pregnant, she was shopping in a department store—oh yes, white shopkeepers are quite prepared to accept *money* earned by other races—and needed to go to the ladies' room. She was told there was a ladies' room on all the floors for whites, "but for you it's on the fifth floor." So she got on the elevator and said, "Fifth floor please," and the white elevator operator told her that since she was not white she had to walk. She walked. I asked how she could stand things like that. She shrugged, "What can you do? Nothing." Well, you could always kill the elevator operator or blow up the department store.

Jock and I heard so many horror stories of South Africa, we were anxious to go and see for ourselves. Also it would have been embarrassing for us to get up on our soapbox in the States to talk about South Africa and then have someone in the audience ask when we were last there. Having to admit we had never been there, would definitely dilute one's argument.

So off we trooped to South Africa—first to Durban which looks like Atlantic City complete with bumper cars, cotton candy, and lots of tattooed people who wear sailor hats which say "Kiss Me Baby." The entire place has the atmosphere of an amusement park, but for us, it lacked any amusement whatsoever.

In 1960 when I went to Zanzibar there were rickshaws, but they have been outlawed now for almost ten years because of the obvious "degradation to man"—and rightly so. However, in Durban there are still rickshaws—brightly painted and decorated and the owners wear elaborate costumes and headdresses to attract the tourists who sit in the rickshaws and are pulled around the city by the African acting as a horse. The only thing missing is a whip. Needless to say, we didn't ride in a rickshaw.

Despising all of Durban, we went to the airport to fly to Cape Town, and in the air terminal we noticed how many white people surrounded us. In fact, we could see only whites—quite an unusual situation in Africa. The airports in South Africa have separate embarkation lounges and are marked accordingly—just as the benches in Durban had been marked . . . WHITE, COLORED, BLACK. . . . and a white person cannot sit on a colored or black's bench—or a black on a colored's, and so on. Cape Town is a beautiful city physically, but the ugliness of racialism erases the enjoyment of it. I know a man in the United States who looks like a Greek God—he is handsome according to anyone's standards— but he is, in fact, a six-feet, four-inch midget, and because he is so mean and nasty and self-centered and unkind and stupid, to name a few of his better points, I really think he is ugly to *look* at. Yet a friend of mine who has a terribly scarred face is beautiful to me because he is beautiful on the inside. Cape Town fits right into the former category for me.

After a couple of days we made our way to Cape Town's all-white air terminal, flew to Johannesburg and got on the all-white airport bus which took us to the "best" all-white hotel in South Africa, which was in fact not elegant at all—just pretentious and "chichi"—fake mink and rhinestone covers on the telephone receivers and all that. Johannesburg is a large city and the buildings try to be modern but just miss—and what is worse than modern architecture just missing? It is a busy city of a million unfashionable white people, all of whom wear outdated clothes, shop in outdated white shops and have outdated white politics. It is as if you were thrown back into the 1950s in Europe or the States again. However, it is one of the wealthiest cities in the world, and it is said that the whites in South Africa, if they are taken alone, enjoy the highest standard of living in the whole world. Only 6 per cent of Africa's total population lives in South Africa, yet it generates 24 per cent of the continent's general wealth. The whites constitute only 17 per cent of South Africa's population yet receive 73 per cent of the income. The Africans constitute 67.9 per cent of the population but their share of the nation's personal cash income is only 18.8 per cent. Nonetheless, they are the ones who man the factories and dig in the mines.

On Sunday morning in Johannesburg, Jock and I went to the famous mine dances staged for the tourists. The stadium, of course, has separate entrances for whites, blacks and coloreds; policemen march up and down between the divided sections and if there is infringement by mistake, the policeman is right there, "Move your foot back!" (Or you vill be shot?) I wondered where the whites sit who are married to blacks? Or perhaps a white who is married to a Vietnamese or an Indian? Well, there are none. It is not only illegal to marry anyone of a different color, but it is also illegal to have any sexual relations with such a person. Chinese are classified as coloreds, but Japanese have been made "honorary whites" because of all the trade that goes on with Japan. So, the Japanese can swim in the white pools but they cannot have sexual relations with or marry a white. When I learned this I thought of a filthy, dreadful white woman we had working for us once in Baltimore as our cleaning woman. She was "real white trash swine from 'Kintucky.'" In South Africa she would not be allowed to go to bed with the Aga Kahn or the Shah of Iran or the Emperor of Japan. Well, I'm sure they would be relieved to learn that.

After the mine dances we asked our white driver about the black miners, and learned that two thirds of them come from the surrounding countries of Swaziland, Lesotho and Botswanaland and earn R18 ($27) per month while the whites in mining earn R297 ($445) per month. I asked if they *had* to live in the mining compounds? Of course they do. No, they couldn't bring their families with them. They have a room twenty feet by twenty feet— home for twenty men. Each man has a concrete bunk.

Jock and I were so depressed when we returned to our hotel we

thought perhaps a movie would cheer us up, but we couldn't find
the movie calendar in the paper. We went to the front desk and
asked the desk clerk if he could tell us what was on at the movies.
He looked at us in horror and said, "Oh my goodness, there are
no films on Sunday."

"Why not?" we asked incredulously.

"The Dutch Reform Church does not believe in it," he answered firmly.

"What about the Episcopalians, the Jews, the atheists?"

"Sorry, NO cinemas on Sunday. No tennis playing either. You
can only go to church on Sunday. You can't do anything else."

"Oh yes we can," we said. "We can leave and go home." And so
we did.

An African driver took us to the airport in a car belonging to
the hotel. We were astonished—he was the first black we had had
an opportunity to talk to—we felt as if were were home in Kenya
again. Jock started chatting to him, and he was polite but very re-
luctant to talk about anything. Finally Jock mentioned that he
was a Kenya citizen and showed him his passport to prove it—the
driver might have thought he was an impostor, since South Africa
is such a police state. His attitude changed instantly. He wanted to
know everything about Kenya and the black/white situation there.
There is no TV in South Africa so people living there know very
little about the outside world. Censorship is very strict, and the
propaganda is worse—so all our driver had heard about Kenya
was that it was in total turmoil since independence. He slowed
down to about ten miles an hour to give us more time to talk on
the drive to the airport, and we managed to have about an hour's
conversation with him. He asked us many questions and we
asked him many. Of course he lived in Soweto—he had no choice.
Yes he was married, but he could not live with his wife because
she was from a different area. Africans working in white areas can
only have their wives with them if the wife is qualified in her own
right to live and work in a white area too—and not many women
are.

After an hour or so we exchanged names and addresses with

Solomon and told him that if he could ever get out of South Africa
to come to Kenya, we would try to get him a job with Percival.
He was very intelligent and would be an asset. But he cannot
leave—his application for a passport would undoubtedly be refused unless he agreed to leave the country permanently. We got
out of the car and extended our hands to him to say good-by. He
looked around apprehensively and then shook our hands saying,
"I did not know there were white people like this in the world." As
we walked into our white terminal, tears were running down my
cheeks, and I went into the white ladies' room, and in protest, peed
all over the "white" toilet seat.

Every plane north was solidly booked but we waited, and after
several hours there was finally a cancellation. When we landed in
Nairobi five hours later, it was as if we were fifty pounds lighter—
the despair lifted and the sun shone again—even though it was
raining.

This was not the end of South Africa for us, but the beginning.

That trip was in November, and at Christmas we got a card
from Solomon—a very special card which he had spent a lot of
time in picking out. It said "To Someone Who Means a Lot To
Me" and inside he had written himself, "I would like to know how
you have travelled from Johannesburg to Nairobi on that day the
20/11/70. With me I can say I have been left with peace and
joy, and you have given me much hope. Greetings to your family
and to your friends. Solomon."

When we were going to write this chapter about South Africa I
wrote to him and asked him if he would like to say anything
about South Africa. On July 11, 1972, he answered, "I would like
to thank your letter which I received on December, 1971. In connection with your book, on which you would like me to say anything about South Africa, I am preparing to say something about
South Africa, I am going to write that for you. I will send that for
you on the 17th of July 1972. And I would like to have your pho-
tos. I will be very glad if you can do that for me. Many thanks of
your letter. Best wishes, yours sincerely, Solomon." We have never
heard from Solomon again.

I read in *Newsweek* (May 1, 1972) how twenty-eight-year-old Van der Sandt de Villiers Smit of South Africa announced his intentions of breeding dogs, slaughtering them and fashioning their pelts into ladies' fur coats. His reasoning was that because of the world crackdown on wild animal skins—no more leopard, cheetah, etc.—he would probably sell a Dalmatian or cocker spaniel coat for $2,600. "Naturally," he was quoted as saying "if someone wanted, say, a Dalmatian coat with small spots, that would cost more because I would have to use more puppies."

The South African Government could see nothing wrong with this and the Minister of Agriculture, Dirk Uys, said, "There is nothing to prevent him from slaughtering dogs. They are his property, so who can stop him? Suppose you feel like cooking your cat today. What can I do about it?"

But soon the white South Africans were up in arms, debating it in Parliament, and one white even offered $40,000 for de Villiers Smit's skin.

With the SPCA and Friends of Animals and every pet lover not only in South Africa but in the States as well putting much pressure on the South African Government, it reversed its stand and announced it would legislate against killing dogs for profit. Villiers Smit was very angry and disappointed—he was sure it would have worked. "Is slaughtering a dog for its skin any worse than killing a lamb or a calf? What's wrong with your wife's wearing a nice Dalmatian or spaniel skin coat?"

"Skin, as all the world knows," exclaimed *Newsweek*, "is a matter of supreme importance in South Africa, and this skin-related problem had many South African whites in a state of moral outrage." It took the Johannesburg *Star* to pose the real question. "When," it asked its readers in the land of apartheid, "will we feel the same kind of compassion for the voiceless people that we so obviously feel for dogs?"

Many Americans will remember when champion tennis player Arthur Ashe was refused a visa by the South African Government. It was, of course because he was black, but the South African

Government claimed that "this American Negro has been involved in the Black Power movement and has made hostile statements toward the government." Can you imagine what American
black would *not* make hostile statements against the South African Government? And every white should. South Africa should be
everybody's nightmare.

There are more than 20 million people in South Africa, and although only one sixth of them are white, that sixth occupy seven-
eights of the land. Of the non-whites, there are roughly 2 million
coloreds, 600,000 Asians, and the rest—the Africans totaling
nearly 70 per cent of the population—have only 9 per cent of the
land.

That is only the beginning.

An African cannot own land among white people and cannot
live in European residential areas, even though he may work
there. Suppose you are a white man, twenty-five years old, and
your baby's fifty-seven-year-old colored nursemaid is sick and
you want to drive her to the bus because it is raining—you can
both go to jail for 180 days under the Immorality Act. It could be
construed as immoral and illegal for two people of the opposite
sex of different races to drive in a car alone together.

The Immorality Act was passed in 1927—and it is under this
act that extra-marital relations between Europeans and Africans
are illegal. Then in 1950 any sexual relations between Europeans
and non-whites of any group became illegal. When Europeans
and coloreds, though not married, have been living together, the
family is broken up and they go to jail for three months. It has
been noted in the press and Parliament that the European male is
often acquitted but his African or colored female partner is found
guilty and sentenced.

The Population Registration Act is a law stating that every
person in South Africa has to register and be classified as white,
colored, Asian, or black. An identity number is assigned to *every*
person. In one year there were 18,469 objections raised by the
persons concerned in the 90,000 borderline cases. There is often
much doubt, and always much individual anguish and suffering.

For example, an old man of eighty-one who had been happily married for twenty-five years was classified officially as African but his wife was reclassified as colored, so they could not remain married or living together.

"Colored" is very difficult to define. In general it is a description applied to persons of mixed race, and it is not used in the old American sense simply for anyone who is not white. Thus, it may be taken to mean anyone who is not African, Indian or European. (European would include white Americans.) The Director of the Census first informed everyone that children born of parents one of whom is African were to be classified as African, but then later on in 1955 the Appeal Board ruled that a man whose father is a European and whose mother is an African is officially colored. The coloreds maintain that race classification is five hundred years out of date, and of course they are right, but the classification continues in South Africa today and the informers have a field day.

A colored school principal admitted that he informed the board that a white family living in a white area was not white. An inspector of the groups area board went to inspect and found the man had lived all his life as a European as had two of his brothers, one of whom was in the Royal Navy. A sister, however, was living as a colored person; therefore he was reclassified as colored and his occupation was then unlawful.

Miss Susan Kirk, blond with blue eyes, has always lived, as her grandmother and grandfather and parents have, as whites. All have white identity cards. Miss Kirk mislaid her card and applied for another. Meanwhile she married a white man. The new identity card stated she was colored, and the officials confirmed she had been reclassified. Her husband then applied successfully for their marriage to be annulled in accordance with the Immorality or Mixed Marriages Act, and she also lost her job.

Mr. Argen Curtin's entire family was classified as white, but after a neighbor complained about the appearance of some of the Curtin's nine children, he was reclassified from white to colored. He took the matter on appeal to the Supreme Court but was unsuccessful. The costs amounted to about $1,500. When it finally decided that he was colored, he lost his job at the post office because it was now illegal work for him. As a white he could earn about R40 per week ($60), but now reclassified, he could earn only R6 ($9) as a farm laborer.

These are actual cases of permanent hardships and heartbreaks, and there are literally thousands like them.

Even though classified as white, ten-year-old Johanna de Bruin was unfortunate enough to have Addison's disease, which caused her skin to turn brown. No school would accept her, so she had to have a tutor to teach her at home.

One entire family in Cape Town was reclassified from white to colored. The eldest daughter had to postpone her marriage to a white man, the second daughter had to leave a white school, and the son's job was threatened. So they all agreed to commit suicide if they could not get the classification altered. On reading their story in a newspaper someone made them an anonymous loan of R500 ($750) to cover the expenses of an appeal, which proved successful.

Apartheid is the Afrikaans word meaning "segregation," and it could just as easily have been called segregation. When it was introduced into the political vocabulary in South Africa in 1948, the English seized upon it probably to suggest, by the use of a foreign word in the English language, something strange and ominous—something so bad there was no word at all in English for it. "Tribalism" sounds worse than "nationalism" doesn't it? and "oath" sounds much worse than "pledge" or "vow." Yet there is no difference between marriage vows or confirmation vows—and oaths—they are all the same thing. "Mau Mau" sounds much worse than "Freedom Fighters" and "apartheid" sounds worse than "segregation." And it is.

Apartheid is very complicated and does not mean total segregation because, carried to a logical conclusion, that means the nonwhites could not work for the whites, and the white South Africans would never agree to this. Although the word "apartheid" was coined in the Afrikaans language in 1943, the policy of segregation goes back into South African history to 1652. From the beginning the Transvaal applied the most rigid segregation while the Cape was, by comparison the most "liberal." Since 1948, though, the policy has been ruthlessly applied throughout South Africa.

Not all whites in South Africa are for apartheid. There are both Afrikaners and English South Africans who oppose it, and it is an erroneous oversimplification to say that the Afrikaners support apartheid and the English South Africans are liberal. As Edgar Brookes said in his informative book *Apartheid,* a documentary study of modern South Africa, "It is very misleading to present the English speaking population as liberals and the Afrikaans speaking as supporters of apartheid. The only measure of truth in this contention is that the British South African, if he supports apartheid, as the majority do, finds himself in opposition to the academic and ecclesiastical leadership of his group, while the liberal Afrikaner minority—and there certainly is such a minority—faces with great moral courage the strictures of the Afrikaans Churches and Universities."

The Government, the civil service and the police force are overwhelmingly Afrikaners, or Afrikaans-speaking, a fact which ensures that the race laws are rigidly enforced. But for whites who break the law, correspondingly lenient treatment can be expected. Mike Arlow, a policeman, was convicted of killing an innocent African. He was fined $100 and given a year's sentence. After his release he was reinstated in the police force. Not many police forces employ convicted killers. Another example concerns a white farmer who beat to death a twelve-year-old African boy who was working for him. The farmer was sentenced to five years imprisonment, and other farmers in the area were so outraged that two thousand of them signed a petition which sought to reduce the sentence because "it was so hard on the man's family." The prevalence of this kind of attitude is indicative of the negligible regard in which an African life is held.

Against such a background the outspokenness of the press is astonishing and many visitors to South Africa are quick to spot the fact. The critical segment of the press comprises English language papers and the Opposition newspapers which hit out hard at many of the iniquities of apartheid, but nevertheless basically agree with some form of apartheid.

Many white South Africans have left their country voluntarily seeing no hope of improving conditions for Africans by remaining. Other opponents of apartheid have seen their duty differently and have remained to take the risks of opposition. One of the outstanding people who constantly speaks out against apartheid is Mrs. Helen Suzman of the Opposition Progressive Party.

In 1965 two hundred colored people were turned away from an Eve Boswell (famous English singer) concert, and many of them had to wait in their cars in the car park until the show was over and the whites had moved their cars. It is very difficult to establish what the criteria are governing admission. Helen Suzman, eloquent sole parliamentary representative of the Progressive Party spoke of the incident, "It started off by not allowing mixed audiences; then one could have mixed audiences as long as there were separate amenities within the hall itself; then one could only have mixed audiences if facilities were not available in the areas set aside for the different races themselves; then one could only have mixed entertainments if the particular event could not be repeated; then one could only have them providing it was only a non-White orchestra with a non-White choir, not a White audience and mixed group of performers on the stage. You have this absurd nonsense which goes beyond words, it surpasses belief."

Until June of 1965 non-whites were spending peaceful leisure hours watching soccer matches and other sports. They are now prevented from doing so. They are not allowed into the two large white stadiums, and Mrs. Suzman says, "What are we trying to do? Are we intent on turning more people into deliquents with no facilities for decent recreation?" No money was spent to provide facilities for the Indian or Bantu sports as was promised when they were prevented from entering the white stadium. However, later in 1965, the Government granted permission for colored people to watch rugby in the white stadium on the condition that a six-foot fence be built between them and the white spectators.

The relocation of Africans is one of South Africa's particularly charming policies. Scattered among the white areas there are numerous little black "islands" where Africans have lived for hundreds of years. Now, in order to tidy the map and to ensure that the white areas are not polluted by the presence of black residents, as opposed to black workers, such black pockets are being systematically broken up and the inhabitants moved forcibly to Bantustans or "homelands," usually arid areas quite unsuited to human habitation.

In the midst of the richest and most rapidly growing economy on the entire continent of Africa, the African is made a refugee in his own land, suffers the most, is riddled with disease, and is compelled to live in arid native quarters, now euphemistically and ironically called "homelands." They are forced away from their homes where they or their kinsmen have lived for hundreds of years, forced to leave their cattle—their only source of income— forced into government trucks and driven, like the prisoners which in fact they are, to arid and ungrazeable bare veldts, and their homes are destroyed after their departure. They are foreigners in their own country, for all Africans not living on native reserves are regarded as foreigners.

The number of Africans living in the homelands rose from 4 million in 1960 to 7 million by 1970, and the trend continues as more and more of them are "endorsed out" of the urban areas and white rural areas and are forcefully squeezed into the 9 per cent of the land that has been designated as theirs—even though they make up 70 per cent of the total population of South Africa.

Cosmas Desmond, an English Roman Catholic priest, witnessed his parishioners being taken from their homes to the native quarter of Limehill. In his book *The Discarded People* he described what transpired. There were uniformed police on the scene during the transfer to tell the priests and the press that it was illegal to take photographs because they were "making contact with the people"—which is illegal—although they were on a public road in what was being forcibly proved to be a "white" area. After the first trucks left, Father Desmond followed them and later wrote, "We found the first arrivals sitting in the bare veldt, surrounded by their belongings, lost and still bewildered. There was a water tank and a pile of folded tents; these people had never erected a tent in their lives. There was nothing else.

"On that first evening there was a heavy rainfall. Many of the tents were swamped, as the people knew nothing about the need for drainage trenches around the tents. Instead they piled earth around the tents which made them insufferably hot during the day and did not keep the water out."

Of course, the Africans and the press had been told that houses would be built for them before their arrival—there would be no need for tents. They were told sufficient communal toilets would, of course, be provided from the first day, none would have to walk more than a quarter of a mile to purchase groceries and fresh vegetables from an established shop, no pupil would have to miss a day at school—a ten-room school was nearly completed. But predictably, when the Africans arrived there was nothing. Instead they were told they were expected to build their own houses and latrines—no sanitary arrangements had been made at all before the removal, nor was there any provision for the people to purchase bread, meat or milk, but there was a general dealer two miles away. The ten-room school was in fact seven miles away and not intended for the Limehill people.

Father Desmond found that 1,200 of these people had all come from Meran where they had been tenants on three African-owned farms. They had lived at Meran for many years and were a well-established community. Most of them had kept cattle and planted corn and a few vegetables. Some of them worked in a town about three miles away and many of the women did occasional work there. There were just over a hundred families, almost all with very neat houses of mud and thatch spaced well apart. Between them they had the use of about 6,000 acres. There was a primary school and a secondary school, too, run by the Mission. The bulldozers demolished these homes where they had lived and they were forceably moved to Limehill.

There they were allocated a tiny plot fifty yards square for each family. No livestock, except chickens, were allowed. There was no land for plowing. The women lost their income from working in the nearby town as the bus fare cost more than they could earn. There were neither shops nor any medical services. Even elementary sanitation was lacking. Most of the men had to work in Johannesburg or Durban, several hundred miles away.

A few months later, not surprisingly, typhoid broke out in the area. Officials of the State Health Department denied there was any serious problem (Just a mild dash of typhoid? Or a touch of leprosy?), yet the priest claimed he had seen the carbon copy of an official notification of a case of typhoid which had been sent to the magistrate. The Regional Director of State Health, appropriately named Dr. Hooey (like some B-rate movie) stated in the Rand *Daily Mail,* November 29, 1968, that to his knowledge there had not been one single case of typhoid, nor had there been any deaths from gastro-enteritis. Churchmen and others called for an enquiry into the health situation, and it was then reported that thirty-three people had died from gastro-enteritis and doctors had reported eight cases of typhoid. Yet again the Ministry of Health denied there had been any serious outbreak of typhoid and said the total number of deaths in the area was only nineteen, a normal figure for a population of 7,500. Yet Father Desmond has a photograph of sixty new graves there, and he learned there were at least six others buried illegally outside the cemetery in Limehill. Most of them were children and they had died between October and December. Finally, late in February 1969, the Minister of Bantu Administration and Development (BAD—ironically) admitted in the House of Assembly that there had been seventy-three deaths. Over the whole of South Africa, half of the black children die before they are ten . . . in the midst of opulence and luxury.

Father Desmond went on a tour of all the "homelands" and time and time again he was told by the Africans, "We are suffering. We have been thrown away. We have nothing. But what can we do? We are only Africans, there is no one to hear us."

This is only one example of what people are subjected to in South Africa for the sake of a political ideology. These poor people are moved because it has been decided that the land on which they had lived for generations is now for whites only. They are not being moved from slums or insanitary conditions—they were being moved to tidy the map, to separate them from contact with whites, to lose them in the remotest, poorest land set aside for Africans.

One of the Nationalist Members of Parliament who visited Limehill remarked that he could not see what all the fuss was about, as there were people living in far worse conditions than at Limehill. And, alas, this is true, but the Government has *created* these grotesque and tragic conditions. There are many Limehills.

Weenen makes Limehill look like a holiday camp. The congestion and squalor was not helped by the law: "No person shall in any way dig into or remove or disturb the surface of the soil, except in such areas as may be designated by the superintendent." Of course there was no superintendent there to do the designating, and yet the people were told to build their own houses.

"Naturally, they were charged rent for these plots—2 rand per month, plus 50 cents for each grown-up child, parent or lodger. In Weenen, which has the advantage over Limehill of not having been removed away from a town and a source of employment, most men earn between 8 rand and 12 rand per month ($12 and $18) and women, 2–5 rand ($3.00–$7.50) per month. There were only four toilets—deep pits—which the people were afraid to use since a child fell into one. The children relieved themselves on their doorsteps. A woman and her ten children lived together in a tent for a year and one of them, a tiny baby, virtually a skeleton, unable to move or even to cry, was covered with flies." Father Desmond had seen thousands of starving, dying children in African hospitals, but he had never seen anything worse than this, so he cut short his tour to take the child to the hospital.

As the months went by more people were moved into Limehill and more tents appeared. It acquired the nickname of *"Mshay azafe,"* which means "beat him until he dies." And here in the Bantustans, the African lives in empty misery in the most opulent country, by the whites own acclaim, in Africa.

Father Desmond said, "The names of other resettlement camps reveal with unconscious irony the bitterness of the experience for those who have to live there. To read the grim litany of these names—Morsgat, meaning messhole; Weenen, place of weeping; and Stinkwater—is to share something of the spirit of the places." For the Government, the Minister, Mr. M. C. Botha, explained, "These names are unfortunate—they are nearly all the names of old farms where the settlements are being carried out."

And . . . "The Bantu people like being moved . . . they like the places where they are being resettled." (*Star*, November 21, 1969.) Can the Minister really believe this? Of course, the people are careful not to complain to the Government officials—they would be listed as "troublemakers" and troublemakers can be put into jail without a trial.

It was reported in *Newsweek*, August 28, 1972, that "Every Sunday morning for the past six weeks, a slight, scholarly priest has left his suburban home near Johannesburg, S. A., to go to church, and each time he has broken the law." Father Cosmas Desmond was put under house arrest shortly after his book, from which I have quoted, was published.

There are roughly two hundred of these Bantustans scattered over areas like these. The Government had moved over half a million blacks by the end of 1968. The rest of the Africans live on temporary sufferance as migrant workers on the white seven-eighths of the country. The Government says the Africans have their rights though. The Bantu Citizenship Act of 1970, for example, states that a citizen of one of the "homelands" may exercise his civil and political rights. However, most Africans have to work in white South Africa where the Deputy Minister of BAD said, "I am afraid to say that the African males from the homelands have no rights whatsoever in South Africa. Their rights are in their own homelands, and they are in South Africa only to sell their labour."

The Government says ". . . the African should only be allowed to enter the urban areas, which are essentially the White Man's creation, when he is willing to enter and minister to the needs of the White Man; he should depart therefrom when he ceases to minister."

The idea is that the black nationalists will have political and citizenship rights in separate states, while South Africa's proud white Afrikaners' race remains pure and dominant. Although the Transkei, for example, was given the trappings of statehood—a national anthem and a flag—it is barred from legislating on military and foreign affairs, and any other legislation, once passed by the assembly, must be approved by the South African State President before it is enacted, thus making a pathetic charade of the whole concept.

The poverty in these territories is unspeakable—it is well below the poverty datum line for a family of five. A white Anglican priest in South Africa forced himself to live on only 5 rand a month ($7.50) for half a year and was on the point of collapse. He chose the sum of 5 rand because this is the pension paid to Africans in Dimbaza, one of the grim resettlement camps in the Transkei.

"I'm just about dead," he said.

During his ordeal of six months—from April to October 1972—he wrote a report each month to Mr. Michael Botha who had ultimate responsibility for camps such as Dimbaza. Botha never replied—publicly or privately. The priest considered himself lucky because he had not needed to buy blankets, clothes, utensils or furniture, nor had he to pay children's school fees, etc. The 5 rand a month seemed easy compared with his life during June when he and a dozen other whites tried to live on monthly rations worth just 2 rand ($3.00)—the same ration given to absolutely destitute people in Dimbaza. During this period he admitted that even his prayers turned to the theme of food.

But grinding poverty is not confined to Bantustans.

Sixty-eight per cent of the families living in Soweto, for instance, have incomes below the estimated minimum costs of survival, which does not include anything for furniture, household goods, reading and writing materials, beer, cigarettes, recreation, savings or personal care. The effective minimum level of income is generally estimated at one and a half times the poverty datum line figure, which means a family of six living at Soweto should have at least 95.63 rand a month (which works out at 16 rand or $24 per month per person). The average income per head in practice works out to 7 rand ($10.50) for the black, instead of the $24 he needs without anything included. The average income per head for whites works out to 95 rand ($144).

Detention without trial. By the General Law Amendment Acts (No. 37 of 1963) police officers may without warrant, arrest and detain up to ninety days on any particular occasion persons suspected of committing or intending to commit or having information about, specified types of political offenses. Apart from a weekly visit from a magistrate, these detainees may be held absolutely incommunicado. There is nothing to prevent the ninety-day period being extended for a further ninety days. There is no appeal to the courts. Thus, in theory, and you can bet your boots in practice from time to time, a police officer can simply arrest and lock up somebody who may have annoyed him even though no law has been broken.

It is an offense to advise, encourage or incite anyone to commit an offense by way of protest against a law or in support of a campaign against any law. Maximum penalties for such an incitement are a fine of 1,000 rand ($1,500), five years' imprisonment, or ten lashes, or a combination of any of these. The penalty for a second or subsequent conviction must include either whipping or imprisonment.

When the Africans or anyone in South Africa have a lawful political meeting the Security Police are there taking notes, using tape-recorders, collecting names and photographing individuals, which is indeed inhibiting. The jails are full of people. After ninety days, many are set free, take two steps out of the jail, are rearrested and back they go for ninety more days, and on and on, and there is never a trial.

Another delightful device is "Banning and House Arrest." Organizations of people who favor racial equality are banned, there is no trial and no appeal to the courts. There is not even an

administrative appeal by which the victim is notified of the details
of his offense and permitted to plead his own case before the
appropriate administrative officer. The South African Government
has stated, "A belief in racial equality is one of the aims of Communism," and the Minister of Justice has deemed that anyone who
promotes any one of the aims of Communism will be banned.
Therefore, it has been possible to ban people who favor racial
equality but are pronounced anti-Communists. Hundreds of people have been so banned—most for a period of five years. There is
no guarantee that it will be lifted at the end of this period, and in
quite a few cases the ban has been renewed.

The banned person is restricted to the magisterial district in
which he lives. He must report personally, usually once a week,
to the police. Banned persons may not communicate with each
other. A banned person may not speak at public meetings, write
to the newspapers, or publish articles or books. To quote a
banned person is a punishable offense. He may not enter any
educational institution, cannot belong to any political organization, and in some cases the ban is accompanied by house arrest,
where you can go only to work and return, but have no visitors
at all—you are a prisoner in your own house. If your father,
for example, is dying, you can apply to the Government to get
permission to go and see him once or twice a year.

Africans are banished from their homes to remote areas where
the banished man finds himself among an ethnic group different
from his own and speaking a different language.

Now, I am not talking about laws that are not enforced. If
we look through American laws I'm sure we could find silly ones.
In Washington, D.C., it is illegal to trim your horse's tail on
Sunday, and Massachusetts prohibits the sale of contraceptive
drugs or devices to unmarried persons. But most people merely
ignore these laws. In South Africa, however, racial legislation is
enforced with fanatical zeal.

A 1969 Survey of Race Relations in South Africa, compiled by
Muriel Horrell states that by July 1, 850 white and 304 non-white
banning orders were enforced for 1969, and that as far as could

be ascertained from press reports since 1950, the banning orders issued since the Suppression of Communism Act became law and up to November 30, 1969, affected a total of 979 persons, 126 whites and 853 non-whites. Many are banned for a second or even third period.

House arrest can also be imposed for a period of five years, and can be extended for a second or third period. There are many people serving life sentences as political prisoners because they believe in racial equality; they are unable to leave their own homes or see anyone except the police to whom, in some cases, they must report every day.

There are "Listed Persons" and "Pass Laws" which the Government will tell you no longer exist, but which, of course, do under the new name "Documentary Offences." Everyone has to have a pass to enter into a white area. In 1968 there were an average of 1,900 pass law offenses *each day*. By 1971 the figure had risen to an average of over 2,830 each day who were being prosecuted, to say nothing of those who were arrested and later released without being prosecuted. Persons equal in number to the entire population of a small town are bundled into police vans every day. The average offender is brought to court after twenty-four hours in jail, and if further investigation is needed, the average time spent in detention is fourteen days, all because a black or colored or Asian might be in a white building without written permission.

There are job restrictions that reserve the more skilled and better-paid jobs for the white workers and the lower-paid ones for the non-whites—which, of course, sets a ceiling on non-white progress. A Kenya African friend of ours, who lived in South Africa for five years while attending a university, told me that the jobs for repairing electrical poles were divided into white and non-white labor—the "skilled" labor being for the whites who painted the poles at the bottom and "unskilled" for the blacks who had the dangerous job of fixing the electric wires at the top. If a colored person owns a taxi, white passengers cannot be transported in it, although white owners who are unable to find white drivers are permitted to employ colored drivers to convey white passengers. Black trade unions are not prohibited but are not recognized in law. Striking by blacks is illegal. The average black wage is one-sixth that of the white.

There is a Prohibition of Disguises Act which renders it an offense for anyone to be found disguised in any manner whatsoever. (What fun would Halloween be?)

There are enough outrageous laws to fill volumes—I am only lightly skimming the surface. But just day-to-day life can be appalling in South Africa. One of Percival Tours managers from the States who was traveling through South Africa told us how he was standing on a street corner when a car came along and knocked down a little black girl standing on the corner holding her mother's hand. He rushed into the drugstore on the corner and said, "Call an ambulance." Outside the child was standing again, but she was shocked and bruised, so he told her to come into the drugstore out of the hot sun and asked the person behind the counter for a drink of water for her. As he was handed some water in the glass the soda jerk saw it was for a black girl, so he said he couldn't give it to her by law. Our manager hollered and raved so much that the man finally ran to the kitchen and came back with a tin can with some water in it. Then the white ambulance came and refused to take the black girl. And on and on it goes.

Since the race problem is basically a moral issue, who are the moral leaders of this country? Nazis? Heathens? Atheists? The answer is Christians. Yes, all of this is done in the name of Christianity. Seventy-two per cent of all South Africans and 94 per cent of all white South Africans profess to be Christians. Those who belong to the Dutch Reform Church, mostly Afrikaners, have twisted Christianity to suit and uphold their political convictions.

The Dutch Reform Church has stated: "The Church allows no equality between whites and non-whites," and, "The Church reserves the right to regulate their membership in accordance with the spirit of Christ." They quote the Bible, "Be ye not unequally yoked together—as an ass with a camel." And so they founded separate churches for non-whites, naturally paying the non-white ministers far less than the white ministers, saying that, "The founding and development of independent indigenous churches for the purpose of evangelising the Non-White races of South Africa was both necessary and in accordance with our understanding of the nature of the Church of the Lord Jesus on earth, and has been richly blessed during the many years that have passed."

Here is an example of the rich blessing:

On February 16, 1964, The Reverend D. P. Anderson, a white minister of the Congregational Union Church in a white area, organized services for Africans in his church after he had been approached by an African minister and asked to do so since the only previous facilities for Africans to worship were in garages in white areas. After the first service the police approached Mr. Anderson at his home and said that the services "had to stop because they would cause property values to drop." Mr. Anderson said there were about 25,000 Africans in the area and there was nowhere for them to worship except for a few "garage services." The police permitted Mr. Anderson to hold one final service at which he told the people that he could not hold any more. A policeman in plain clothes attended this last service . . . with the spirit of Christ.

Dutch Reform Christians say, "The establishment of separate churches is for the sake of good order and more efficient ministry to members from different language and cultural groups and is also in accordance with the Scriptures." They prefer to think of apartheid as "Christian guardianship."

The Dutch Reform Church is Calvinist in doctrine and Presbyterian in discipline and church order, and is one of the strongest influences in South Africa favoring apartheid. The Afrikaners are a believing and church-going people, to a much greater extent than the British South Africans, and so the Church leads them to feel that their national policy is deeply rooted in morality and religion. To the world outside and to the wider Christian Church, which is generally opposed to apartheid, the Dutch Reform Church has become something inexplicable. In 1960 it withdrew from both the World Council of Churches and from all official contact with the other Protestant churches in South Africa. Christianity has more adherents than any religion in the history of the world and a third of the world's population are Christians, but the Dutch Reform Church no longer truly belongs.

The Dutch Reform Church has been a scandal, a stumbling block, and has been counter-productive in the sense that its bigoted narrowness has fostered Communist notions among Africans. If the attitude of the Church leaders would change, the whole South African situation would be transformed. I can hardly express the loathing I have for the Dutch Reform Church, which the Africans so aptly call the "Dutch Deform Church"—and God must really despise it too.

Edgar Brookes, former Senator and principal of Adams College, the 103-year-old Bantu School that was recently closed by the Government, has much excellent material in his book *Apartheid*. I found it a most useful source, and not only have I paraphrased portions of his book, but from time to time I quote from it directly.

In understanding the history of the Afrikaner and realizing that the Church has encouraged his feelings, it is not difficult to see how such a hideosity as apartheid took hold and still sticks in a world that "mostly considers race distinction as obsolete, discredited and wrong."

It all started in 1652 when Jan Van Riebeck landed at the Cape with only soldiers and petty officials of the Dutch East India Company, rather than a select band of cultured immigrants who might not have had as many prejudices. The local people spoke a language that seemed extremely queer to the settlers, so with the superiority of the white man and because of its stammering sound they named the inhabitants "Hottentots." Soon it became the "stinking and lazy Hottentots" since the tribesmen saw no real advantage in working for the Dutchmen. Besides, they were busy fighting the only other indigenous people in South Africa at the time, the Bushmen. Thousands were killed on both sides, although the South Africans estimate there were only about 40,000 Hottentots and 25,000 Bushmen when they arrived in 1652. They also claim the Hottentots and the Bushmen were not blacks but coloreds who were brown and had been brought to the Cape at various stages from Malaya, India and Ceylon, along with Negroes from West Africa, East Africa and Madagascar. In 1658, 170 slaves arrived from Angola, and from its very earliest days South Africa thus came to depend on colored slave labor, and color, as in every slave state, became identified with inferiority. The first meeting of the blacks and the Afrikaners was not for 150 years after Van Riebeck's 1652 landing.

Although the original settlers had been ruled from Holland, they took on a personality of their own, asserting themselves against the tyrannous and arbitrary acts of the Dutch authorities —more specifically the Dutch East India Company which originally ran the settlement at the Cape as a commercial enterprise. They began speaking a brand new language first written in 1861 but not officially recognized until 1927, and they also began calling themselves, not Dutch, but "Afrikaners" meaning "the people of Africa."

The Asians arrived from India as indentured laborers between 1800 and 1911, and in 1806 the British arrived and started their usual British take-over operation. Soon afterward began the historic Great Trek, which was the Afrikaners' movement north to get away from the British. Poor and backward, these Afrikaners or "Boer" people as they became known after 1800, forsook the world of books and of changing thought, going farther and farther inland and northward and creating their own republics and forms of government hundreds of miles away from the Cape. This is when they met the Bantu, of whom there were many more than the Bushmen or Hottentots, who were more advanced in organization law and government, and wicked fighters as well. The British were prepared to help the Afrikaner farmers fight the Bantu, but they also claimed the right to pass judgment on frontier disputes, and to the fury of the farmers they didn't always rule in favor of the Afrikaner. Thus began the "war on two fronts"—the struggle against the British and the struggle against the Bantu.

Largely, the British were no better than the Afrikaners in that they were all for white supremacy and cheap labor too.

Then at the end of the nineteenth century came the Anglo-Boer War. The British won the war theoretically on the battlefield, but it was lost in the minds and the hearts of the English-speaking people, as well as Britain, and only eight years after the war complete internal self-rule was given to the Afrikaans-speaking republics on the Transvaal and Orange Free State which joined with Natal and the Cape Province to create South Africa. In 1902 when the peace treaty was signed, it promised that no franchise would be given to "Natives in the former republics until after the introduction of self-government" and although apartheid didn't actually come into being until 1948, it must be understood that for 300 years the principle of segregation has been the premise of every policy.

There is nothing much in the beginning of the Afrikaners' history that could not be paralleled with the history of Virginia or the Carolinas, but it is not in its origins so much as in its long and uncritical continuance that the South African way of life is especially open to criticism.

The South Africans will tell you that as children grow and develop a will of their own, their wishes have to be taken into account in the affairs of the family, and that is what they themselves are driving at. But who has ever heard of a 350-year-old kid? And with your children you encourage rather than discourage proper education. This is just a sample of the type of argument you get from South Africans.

The Government spends ten times as much on the education of whites as it does on blacks. The blacks must pay for their education. The whites who can't afford private schools get it free. An official statement says, "Education plays its essential part in the general advancement of the Bantu people." What this really means is that the English language is forbidden as a medium of instruction and that Africans have a different curriculum from white schools. African schools ignore history, geography and most of the sciences, and instead children in the upper primary school—the select minority who will supply the leaders of the future—spend six hours per week on just three subjects—tree planting and soil conservation, gardening, and handwork, which means planting reeds and grasses and making useless articles out of scraps of waste, wire, beads and so on. Children so trained can be guaranteed non-competitive. "Bantu education" says Edgar Brookes, "fails not only to prepare African children for life in the general economy of South Africa, but fails even to provide the technicians and artisans required by the Bantustans. There is no need, we are told, for Bantu engineers. Poor Bantustans!"

The late Prime Minister Dr. Verwoerd said, "What is the use of teaching the Bantu child mathematics when it cannot use it in practice? It is absurd . . . there is no place for the Native in a European community above the level of certain forms of labour . . . It is of no avail for him to receive a training which has as its aim absorption in the European community . . . teach them . . . that equality is not for them."

Brookes went on to say, "In the narrow context of poor Whitism a generation or two ago talk like that may have sounded sensible. It was certainly good electioneering tactics. There was no excuse for it in 1954 and there has been none since. In the Africa of 1962 it is madness." And, of course, in the 1970s apartheid, more strongly enforced than ever, is utter lunacy.

Tom Stacey, a schoolmate of Jock's at Eton and former chief roving reporter of London's *Sunday Times,* once said that the critics of South Africa fall into two groups—the ignorant or the all-but-ignorant, and I suspect I fall somewhere in between. But I decided I had to read not only the books against apartheid, but those for it too. It was with great fear I picked up *The Case for South Africa* by Dawid de Villiers and began to read it. I have such a weak mind and am so unknowledgeable in facts, almost all facts, that whatever I read seems to convince me. The opposing side always seems equally right to me. I could never take a stand on capital punishment for example; I agree with it when I'm talking to intelligent people who do, and I'm against it when I'm talking to intelligent people who don't. I couldn't decide whether to tell you the following or not, but I'll come clean . . .

I am loathe to admit that in 1960, after my second trip to Africa when we sailed from London to Dar es Salaam, I was taking an English course at Johns Hopkins University and had to write an essay which I entitled "Apartheid's All Right With Me" (on which I got an "A"—which makes it even worse). Before then I had never even heard of apartheid, but during the twenty-eight days on the Mediterranean, the Suez Canal, the Red Sea and the Indian Ocean, I was totally brainwashed by some Afrikaners, saw only their point of view, and meant every word I wrote. Their arguments are powerful and certainly convincing, especially if you don't know any better.

The South Africans will tell you the races live separately and that that is the choice of the blacks too. That each group has its own rights. That it is separate but equal development.

As the years went on various people began to straighten me out, especially a good British friend, Patrick Arton, who had lived in South Africa for ten years, and much of whose advice and thinking is reflected in this chapter. (Another friend and author, Quentin Crewe, who has written on South Africa in the British press has also helped, and indeed the chapter title "The Cruel Paradise" we actually stole from him.) However, I did a complete turn about and, alas, reacted emotionally, for which I am not apologizing because apartheid *is* a very emotional situation. Perhaps I overreacted to the point where I let my emotions carry my mind away and publicly accused South Africans in the *Women's Wear Daily* of being just like the Nazis (which Patrick also convinced me was incorrect). Edgar Brookes in his book, which is against apartheid but is also fair and just in presenting the other side, says, "To accuse the Nationalists of being Nazis is an exaggeration and an affront." However, he does go on to say that although every Nationalist is not a Nazi, every Nazi would most certainly be a Nationalist. (Balthazar J. Vorster, now Prime

Minister, was an admirer of Hitler. During the war he was imprisoned because he was a general in a pro-Nazi organization that carried out criminal sabotage.) Thus, I have been guilty of everything when it comes to apartheid. I have applauded it and abused it unfairly, but I have tried in this attempt to be objective and fair and factual.

Therefore, I am pleased to be able to tell you that *The Case for South Africa* did not sway me at all. Dawid de Villiers is an intelligent, forthright and articulate man who has tried very hard to be fair, and I believe he may even be a kindly man—he is merely wrong.

He tells us we will find that South Africans who are black, colored or Asian enjoy higher standards and have advanced further in almost all respects than their fellow Africans in the rest of the continent, and that this is so in living standards, in housing and health services. I'm sure he believes this, but he doesn't go far enough to define "living standards"—isn't freedom the basis for "living standards"? How can a pair of shoes compensate the wearer for his loss of freedom?

He said he had written his book not as an apology or an attempt to gain converts, but for those who want to know how South Africans think, and he hoped that he might add a little understanding and perspective. He has succeeded there—in that I now understand the fears of the Afrikaner better, and it added a lot to my perspective of the limited, if not *always* cruel, mind of the Afrikaner. The Africans and the Dutch did arrive in South Africa at about the same time, but the Dutch did not regard the entire population as one nation and try to integrate into one political and social structure because the "White Africans," as De Villiers likes to speak of himself, would have been politically overwhelmed by the sheer weight of the non-white numbers; and this overwhelming would have involved not only the whites but the smaller non-white population. Today, the Pan-Africanists on the other end of the scale don't want a democratic society either, they want an all-black society, and for 17 per cent of the population to agree to one-man, one-vote would certainly be the end

of them. I can understand their fear. One of the arguments put to
me in 1960 is, "Would you Americans give Manhattan back to
the Indians now? Isn't there such a thing as *earning* a right to a
country?"

Also, if they were swamped, they couldn't just pull out and go
back to a safe metropolitan haven as the British colonialist could,
or as I could return to the States any time—they have to sit it
out in South Africa, because they have no other home.

Though this might have excused them a few hundred years
ago and makes their fear understandable today, it certainly does
not make them right.

About their history, they will tell you that South Africa is not a
country, "in which an indigenous population was dispossessed to
make way for alien settlers, nor can one think of its population as
true inhabitants and others as temporary guests. Each has a
right to call South Africa home."

They will tell you how their assertion against the tyrannous
and arbitrary acts of the Dutch authorities in today's idiom was
clearly the start of an anti-colonial movement, the first in Africa,
and this was two and a half centuries ago. They will tell you how
their fighting with the British was not a struggle for power in the
scramble for Africa, but "the first anti-colonial war in Africa of
this anti-colonial century." Perhaps they believe it.

They will tell you there are no "Pass Laws" any more. Just
"Documentary Offenses." As I mentioned before, every South African is obliged to carry identification documents, and the black
African's document is a reference book to see if the holder has the
authority to work in a white area, and the reason they have them
is to "prevent urban areas from becoming overcrowded with unemployed people." To the charges of the hardship, inconvenience
and indignity caused to Africans, a standard answer, which you
hear over and over again, is, "You cannot make an omelette without breaking eggs." But Africans are not eggs, they are human beings, in case the South Africans haven't noticed. Mr. de Villiers'
answer to the accusation is, "These I am afraid cannot be denied,
but it is so important to note that the hardships are neither planned

nor desired as such. They are rather to be seen as by-products of measures which have on balance been considered necessary in serving the greatest good for the greatest number."

Wow! They sure have a lot of bad by-products.

Blacks have no claim to remain in any town. They cannot stay in a town unless they have been born in it and unless they have remained in it continuously. If they leave it, or are turned out, even having been born there, they have no right to come back. Suppose a child goes away for more than a year to live with his grandparents and cannot prove he was at school there, he may not return. There is a case of a sixteen-year-old girl who went to live with her grandmother when she was eight. She says she went to school there, but there are no records. So now, for something that happened half her lifetime ago, she is illegally in her town, and since the officials have found this out, she must leave; leave her mother, her father, her twin brother. Her grandmother is dead. Where will she go?

No African has the right to seek work where he wants to or of the kind he desires. At every stage he requires a permit. No white employer may strike his own bargain with an African employee to whom he would like to give work. He must apply through the local labor bureau. The wife and children of an African laborer may not reside with the husband or father, unless the latter has been born in the urban area and resided there continuously since birth, or unless he has worked in the same employment for not less than ten years. So you can see the entire life of an African worker is hedged in by regulations and permits.

White South Africans, Afrikaners and British, will tell you over and over again how happy the African is. I simply cannot imagine how they can still their consciences or by what astonishing mental gymnastics they are able to reach such a conclusion. They will tell you how South Africa continues to be one of the few peaceful and stable areas in a world of mounting tensions, strife, political unrest and upheaval, even of genocide. Just ask the African in South Africa if he were not ruthlessly policed, not simply into "peace" but acquiescence, whether he would not create tensions, strife, political unrest and upheaval, to change his wretched lot. Why, if South Africa is one of the few peaceful and stable areas in the world, is government maintained under a "state of emergency"?

Whites will tell you that the Communists are stirring up conflict and revolutionary upheaval, disguising it in the name of "casting off the yoke of oppression and slavery," and therefore there is an emergency which in the rule-of-law concept carries in itself a provision for extraordinary powers and action in emergency.

Thus, in June 1967 the Terrorism Act was passed. Terrorism is defined as "Acts inside or outside South Africa committed with intent to endanger the maintenance of law and order in South Africa or to embarrass the administration of the affairs of the state." In addition, police officers above a certain rank have been given powers to detain and interrogate persons suspected of terrorism or of withholding information about terrorists. Now comes the punch line—the onus is on the accused person to establish his *innocence*. In terms of the Act, he is then required to establish beyond reasonable doubt that he did not have the intent to endanger the maintenance of law and order or bring about what the Act specified. If he cannot completely prove this, he is charged with terrorism. Inasmuch as the death sentence can be imposed in extreme cases of terrorism, this has caused people to say that a person can be sentenced to death in South Africa for "embarrassing the Government." Anybody trying to bring about political, economic, or social change is guilty of "Communism" as defined by the Suppression of Communism Act.

In the last few decades it has been a long slide backward, particularly since the Nationalist Party came into power in 1948 and apartheid was born. Although the Immorality Act was passed as long ago as 1927 (no sexual relations between blacks and whites), in 1949 came the Prohibition of Mixed Marriages, and in 1950 sexual relations between whites and colored or non-whites was outlawed. The year 1950 also brought the Group Area Act, compulsory residential segregation and banning. Banishment came in 1956. The "90 Day" clause was enacted in 1963, the "180 Day" clause in 1965. The jails are filled with political prisoners locked up in this "peaceful" country which is in the "state of emergency." And on and on and on.

Dr. Edgar Brookes said in his book which was published in 1968 that there have been more examples of *"klein"* (small) apartheid progressively each year, and, "In no other year since the Nationalists came into power in 1948 have so many apartheid notices been put up or has so much money been spent on separate entrances, toilets, seating arrangements and other trappings of apartheid." Then he lists some of the many "pinpricks" that were reported in just one year:

1. Louis Armstrong being refused a visa to visit South Africa by the government.
2. The directive to scientific bodies—such as the South African Bird Watchers' Society—to exclude non-Whites from their membership.
3. The announcement that an apartheid investigation is to be held on the rocks in the sea—anglers of different colors should not be allowed to fish from the same rock.
4. The cancellation of a proposed visit to Cape Town of the U.S. aircraft-carrier *Independence,* after the South African Government had insisted that its pilots who landed in South Africa must be white.
5. The prohibition of Whites from watching a non-White golf tournament on a White golf course because an Indian champion was taking part.
6. The considerable inconvenience caused to a blind white girl accompanied by a colored maid after she had been told by a white taximan that he would not carry white and colored passengers in the same car.
7. The refusal of permission for an Indian couple to bring their baby, born prematurely during a visit to India by its mother, into South Africa.

The Minister of Community Development said in answer to a statement accusing South Africans of arbitrarily uprooting people from areas where they have lived for hundreds of years and placing them in new areas, "Can anyone give me an example of a peaceful area which is a mixed residential area? Give me one example in the world. Take England and America; mention one urban area to me where there is peace and quiet in a mixed residential area."

Jock and I and about four hundred other people we know live in a mixed area, and have for years, and it is 100 per cent peaceful.

The Afrikaners will tell you how one step can so easily and logically lead to the next. Receiving non-white cricketers in South Africa as members of a touring side will, "almost inevitably encourage the idea that South African whites and non-whites would sometimes play cricket against each other in South Africa." Now it may well be, as the Cape *Times* has suggested, "that the heavens will not fall if a coloured side were occasionally to play cricket against a white side." But then, as a Government spokesman said, "what about rugby, which is a *contact* game, in which incidents are known to flare up, sometimes between spectators, sometimes between players? Where does one draw the line? And on what grounds? These problems go right to the heart of the South African situation and South Africans have to sort them out in their own way and in their own good time." (They've had more than 300 years.) That is one of the most extraordinary paragraphs I've ever read. So when De Villiers says a little later on in his book that South Africa's problems are easier to criticize than to solve, one figures that it wouldn't be all that difficult to solve many of the problems. Simply let the people play cricket with one another, allow them to watch each other on golf courses, or to fish off the same rocks, or have sexual intercourse if they want to, or enter the building through the same door.

And so, by the time I had come to the conclusion of Dawid de Villiers' book, *The Case for South Africa,* and he had said the critics of South Africa say apartheid is designed to perpetuate the evil of white domination and the exploitation of the non-white majorities, I had come, wholeheartedly, to agree with the critics, and I was able to fault out all his arguments for apartheid.

Another standard white South African statement is: "Among white men all over Africa, one comes across many who will insist that the Africans are much happier when they are 'kept in their place,' without much education, without political ideas or notions of progress and competition."

There is a certain truth in this view, with which I too would have to agree, and that is that the African may be happier, in fact *anyone* may be happier "not being concerned about relative capabilities," and indeed the youth of today are prescribing a reduction of competitive attitudes. In elaboration of this theory, Tom Stacey, who wrote the introduction to De Villiers' book, says: "The African, the tribal African, the peasant African, accepts the world as he finds it, and if he is spared natural disaster he will live on in contentment, submerged in his environment and in his group with all its ancient and subtly evolved sanctions and unquestioned disciplines, even if these are in part applied by white strangers. Life is secure, intuitively apprehended, and governed by forces that are never challenged." With this I agree. BUT this is where the supporters of apartheid stop, and with such reasoning they justify apartheid. They do not carry their thinking through to the next stage which is the only thing to be really considered; that if the African *desires* freedom, he certainly has the right to have it, even if it does destroy his "happiness." For what is happiness? Ignorance, and being spared natural disasters? Perhaps, for some who know no better there is nothing more, but that certainly is not enough for me nor for you, and most certainly not enough for anyone who wants more, as millions of Africans do. The non-white, who has at least as equal a stake to the claim of South Africa as the white, has the right, even if it will destroy his happiness, to "progress" if that is what he wants. The whites have no right to impose their judgments on him and tell him he is happier without freedom, without education, opportunities, progress and so on. Even if it were true—and no human could ever convince another that it was—they would have to find out for themselves. If the Africans are wrong in wanting these things, then they must be allowed to be wrong. They have the right to be wrong—in common with every other human being since the beginning of time.

Perhaps I am particularly stupefied by apartheid because this grotesque monster has been created by WASPs like me. When the Chinese torture someone or the Koreans do something dreadful, I am inclined to think, "Well, those Orientals, I never could understand them." And when 250,000 Africans slaughtered each other in Burundi in 1972 I am ashamed to admit it, but I felt practically nothing emotionally and dismissed it with an imperialistic sort of "savages" shrug. Yet if I claim to hate killing for its own sake, if I claim that what I hate is the inhumanity—all killing—then why do I feel enraged when South African whites machine-gun 69 defenseless blacks to death at Sharpeville (for tearing up their passbooks) yet feel little when 250,000 Africans butcher one another in a tribal war in Burundi? If it is all killing the larger the number, the larger the atrocity should be.

Guilt is the answer, you will say. I thought you'd say that, so I thought about it for a while and then dismissed it because I absolutely refuse to accept any blame whatsoever for something I had nothing to do with. I adamantly refuse to be responsible for what some dopey strangers who might have happened to be my ancestors did to the American Indian or the American slaves. I wasn't there, I didn't do anything, and nobody even asked me what I thought about it. I cannot accept the guilt of my ancestors any more than I can accept credit for their good deeds, if they ever did any.

Then what is this ambiguity of minding about whites killing blacks more than blacks killing blacks? Well, I think it may be because the Chinese are so unknowable to me, as are many Africans—primitive peoples—that I assume "they" must have different standards and values and even qualities which I would never be able to understand. But white South Africans are supposed to be *civilized,* they are not wild nor primitive, and they are supposed to be *Christians,* not some mysterious kind of sect.

They are people like *me,* and there is just no excuse, no justification for them—there is nothing but the wrong.

I was not present when the American Indians were wiped out or the blacks were enslaved, but I *am* here now, and there *is* something I can say and do about it, and so it *is* therefore, my responsibility.

It is also time for us to stop tolerating things that are intolerable.

What can we do? What is going to happen?

As Edgar Brookes says, "To change, the Afrikaner would have to undergo an experience no less extraordinary than a miraculous religious conversion. Apartheid is more than a law, it is a fundamental premise, a philosophy of life, in which the prejudices are rationalized and apartheid becomes moral principle. So the concept of racial equality will not come to the Afrikaner through his insight or conscience."

What about revolution? Because I have always been drawn to extremes and have always liked blacks or whites but not grays, I was initially attracted to the idea of a forceful takeover by the black African majority. But I am now convinced that this is stupid—at the moment—that there is little likelihood of successful violent revolution within South Africa because of the massive and ruthless security forces, informers, detentions without trial, and all the rest. It has been said, and I suspect it is true, that if all the countries in Africa got together to fight South Africa the attack would not stand a chance because South Africa is so strong militarily. If the great powers intervened, they could undoubtedly win, but whether one likes that idea or not it is patently not a realistic possibility, and if it were it might lead to a third world war. Anyway, outside intervention might bring untold suffering to the people it was meant to help—the blacks, coloreds and the Indians. So force, for many reasons, would simply not work.

What then?

Depressingly, there is not too much we Americans can do, and the frustration one feels when asked to make concrete suggestions about South Africa is just one more infuriating feeling the place is able to generate among its critics.

People talk of boycotts, of cutting off all trade with South Africa, but, realistically, it is not going to happen. Even if America were to sever connections—highly unlikely since the United States investments total over a billion dollars—it is even more unlikely that Britain would since they have a much greater stake than we do, and there are many other countries too who will keep on buying and selling. Thus American withdrawal would certainly not cause the collapse of apartheid.

Then there is another thing. Who would the boycotts hurt? The whites, insulated as they are from immediate physical hardship, could tighten their belts and not really be affected by a little bit of boycott. For the majority of Africans whose struggle for survival is a matter of daily anxiety, even a slight reduction in economic activity could cause great hardship. In black African countries, where the vast majority of the people live off the land, the prospect of economic sanctions is not too alarming, but in South Africa, in case you have forgotten, 70 per cent have only 9 per cent of the land—and it is arid and useless land at that. What would happen to the wretched Africans who would be laid off and deprived of the pittance they now earn? You can argue that their state can hardly be diminished to anything worse and that they have nothing to lose. But do they feel this way, and who has asked them? Can outsiders make such a decision on their behalf?

Forget about buying and selling for the moment. What of the American companies that have factories in South Africa and make good profits from them? Companies like I.B.M., Mobil, General Motors, General Electric, Firestone and many others come to mind. Remember that American shareholders are growing rich as a result of some of the exploitation described in this chapter, but oddly enough, a tiny glimmer of hope has emerged *because* of the presence of American business. Enlightened American shareholders, many of them blacks, have put pressure on the parent companies in the States. Some of these companies revised their policies in South Africa and committed what is tantamount to heresy—

they promoted able Africans, they installed interracial cafeterias, and in one case appointed a black supervisor over a partly white assembly line. They have broken down racially stratified wage structures and are moving toward wage parity. Their actions in so doing have in some cases actually been illegal, but the Government has not yet—and may never—challenge them.

Soon the ideas may spread to other companies. Many industrialists—even South Africans—would welcome the chance to promote Africans because sheer economic common sense dictates that already there are insufficient whites to man the jobs that are reserved for them by law, and expanding industry will have to tap hitherto untouchable African reservoirs.

As I said, it was American shareholder pressure which started the trend and it is that same pressure which must continually be exerted to make the tiny beginning into the accepted commonplace. Gillette and I.B.M. are quite daring in setting the pace, and others must be goaded into line also so that it is impossible to stop the tide—so that even a below-poverty-line African from Soweto may find himself the recipient of a respectable wage packet, a fair pension and a chance for a piece of the action.

Lest we Americans feel smug because a few of our companies have broken ice in South Africa, here are some facts to ponder. A recent survey of the 292 United States companies in South Africa showed that three quarters of the American businessmen approved of apartheid, only 20 per cent opposed it, and only ten out of the 292 companies felt it was "all together wrong."

In 1970 the managing director of the International Harvester subsidiary in South Africa told a visitor from New York's Council for Christian Social Action, "I am sympathetic to what the South Africans are trying to do. I don't want hundreds of Africans running around in front of my house."

The very system of subsidiaries is not exactly conducive to enlightened social action. A bright young man is often sent abroad by the parent company for a "tour" of four or five years. For him it is a stepping stone in a career, and if he can show increased profits by the end of his tenure, promotion is ensured. Why should he pay equal wages for equal work or introduce an expensive medical or pension scheme? Hiding behind the South African policy of "job reservations" and current wage structures most managers do nothing much and so become "partners in apartheid."

It requires much detailed knowledge to argue with articulate South Africans or those who choose to function blindly within its system, and one must be aware of the facile semantic approach they often use to get off the hook. Managers of companies will say, "We pay people for the job regardless of race." The statement sounds good but examine it. Colored electricians, for example, may not be called electricians but "electrical assistants." Further, they may not work from a blueprint, but to work from a *photograph* of a blueprint is O.K. Thus, by a childish schoolboy ruse the coloreds are denied the title and the money to go with the job, though they are engaged in identical work with a white. "Oh, no," says the company innocently, "we don't have any colored electricians as it happens, but if we did we would pay them the scale for electricians." That kind of puerile cop-out revolts me.

But Americans who are shareholders in companies with subsidiaries in South Africa, and I list the companies in the Appendix, can bring real pressure to bear on the parent corporation simply by writing and asking for details of what is being done to ameliorate conditions and terms for all workers in the South African plant. A good example is that until recently Ford in South Africa gave medical coverage to whites after three months employment and to blacks after ten years! Since 1972, because of an anticipated outcry and consequent bad publicity, all families who work for Ford are now covered after three months.

For those readers who may not own shares in such a company, as well as for those who do, there is always the opportunity to contribute financially to organizations whose purpose it is to fight for the rights of non-white South Africans, and one of the most energetic in this regard is the South African Institute of Race Relations, the address of which is also given at the end of the Appendix.

In 1973, as a result of an exposé in the British press, many

English companies which make substantial profits out of South Africa are being forced to examine the conditions of their black and colored workers. May the trend continue, may it spread to all countries with South African investments, and may its effects be the edge of the wedge that will bring real change and real opportunity to millions of oppressed humans in South Africa.

The next step, and there are signs that it has started, is for the black and colored and even sympathetic white workers to begin withholding their labor and use that power to negotiate. So much for the corporate world.

What else can an American do? Well, South Africans are very sports minded, and lacking any fine culture of their own they also love importing entertainment—from opera singers to rock groups. This is where boycott can hurt. No entertainer or sportsman of any kind should set foot in South Africa until he may sing or run in front of and together with South Africans of all races. This would be a blow badly taken by South Africans and each time it happened it would force them to re-examine themselves.

All right, you agree to help. But if we Americans write letters, create shareholder fuss and so on, what are the Africans going to do to help themselves? And what are the South African whites who disagree with their Government's policies going to do?—there are quite a few of these. As I mentioned before and as Dr. Brookes pointed out in his book, for a British South African to disagree with apartheid, he has his church and his universities also on his side. But when an Afrikaner disagrees with apartheid, he has not only his Government but his church and his universities opposing him as well as his own community. Unfortunately, those people, white or non-white, who oppose apartheid can't actually do as much as you and I can because any public opposition to South African Government policies is attended with grave personal risk, and this must be remembered when comment is made about the silence of "friends of civil liberty" within South Africa. There are so many informers and the police state is so effective that few, understandably, are willing to give public expression to their feelings.

South Africa is more self-sufficient than many countries and in a pinch could get along in a fashion without the rest of the world, so attempted economic isolation is not only impractical, it might even be counter-productive. I believe that the more the enlightened breezes of the outside world can blow through the musty outdated corridors of Pretoria, the capitol, the better chance there is that South Africans will see themselves as others see them and will begin to change. But make them aware that they are way out of line by denying them international sport and entertainment. With that exception, the more that South Africa can see and be seen, the more chance there is that that most valuable international currency of all—ideas—will seep and spread into the dark corners of rigid little South African minds.

Most travelers to South Africa do not see what they are looking at, but it is not really their fault because the Government is at pains to hide the hideosities not only from the outside world but from their own community. It is hard to believe, but true, that there are countless whites in South Africa, living in their own tight little circle, who do not really know what goes on in their own country. They believe that ". . . the Government is taking care of the Africans" and they are told of schools and housing schemes and health projects and they feel warm inside for a minute and they don't think about the subject again for six months. The traveler is even conned by a fake overtness, an example of which is the city sightseeing bus which includes Soweto on the tour of Johannesburg. Visitors are shown a small, deliberately well-kept showpiece section of Soweto, given a booklet called "Happy Living," and the accompanying commentary by a white is designed to forestall questions about the lot of the African. But let the visitor try hiring a car and going off to explore Soweto on his own—oh, no indeed. But a tourist in Nairobi can go anywhere he wants in the whole city at any time of day or night.

Thus, a visitor can leave South Africa with the feeling that all is nice and clean and well ordered, and he may even have picked up a few propaganda clichés from the white driver or the white hotel clerk since, largely, he will only be exposed to white people during his stay. Some will go having read this book. Some may read this after they return. Most, of course, will never read this at all. But there is other material, there are articles and news items and documentaries and it is a fact that anyone who has ever visited a country carries with him a little corner of interest about it for ever.

Those who are forewarned and do know the facts about South Africa before they go there, are surely obligated—if only to themselves—to speak out against it there to drivers, escorts or to South African acquaintances.

In a small way Jock and I do what we can. When tourists who travel with our company arrive in Kenya, if South Africa is on their itinerary, we tell them about it—perhaps more than they want to know. Whether they agree with us or argue (if the latter, it is usually a parroting of arguments they have just heard from the white South Africans), we do find that there is intense interest in the subject *because they have been there*. Cutting off South Africa, amputating it, so to speak, from the world is not the way to bring about change. Even the African nations who so bitterly oppose the hated regime should leave the lines of communication open to the Government, to the people, and above all to their own oppressed brethren. And if white South Africans could travel through the rest of Africa they might lose their fear of Africans. Let them explore Nairobi to their heart's content. Let them ride on safari for a week with an African as a driver and escort and dinner companion. Let them feel what it is like to move freely and easily alongside black people. In the absence of other realistic solutions to the problem of South Africa, communication could be the best way of helping the trapped people of that sad country to advance toward a peaceful evolutionary goal of racial equality.

Perhaps a few white South Africans have already had a change of heart. Maybe some who have traveled abroad have met people of other races on a social level, with whom they have become friendly, and have discovered that they aren't so different after all. Perhaps those South Africans who have talked to American black diplomats who from time to time have been allowed into South Africa, realize that the difference in the color of skin is about as important as the difference of the color of someone's eyes. So, perhaps there have been a few who have had a change of heart. But in the words of Edgar Brookes, "Until there is a change of power, all of us inside and outside of South Africa who value human rights and respect all men, white men included, must work for better things. We cannot just leave the situation as it stands."

There remains the haunting cry, "We are suffering. We have been thrown away. We have nothing. But what can we do? We are only Africans. There is no one to hear us."

Most of the world does seem to be deaf, but speaking of Americans generally—not the politicians and businessmen who have supported South Africa—I believe it is not that they are deaf but that they have never been told the words. I believe that the majority of the world just do not know what actually happens in this "cruel paradise." Can you imagine how euphoric the black South Africans, the voiceless people, will be when they get an answer, perhaps for the first time from us, "Yes, there is someone who hears you."

How Do You Pronounce Kenya?

MAINLY BY JOCK

People ask us questions ranging from, "How do you pronounce Kenya?" to, "What do you think is the future of Africa?"

"Ken" to rhyme with "pen" is the answer to the first, but the second question is as big as the continent, and it is a bit like asking, "What is the future of the world?"

As with a lot of questions, we spend the first few minutes trying to elicit from the questioner what he means—which part of Africa? Does he understand the continent is divided into at least three broad areas, North Africa, sub-Sahara Africa, and South Africa—and that the answers are totally different for each? Next, what kind of future? Economic? Role in world affairs? Political? Then we have to work out the questioner's own point of reference. No, sir, there are probably not a lot of opportunities for a New York taxi driver in independent black Africa. Yes, miss, the Salvation Army does a good job in Uganda, but we don't really know about their plans for Algeria. No, I was not aware that the Baltimore Colts had considered playing a benefit match in Somalia in 1975—are you sure you have that right, sir?

The future can mean many different things to different questioners. There are too many factors beyond the control of Africans themselves for them alone to dictate what happens in the next twenty years, and increasingly no country will be able to function in isolation. But here are a few things to ponder.

The population explosion in many African countries is such that it outstrips economic expansion in the sense that each year there is less "butter" for the government to spread per person rather than more.

Although there is development and progress in Africa, its rate is slower than current development and progress in industrial nations, so although the African countries might seem to be moving forward, the gap between them and the rich nations actually grows wider—not less—with each year that passes because the advanced countries are accelerating at an ever-increasing speed.

While education is regarded as a priority, in many countries the scholars and intellectuals often have a hard time. Thoughts they may have can appear as threatening to entrenched leaders of lesser mental agility whose main preoccupation is to stay in power. The persecution or shunting aside of intellectuals may follow, and the working conditions and opportunities open to the *crème de la crème* of Africa are often insufficient inducement for them to stay.

This might make a scary picture but there are other factors that have a bearing. For a start, the rest of the world is not going to let Africa go to sleep. Already there is too much involvement, too much awareness of the problems. People will not starve by the thousands because foreign agencies will ensure, one way or another, that they don't. The soaring affluence and technical ability of the richer countries will be available to solve problems that exist in Africa, and increasingly so. Don't forget that a restless, impoverished and troubled Africa (or Asia or South America) is a form of threat to those who are better off, and often out of self-interest, disguised of course as altruism, massive loans, massive projects and no little influence for "good" will be brought to bear. Financial assistance to developing countries has been cynically described as ". . . taking from the poor in the rich countries and giving to the rich in the poor countries." No smoke without a fire and all that, and it is true that low and middle income brackets are the most heavily taxed in the States, and it is true, too, that some assistance cash has now and then been diverted into a second or

third Mercedes Benz for an already prosperous African government minister. By and large, though, money given to developing
countries is well used, and without aid programs and loans I dread
to think what state the continent would be in.

Some of the aberrations that afflict African regimes at the present time will ultimately be seen in perspective by the electorates
of their countries as damaging and stupid, and leaders will not be
allowed to get away with much of the nonsense they put over on
their people now. The other side of this coin is that those African
countries that have chosen the route of reason and hard work,
and I would include Kenya among them, will serve as an example
to others. Jomo Kenyatta, for instance, has been truly remarkable
in that he not only led a successful revolutionary movement and
became leader of a sovereign state, he then *did* something with that
state, giving it stability and the chance for real progress. It is easy
to lead a revolution, but how many can then switch and lead a
country in the right direction when the excitement is over? Almost
none.

What will China be up to in Africa in twenty years' time? What
will Russia be doing? Is it inconceivable that China and Russia
and the United States will be jointly involved in a massive plan to
aid less-fortunate countries? I am glad that I will still be alive, because I can't wait to see what is going to happen.

In our travels through the States we are often questioned by
people who have been on safari in Tanzania as to why there are so
many Chinese there. It is a funny thing, but many otherwise reasonable and kindly people have a blind spot when it comes to this
subject. (This is not a political book, but you may have noticed
that every now and then we try to sneak in a little serious information, just quietly sliding it in between the lighthearted bits.
Ready?)

Tanzania needed a railroad, or to be accurate, another railroad.
Communications in the southern part of the country were not that
great, and there was no rail link between Tanzania and land-
locked copper-rich Zambia to her south. Because of the copper
(Zambia hates to use her only other access to the sea through

Rhodesia because it means paying money to the racist Smith—more about that next) a Tanzanian railway can be kept busy, will be profitable and will help the people living within reach of it on its way to the sea.

The Tanzanians sought the money, £169,000,000 ($405,-600,000), for the project from the West, but Europe and America kept saying they could not afford to help. For about five years they kept asking and they said that if the West was not prepared to help, they would get the cash from China—which suggestion caused much derisive laughter in London, Bonn and Washington. That is, until the Chinese put up the money and the technicians and the equipment.

And when, a few years ago, the Chinese ship *Xuan Huo* steamed into Dar es Salaam harbor bearing red flags and a banner that read, "Long live the Friendship between the Chinese and Tanzanian Peoples," small children on the quay were told, "This is the first time a Chinese ship has ever been here."

What they should have been told was, "This is the first time a Chinese ship has been here for five hundred years," and they first came over 2,000 years ago. The Ming Dynasty of the fifteenth century had built a huge and efficient navy whose motives for going to the utmost regions of the known world was to enhance China's reputation in foreign lands and to seek tribute acknowledging the distant authority of the Emperor. The emperors regarded themselves as the Sons of Heaven, and they wished their eminence made known to "barbarians," as they called foreigners. Those who offered tribute were left in peace, and those who didn't were captured and sent back to China as "devil slaves." Some scholars say a further reason for African exploration by the Chinese was for the *tsu-la*—giraffe. The ruler of Bengal received many giraffe from certain African rulers, and he passed one on as homage to Emperor Yung-lo, which he received in the great Hall of Receptions reserved for the most distinguished guests. From the minute it strode into the Emperor's court it caused a great sensation and became the emblem in China of Perfect Virtue, Perfect Government and Perfect Harmony. It was Yung-lo who commissioned the most daring of all sea adventurers—the eunuch Cheng Ho—who made seven voyages and "traversed more than 100,000 li (Chinese mile—633 yards) and "made manifest the transforming power of the Imperial virtue to barbarian rulers." Then, in 1430 Yung-lo's successor ordered the disbandment of the navy, all shipbuilding stopped, and Confucian thought prevented all interest in the world outside China. Historians destroyed documents relating to overseas exploration so those "expansion" policies would not resume again. Teobaldo Filese, who wrote *China and Africa in the Middle Ages* (translated by David Morison), sums up these medieval voyages thus:

". . . the Chinese confined themselves to appearing on the coast of East Africa, without any aim of exerting direct influence on the life and destinies of the local populations.

They were neither conquerors nor emigrants in search of new homes, but only able navigators and merchants who made known to remote countries the illustrious name and gracious commands of the Son of Heaven.

The commands are now called Thoughts, and the Son of Heaven had become a Chairman: perhaps the messages carried on the side of the *Xuan Huo* were not all that different from that brought across the "immense water spaces" by Cheng Ho 500 years earlier."

Today there are thousands of Chinese in Tanzania and millions of copies of the thoughts of Chairman Mao. People say, "The Red Chinese have taken over Tanzania and they will soon spread like a plague over the rest of Africa."

Well, the facts don't actually bear that out yet. For a start, the Tanzanians have just got rid of one bunch of colonialists and are not about to saddle themselves with another. They are jealous of their sovereignty, conscious of their new nationalism and a little wary of the Chinese. The latter, so it would seem, are not exactly at ease among the Africans. The "black and yellow and brown men of the world, united as brothers against the neo-colonialist imperialism of the white oppressors" sounds seductive in Afro-Asian conferences, but doesn't seem to work out in practice. The

Chinese in Tanzania appear to keep very much to themselves, do not fraternize with the locals (who don't exactly line up to fraternize with them, either) and do not appear to be meddling overmuch in day-to-day politics. Maybe they are frightened of backing a loser (Peking backed an African politician who blotted his copybook in Kenya, thus spoiling their chances for any kind of a Kenya foothold for the time being), and maybe they are just keeping a very low profile and playing a long-term waiting game— which would be in keeping with their methods.

Certainly President Nyerere of Tanzania has taken a highly socialistic line with his country's affairs, but for those who have observed him over any length of time this represents no sudden change. Who knows, Chinese advisers may have influenced the degree of his socialism, but on the other hand it is not known for sure that he even seeks or listens to their advice.

Meanwhile, the railroad nears completion, and we all watch to see how many Chinese workers and technical experts go home when it is finished and how many stay to invest their energies in other activities. The annoying part is that we will probably never know for sure because Chinese comings and goings in Tanzania seem to be shrouded in secrecy and no Tanzanian officials will answer nosy questions about them.

One hears rumors from time to time of Chinese arms and military advisers, destined, perhaps, to help unseat Rhodesia's Smith. But to be fair, there are British and French and probably American and Russian arms floating around in various parts of Africa and nobody gets too uptight about them.

Probably, the Chinese will work very hard, will keep their noses very clean, and when they have become part of the scenery in twenty years' time they will rise up and take over the entire continent from Morocco to the Cape of Good Hope. And then again they may not.

Another serious-type question we are called upon to answer and explain from time to time concerns the Asians who live in East Africa.

"Why," our questioners demand, sometimes with a tinge of hostility, "did the Governments throw out all the Asians?"

Well now, to understand all this we must go back a bit. Remember—most of the original Indians were coolies brought over from India to work on the railroad construction at the beginning of the century, and when the project was complete they stayed in the country, multiplied, sent for relatives from India, and spread all over either as tradesmen or artisans—builders, plumbers and the like.

They were thrifty, hard working and acquisitive. The Indian *duka* (store) became a part of everyone's life. Europeans bought groceries at *dukas* and Africans bought sugar and blankets and oil lamps. Most of the country's wholesale and retail trade was in Asian hands and practically every contractor was an Asian. Some became rich and powerful and nobody can deny that their energy made a real contribution to the growing Kenya, and to Uganda and Tanganyika as well.

All the while, however, the Indians were accumulating bad marks from an African point of view. In the first place, all Indians are very community-minded (their own community, that is). They hardly mix with Indians of other Indian communities, let alone with Africans or Europeans. The communities in this sense are not so much based on physical dwelling location as upon religion and custom and caste. There are Oshwals and Khojas and Ismailis and Sikhs and all sorts of confusing Indians, whether Hindus or Muslims, and they like to consort with their own kind. This is fine by me (frequently a relief, actually, since we are not fond of Asian movies and entertainment, and although we hardly drink at all, the very sight of grape juice and no option brings out the perverse in both of us and we instantly want to get drunk), but the Africans, who are not really on very strong ground themselves since they are inclined to be rigidly tribal, interpret Asian community-mindedness as standoffishness.

The next thing is that the Indians are not renowned for parting with money or for giving generous or reasonable deals. Simple, commercially unsophisticated Africans were easy prey for the

sharp businessman, even at the trading level of a blanket and a
few pounds of sugar. Asians also paid their workers something
less than minimum wages but demanded more than a standard
day's work—probably (I'm being charitable) because they work
so hard themselves. Their instructions to African employees were
often delivered in a high-pitched and garrulous manner, which
in part reflected an attitude and in part (more charity) is simply
what an Indian sounds like when speaking broken Swahili.

Skilled Indians tend to be jealous of their crafts. This in contrast to the British who can't wait to have everyone around them
operating with maximum efficiency and skill and who adore the
talented protégé. Swelling with vicarious pride, white farmers
would boast to one another about their tractor driver who could
plow as straight as an arrow or the farm mechanic who could
build a new fuel pump out of a condensed milk can and an old
inner tube. But the skilled Indian plasterer or cabinetmaker saw
the clever African workman as a threat—as somebody who might
be able to replace him or do him out of a job.

Related to this factor was another. As the African did acquire
skills, or aspired to be a trader, or edged toward a middle-class
existence, who was standing in the way? Shah or Patel or Singh.

Politically, the Asians tended, in pre-independence days, to be
more hooked up with Africans than with the British. After all,
they had been dominated by the British in India and they felt the
same racial slights as colonial subjects in India. But ironies creep
in everywhere. Rather in the same way that Jews have been
vilified by American blacks, even though they have long supported black hopes, the fact that they were also landlords of black
tenements and owned the corner store meant that black Americans
came into contact with them in their daily lives, and had to hand
money over to them for rent and food. Thus, the Jews ended up
being the ones whom the black Americans hated most, even
though they had been politically helpful. And so it is with the
Indians in Africa.

All this has just been background. Now for the nitty-gritty. At
the stroke of midnight on the respective independence dates of

Kenya, Uganda and Tanzania, as the British flag was lowered and the new national flags were hoisted high, at that actual moment all the indigenous peoples of those countries, Africans and Arabs (who were regarded as indigenous) became Kenyans, or Ugandans or Tanzanians. Previously Africans had traveled abroad on British passports. From this moment on they would have their own. The "expatriates" retained their own nationalities.

The new Kenya flag, fluttering bravely, was interesting in its composition. There was black for the people of Kenya. There was red for the blood shed on the path to freedom. And there was green for the fertile land. These colors, and this is really nice if you think about it and take all the circumstances into account, were separated one from another by thin white lines, which represented the minority communities who lived in the country, who had helped to build it and a percentage of whom would in all probability remain. As midnight tolled out, an offer made by Kenyatta's Government to the expatriates came into effect. Subject only to suitable proof of residence, any member of a non-indigenous minority (i.e., British, Indian, French, Italian, anything) could, with no formalities other than the renunciation of their former citizenship, become a full Kenya citizen. The offer was to remain open for a period of two years after which the adoption of Kenya citizenship, unless you had been born in the country, was going to be a lot harder and approximately in line with requirements of most countries in the world. Similar offers were made by Tanzania and Uganda. Jock, and many like him who had lived here all their lives and had their houses and businesses and interests in Kenya, quickly became citizens. So did a fair number of Asians, who, in conformity with the offer, were given new passports without difficulty.

Many of the Asians, however, sat on the fence. After all, they could still live and work in Kenya, though there was some talk of trading licenses only being issued to citizens in the future. But for the time being all was well, though it had dawned on most of them that the Africans did not love them like brothers. However, if things got rough or too difficult, they could always move to Eng-

land since they were still British subjects with British passports.
Then the bombshell.

Britain passed a Commonwealth Immigrants Act in 1968 which
for the first time differentiated between English, Welsh and Scottish
British on the one hand, and the other kinds of British passport
holders from around the world on the other. They agreed not to
disturb Jamaican or Pakistani British for example, already resid-
ing in England, but no newcomers would be allowed in other than
as visitors. The "insurance policy" in the shape of a British passport which the East African Asians had been banking on was
suddenly valueless. However, and this is the real nub of the matter—what I have been building up to all through this explanation
—the Act was not to pass into law until a certain specified date.
Realizing that if they could get into England before that date they
could claim to be residents under the existing but about-to-be-
changed law, more than 20,000 Indians in Kenya packed up and
left in a matter of weeks, squeezing into the British Isles before
the gates clanged shut for ever.

Incredible as it may seem, much of the world press did not
bother to get the facts straight, and articles appeared from Stock-
holm to São Paulo about Asians fleeing from Kenyatta's African
Government. They weren't fleeing *from* anything, they were fleeing *toward* Britain while they still could.

The spectacle in Nairobi was amazing. The airport looked
like a disaster area, with charter aircraft and scheduled flights
taking off in squadrons, groaning with human cargo. Rich merchants who had lived on a grain of rice a day until they could afford a Mercedes (a typically Indian peculiarity; apparent shirt-
tail poverty to instant opulence at the moment of surpassing a
self-set target of a magic bank figure) were virtually giving their
cars away. Heads of families bid farewell to hosts of women and
children who were to remain behind winding up the business
while Dad established his residential qualifications in Earls Court
or Croydon. Master masons walked off half completed building
projects and scrambled on to anything that would fly them to the
golden gates of Heathrow. Shops that were fully functioning on

Monday were closed for good on Tuesday. It must have been one of the biggest mass movements in history that took place without being sparked by any desperate danger or crisis. After all, nobody was being shot at or threatened or physically persecuted, or even asked to leave.

And that was "the Asian exodus" from Kenya. There are, perhaps, one or two footnotes that may help to complete the picture.

In the first place many Indians had actually applied for Kenya citizenship before the exodus took place but had not had their papers processed. This could be interpreted as deliberate on the part of the Government who did not want a glut of Asian citizens, because, as shown above, there was not a lot of love lost between them.

Secondly, people often ask why they didn't simply go back to India. The reason is that the Government of India took a quick look at the problem and said to themselves, "But we already have 400 million Indians and we feel that's about enough, thank you very much." Actually, India felt, quite understandably, that those who had lived outside her shores for three and four generations and had carried *British* passports all the while were not really their responsibility. After all, if life suddenly got hot for third-generation Italian Americans, for example, do you think Italy would reabsorb them all just like that? Patently, prime responsibility for British Asians in East Africa rests with Britain, and the problem is by no means over yet. Those Indians who left it until too late cannot live and work in East Africa, but no other country will accept them either. In effect, they are a displaced people, lost souls without a country, and that is a truly sad condition in which to find oneself.

Finally, I must tell you that those Asians who did not fence-sit and who took Kenya citizenship when it was offered, have been absorbed into the life of the country, have their jobs and their stores and their homes—and, I should imagine, give thanks to their sundry gods daily that they are not afloat in limbo.

The matter of the Uganda Asians during 1972 attracted much more world-wide attention than the relatively mild exodus from

Kenya a few years earlier. The wild remarks and mercurial behavior of Uganda's military dictator, General Amin, who started
the purge without warning, made the airlift of 30,000 Asians in
ninety days headline material around the world. It is not the fact
that Amin wanted the non-citizen Asians to leave the country so
much as his extreme methods and unseemly haste that caused the
furor.

Not only was much suffering and anguish caused to those who
had to uproot themselves and flee penniless to heaven knows
what future, but almost total disruption of the Ugandan economy
resulted. Amin acted on emotional impulse, and the non-thinking
African masses applauded him. After all, if the Asians were to
go and could not take their money and businesses, naturally
what they left behind would become theirs.

"The Asians have exploited us for seventy years," they cried.
"Now we will have what should have been ours all along." What
the ordinary man could not be expected to understand, and what
the intellectuals kept quiet about for fear of attracting the wrath-
ful attention of Amin, was that the Asians are among the most
competent people in the world, diligent and effective in almost
any undertaking. The Uganda economy ticked because they
were an integral part of it. Without them, like a car out of fuel,
the country gave a weak shudder and quit.

To digress a moment. It is a particularly African trait to look
at another man and to assume in full confidence that it would
immediately be easy to do what he does, given the opportunity.
Westerners tend to be more realistically cautious, to understand
that it usually takes years of dedicated application, attention to
detail, self-discipline, and other boring things like that to reach
the top. A degree of self-confidence is vital to success, of course,
but where does it get you if the books are not kept up to date,
letters lie around unanswered and office time is spent cruising
around in the Mercedes? I sometimes feel that what some Africans need to bring to a job is a bit more self-doubt—not self-
confidence—a little realistic appraisal of the facts that spell viabil-
ity, and a bit less adulation of the academic degree which is so

much paper unless its acquisition is followed by a rolling up of the sleeves and the recognition that a qualification only gets you to the starting gate, so to speak, not the end of the race. An African with a degree, by comparison with other Africans, is a god at this period in history. But what kind of measure is that?

"How's your wife?" a man asked his friend.

"Compared to whom?" he replied, with a fine regard for perspective. I have heard that more than 50 per cent of Americans under thirty have been to college but that less than 3 per cent of the jobs in the States actually need a college education. This means that there are some very smart people working on building sites, in the clothing business, in agriculture and so on, and their brains and perspective are bound to enhance their respective industries even at a menial level. If they lived in Africa, however, every one of them would hold a senior position in a Government ministry or would be in the process of being groomed by private industry to head the corporation in five years.

Quite understandably the law of supply and demand has thus given the possessors of degrees in Africa an inflated sense of importance—but "compared to whom?" Surely one of the main purposes of higher education is to produce people who have not only a degree in a subject but a proper sense of perspective of the world as a whole.

But to get back to the main theme, Amin's miscalculation was that Ugandans could simply replace the Asians and that the economy would then be in the hands of citizens—a perfectly laudable premise in itself but doomed to failure as an overnight policy. His action, therefore, not only caused all kinds of misery for the Asians concerned but resulted in unemployment and despair for hundreds of thousands of Africans who found themselves without work and hope. At least the Asians stood the chance of a new life in England or Canada or India, but the unemployed African has nowhere to turn. Even so, and this is one of the main things in the understanding of Africa, the vast majority of the population lead the life of subsistence peasants, eating what they grow, building their houses out of sticks and

thatch and mud and getting their water from a stream. What
difference does "the economy" in the modern sense make to
them? Almost none. They may have to hold off for another six
months before buying a new blanket. The dispensary may be
short of drugs and new bicycle tires hard to come by, but because their lives are not geared directly to the economy in a
modern sense they hardly notice any difference when the economy "collapses." And they still think Amin did the right thing.

The bad guy in the eyes of the world, if not among his own
people, has been General Idi Amin Dada, the ex-sergeant and
heavyweight boxer who overthrew Uganda's elected President
Milton Obote in a military coup. His erratic behavior and wild
pronouncements have brought chaos and bloodshed—and occasionally a laugh or two. Imagine President Nixon saying he
would have married Kosygin had the latter been a girl. That is
exactly what Amin said in a public statement addressed to Tanzania's President Nyerere who at the time refused to recognize
Amin's regime and who the General was trying to win over. Another time the paranoid Amin accused Britain of planning to in-
vade Uganda "by land, by air, and by sea." When asked to
clarify "by sea" since Uganda is five hundred miles from the
ocean, Amin's retort was that the planning of a sea attack in
the first place displayed the ineptitude and ignorance of Douglas
Home, Britain's Foreign Secretary.

Even some of the luckless prisoners—a number of Europeans
were arrested in September of 1972 for no reason at all and
released ten days later, also for no reason—had humorous things
to recount. One group, thrown into a tiny cell that was so small
they had to take turns lying down on the floor to sleep, were in
fear of their lives and were sure they would be dragged from
their prison and shot by the soldiers. Sure enough, on the first
night men appeared with machine guns and marched them from
the cell. At gun point they were escorted through the streets to the
Grand Hotel, where they were seated at an elegant table and
were served a five-course dinner. Their armed escorts sat at a
nearby table and drank. Music played and people danced. After

dinner they were marched back to the cell, and so it was every night until they were released. Either the prison had no supplies of food or they were not certain what to feed the Europeans. Uganda during that period was a kind of tragi-comedy, like an excerpt from *Mad* magazine.

The good guys in the Uganda Asian saga turned out to be the British. Faced with the situation the British Government in a sense reversed itself by recognizing responsibility for British passport holders, albeit not British born, and with typical crisis-induced British efficiency arranged to absorb the vast bulk of the evicted Asians. Others to be applauded for their humanitarianism are the countries who agreed to accept at least a number of Asians, and India, Canada and the States are among those who rose to the occasion.

But what of Uganda's future? At the time of writing it is hard to see how someone as limited intellectually as General Amin can revive the country he has plunged into near bankruptcy. True, he can anticipate substantial aid and loans from his fellow Muslim, Libya's Quadaffi, but one country cannot simply bankroll another —at least not for any length of time. Logically, he should allow some very able Ugandans, and there are a number, to revive the economy for him even though it would take some years. But anybody capable of that would probably, in Amin's eyes, be a threat to his own supremacy, and it seems to be the retention of power at any cost that motivates him.

In Kenya the ordinary rural man (about 95 per cent of the population) is very like his Ugandan counterpart. Most of them probably think the Kenya Government should get rid of the remaining Asians too. Knowing this, the Government is likely to speed up the process, which is already quietly under way. There are enough good people in the Kenya Government today with an understanding of how a country works who can see how easily things can be thrown off balance. Such men also have sufficient humanity not to wish undue hardship on fellow human beings. The pressure will be slow but inexorable, and in a few years probably the only Asians left in Kenya will be those 40,000 who hold Kenya nationality. The British Asians will have gone and they will dribble into England and Canada and Europe and India in a manner that will not attract attention, will not cause dangerous waves, and will not, above all else, disrupt the economy of Kenya.

In actual fact, since independence ten years ago, Kenya has quietly but steadily been doing what Uganda did in a rush—but nobody has really noticed and even though Amin's action will speed up the process in Kenya—they must not be seen to lag behind—there is a chance that the exercise will be completed in the next two or three years without anybody but the Asians concerned really being aware of the movement.

At our lectures in the States we are also often questioned about Ian Smith and Rhodesia.

Until six or seven years ago, Rhodesia, which is about the size of Texas and which borders South Africa, was an appendage of Britain without being exactly a colony. In other words, Britain allowed Rhodesia to rule herself internally. (That amounts, if you can imagine it, to something like one of the American states having very wide state laws with no federal interference, but still "belonging" to the federal whole and thus being unable to go to war or to relate to outside countries by itself. And ultimate responsibility would be with Washington, because the autonomy was granted by Washington in the first place.)

Now, white Rhodesians are similar to white South Africans in attitude. They are attracted to the concept of separate development for the different races, which in the case of both countries means a small percentage of white people (17 per cent in South Africa—4 per cent in Rhodesia) living on the bulk of the land, having all top jobs and telling the millions of Africans where to work, where to have their homes and what to do. By denying them any real say in government and by ruthlessly controlling every aspect of their lives, the white population effectively controls a vast cheap labor force from the sweat of which they grow rich. I am not indulging in easy polemics. What I am telling you is true, is well documented throughout the world and is so incredible in 1973 that people really find it hard to believe. South Africa and Rhodesia are beautiful, industrially progressive, luxurious countries, offering the good life to anyone who is white—and can deaden his conscience.

During the past fifteen years Britain has granted independence to almost all her former colonies and overseas possessions. Rhodesia's Government of whites felt nervous. They felt sure the country's turn was coming and the British settlers feared that they would be swept aside as Africans attained political power. Since they already governed the country internally, they reasoned, why not go the whole hog and declare themselves a sovereign state and to hell with the constitutional legalities of it all vis-à-vis Britain. Britain never believed they would do this but one fine morning they woke up and found that Rhodesia had had the gall to declare U.D.I.—Unilateral Declaration of Independence.

For a moment the British Government contemplated sending troops to wrest power back from Smith, but they shirked the issue, fearing that English soldiers might mutiny rather than fire upon other Englishmen who might even be their cousins or friends. In actual fact, if Britain had arrived with a show of force, paratroopers and so on, within forty-eight hours of the break, they could probably have gained control of key installations in Salisbury without having to shoot at all—but the moment was missed, and after a week they felt it was too late even to try.

All the African states that had been given their freedom by Britain were outraged at her lack of guts. If any of *them* had given an ounce of trouble (and some of them had, prior to their independence), Britain had immediately sent troops to straighten things out. Now they could see that the former colonial power had always been prepared to shoot and detain Africans in the name of law and order, but it was a different matter when the white folks stepped out of line.

The Africans in Rhodesia were dismayed for the same reason. They were sure that Britain would not countenance the act of rebellion—that she would quickly reassert her rightful authority. An understanding of African reactions both inside and outside Rhodesia is essential if the whole mess following U.D.I. is to be grasped. None of them, not the Rhodesian Africans or leaders in other African countries suggested immediate African majority rule of Rhodesia as a solution. They all said the same thing— that it was up to Britain to unseat Smith and to establish her authority through the now powerless and emasculated governor. Then, a constitution should be devised which would, over a period of five or six years, lead to true independence on the basis of one man one vote, exactly as in Kenya, Ghana, Nigeria, Uganda, Malawi, Zambia and many other countries formerly ruled from London. What was so special about Rhodesia, they asked, that warranted a different formula? Of course in their hearts they knew the answer and so did Britain. There were more white people living in Rhodesia than in the African countries mentioned, and Britain lost her nerve when faced with having to rap their knuckles.

So what happened? Britain rushed around among her friends throughout the world and with an embarrassed clearing of the throat said, "Look, chaps, our cousins in Rhodesia are giving us a bit of the old grief. Be a good sport and don't buy anything Rhodesian or sell anything to them and we'll have them knocking on our door to come back in after a few months. Then we'll solve the problem right away. We are so opposed to violence and war, and this way we can achieve the same ends with no bloodshed. (They meant no British blood or white Rhodesian blood.) Be a good sport and go along with us, O.K.?"

All the African countries severed ties with the rebel government immediately. Most of the rest of the world did too, but it goes without saying that the most important, the most vital element in the survival of Rhodesia, neighboring South Africa, did not. So the sanctions, while annoying, of course, had little real effect. Some thought that Rhodesia might even merge with South Africa, but the South Africans, though possessing mostly negative characteristics, are not entirely stupid. Union for them would have meant gaining a couple of hundred thousand white kindred spirits but also 11 million more Africans and their overall black/ white ratio would have been worse, or blacker—in both senses of the word as they understand it. Further, as independent Africa gets madder at South Africa with each week that passes, it is comforting for the Boers to know that there is a buffer state to the north of them.

The sanctions dragged on and people got bored and quietly resumed trading with Rhodesia through loopholes, usually South African loopholes. From time to time Britain made feeble attempts at talking to Smith and his cronies. If only he could be a little bit reasonable, if only, if only . . .

Meanwhile, Smith and his gang started to work on their world image and America was one obvious place in which it seemed important to have friends. It was as if they hired a good P.R. man and he came up with, "How about this, fellas? 'Smith deserves the support of all true Americans. He seized his independence from the British just as we did. He is a latter-day Patrick Henry.' How does that grab you?" Well, it grabbed a number who had not the wit to understand that what Patrick Henry wanted was "Freedom for *all*"—in contrast to Smith and his lads who want freedom to continue dominating millions of Africans undisturbed by winds of change or the breath of enlightenment.

"How about another good, blood-pressure raising, infallible publicity ploy?" said the P.R. man. "I've got it! Communism! 'Smith and the Rhodesians are the bastions against Communist-inspired aggression from neighboring African states. He is the protector of Western ideals in a morass of black insurgency.' " Yet it was precisely because of Smith's action that the neighboring African states have sought to help their brethren to escape his domination and to overthrow his government, which, being illegal, they do not recognize. Since no help was forthcoming from the West and especially from Britain, who had patently ducked her obligations, they were accepting help from wherever they could get it. The only people who seemed to want to help physically happened to be part of the Eastern bloc. The irony is that but for Smith they wouldn't have had such an opportunity to be invited to Africa.

"We need one more heart clutcher and I think I have it. 'Smith was a fighter pilot during the war and he fought those Nazis. It is because of people like him and other members of his cabinet that the world is a safe place today.' Boy, that should get anybody who may not have fallen for the other stuff."

Does an action of twenty-five years ago, however admirable, exonerate a man from fulfilling his obligations of today? But just as important, what of the black African Rhodesians who fought on the same side as Smith during the war against the same enemy? Where do they stand, and who recalls their bravery and the debt owed to them by Britain and the allies?

No, the pro-white Rhodesian arguments simply do not stand up to informed examination. Even the wail from Smith's followers that the white man has been eliminated from independent Africa and that they will be wiped out if they give in is not borne out by events elsewhere. The white population in most African states has remained roughly static in the years following independence. True, there has been a shift of emphasis and many farmers have left or been bought out (not "thrown out" as Smith supporters say), but they have been replaced by technicians, advisers, teachers and so on who are white. Other than in Zaire (previously the Congo), which was a disaster for a whole series of other reasons, the Africans have been very reasonable toward their white minorities, mainly because they need their capital and expertise and are not yet able to run their countries from an economic standpoint without them.

Anyhow, to get back to the main theme, Britain and Smith kept talking from time to time and eventually they both agreed upon a constitution that would ultimately lead to majority (i.e., African) rule in Rhodesia. But it was so "ultimately" and so hedged around with unrealistic safeguards (for whites) that it was a non-starter as a solution. To give you an idea, it was roughly equivalent to telling American blacks that if they were very good and did everything they were told to do, they could vote and elect representatives in, say, 2000.

Having reached a form of agreement with Smith, but without having talked to any Africans about it, the British lost their nerve and decided that they should at least try to cover themselves if it turned out that the Africans didn't like the proposals. They appointed a commission with Lord Pearce as its leader, to ascertain the true feelings of Rhodesians of all colors about the proposals. The findings of the commission could have been predicted by anyone with even a glimmer of understanding of Africa. The white people accepted the proposals (they had helped to draft them) because they lost little or nothing under the new constitution, and the Africans rejected them for exactly opposite reasons—they gained little or nothing from the document. Pearce reported these truths and returned home, his task well done.

Britain shrugged helplessly, the white Rhodesians screamed that the Africans really loved the plans but had been intimidated into telling Lord Pearce the opposite, and Smith continues to rule illegally under the same "constitution" and oppressive emergency powers that he introduced at the moment of U.D.I. The United Nations sighed and resolved to tighten up the trade sanctions all over again.

At that moment the United States Senate voted by a majority of forty to thirty-six to buy chrome from Rhodesia, thus breaking the embargo and helping to prolong Smith's tenure. This was a blow badly taken by developing countries all over the world. America was seen as merely a verbal supporter of freedom and democratic rule, but as a country that would cynically disregard such ideals where her own commercial interests were involved. Too bad, since America does so many good things throughout the world, that more than half the senators demonstrated so little understanding.

Senator Byrd of West Virginia led this move to renew trade with Rhodesia, and we wrote to him describing the feelings of many in Africa on the subject. We also wrote to Senator Mac

Mathias of Maryland, who replied that he agreed with us. But from Byrd we never heard a word.

About the time all this was going on, Henry Loomis, then deputy head of the U.S.I.A., was in Nairobi on a private visit and we questioned him about the role of America in the context of Rhodesia and South Africa. In front of a number of black Kenyans and black Americans (Betty and I, along with the Loomis family, were token whites at an otherwise black dinner party) Loomis replied that Rhodesia and South Africa are the only countries on the entire continent that are of any importance to the United States. He said that South Africa is important to America financially and strategically, and that is why we keep on good terms with them. Betty said that for the first time in her life she was ashamed to be an American.

Well, we in Africa continue to watch and hope. Rhodesia's neighbor, Zambia, whose main access to the sea is a railway running through Rhodesia, is the worst affected, especially since Rhodesia has now denied them the use of the line. When completed, the Chinese railroad through Tanzania will carry Zambia's copper to the ships, so one problem, anyway, will soon be solved.

A bad side effect is that anti-Smith feeling among Africans is easily fanned into anti-white feelings in a much wider sense. Those of us who are white and who live in independent Africa are thus obliquely threatened by Smith's actions. Also, African countries who are importing Eastern arms and military advice to unseat Smith are subtly threatened for the future; will the arms and advice be used against Smith alone or may the countries be tempted to use the foreign forces against one another?

The Western world, particularly Britain, appears in a bad light because when it came to the pinch she was seen not to mean what she said about freedom and the equality of man. America looks bad because of buying Rhodesian chrome, which she could just as easily have bought from Russia, even though it would be more expensive.

So you see, Smith's action did not only affect Rhodesians. The ripples and the consequences adversely touch the lives and thoughts and hopes of millions. But the end result is as certain as sunrise. There will be African rule in Rhodesia. Why cannot Smith and his band see this? Why can they not help and nurture and build a new kind of Rhodesia with full participation for all, instead of allowing the country to be torn apart? Why not choose the path of good will and co-operation—when the alternative is bitterness and blood? But then why are human beings as they are?

When This Was Africa

Jock and I were driving through Swaziland to South Africa in a rented car we had picked up in Mozambique. Since it was cheaper to have a driver go with us than pay for his air fare from Laurenço Marques to South Africa to fetch the car to drive it back (no drop-off-in-another-city service in Africa), we had a very nice old Portuguese driver with us, named Fernandes. The first thing we did was to get in the front of the car and chauffeur him because Jock throws up if he doesn't drive. Alone in the back seat he kept asking if we didn't want to go to the Cathedral, the historical monument, City Hall and the Botanical Gardens, and we kept saying no, no, no. He was becoming so disappointed that finally we agreed, under duress, to go to the museum. We were right in the first place—we should not have gone. The museum in Laurenço Marques has twenty-two progressing elephant foeti in a row of bottles from the first months of gestation up to the last (which is twenty-two months for a boy elephant and twenty months for a girl). To acquire this collection—the only one of its kind in the world, mercifully—they must have had to shoot about forty million prospective elephant mothers to find pregnant ones in the first place (I have never seen an elephant that *didn't* look pregnant) and then to find the foetus in each stage of gestation. After that revolting display we continued on to Swaziland where we spent the night; then on to Durban—a two-day trip in all. We enjoyed Fernandes and he enjoyed being driven and the switched roles, with him playing client and us the tour leaders. During one meal he talked about his father who had arrived in Africa in 1898 and how he had walked with porters from Dar es Salaam to Mombasa and how he had gone into the interior, walking another two hundred miles and how he had done this and that "when this was Africa."

The phrase struck me—the truth of it. Today in Africa we have supermarkets and Woolworths, Holiday Inns, and paved highways. And even in the bush today there is the comfort of the Flying Doctors who can haul us out if we get sick, and helicopters to spot us if we get lost, and radios and other utilities which I suppose are a good thing. It is, nevertheless, a little sad, a little less romantic, and with every inch of tarmac which covers a terrible dirt road, my heart saddens, because in burying the earth road a part of Africa is buried with it, and soon the Africa we were raised to think of will be gone and will never return. With it will go many things, like adventure. When this was Africa it gave many people the gift of being brave and intrepid and adventuresome and of exploring the awesome unknown—things that are only possible on the moon for astronauts now.

In addition to the Spekes and the Burtons and Stanleys and Livingstones, idealists and reformers, there were bloodthirsty hunters and exploiters as early as 1843. Roualeyn Gordon Cummings, son of a Scottish baronet, and Michael Norton, who claimed to have killed over 2,000 elephant, were two examples of ruthless individuals who shot all the game they could find, sometimes by sitting at water holes just waiting for the animals to come to drink. Finally, Courtney Selous, who had hunted elephant on horseback for ivory, revolted against the terrible destruction of wildlife, and so helped develop early game regulations and launch the profession of being a "white hunter"—one of the world's most glamorous jobs even today. Selous Reserve in Tanzania is named after him.

In those days not only fortune seekers and hunters arrived, but some came just for the sake of the unknown. In 1895 a young Scottish surgeon, Mungo Park, made a journey trying to explore the Niger River, but everyone except him in his party perished so he returned alone with only his horse. During the next ten years he gathered together thirty-five soldiers and two sailors and set out again, going 1,000 miles into the interior and losing all but five along the way. Finally, these five were attacked on the river by a hostile tribe and all were drowned, including Park, but one slave survived to tell the story. How many expeditions must there have been with no survivors to tell the world?

Winston Churchill arrived in 1907 to inspect England's new protectorate, Uganda. (Kenya was a colony, Tanganyika a territory and Uganda a protectorate—each a lesser degree of settlement and responsibility and exploitation.) He went up the Nile with his personal physician, four colonial officers, two hunters, a hundred African helpers and a detachment of the King's African Rifles. Each morning twenty porters in each group would load up with what had been decided they could carry—sixty-five pounds each. Churchill wrote about his safari: "It compromises yourself and everybody and everything you take with you—food, tents, rifles, clothing, cooks, servants, escort, porters—but especially porters. This ragged figure, tottering along under his load, is the unit of locomotion and the limit of possibility. Without porters you cannot move. With them you can move about twelve miles a day if all is well. How much can he carry? How far can he carry it? These are the questions which govern alike your calculations and your fate. The elephant grass on each side of the trail rose 15 ft. high. In the valleys great trees grew and arched above our heads, laced and twined together with curtains of flowering creepers. Here and there a glade opened, and patches of vivid sunlight splashed into the gloom. Around the crossings of little streams butterflies danced in brilliant ballets . . . the jungle was haunted by game—utterly lost in its dense entanglements. And I think it is a sensation all by itself to walk on your own feet, staff in hand, along these mysterious paths, amid such beautiful, yet sinister surroundings and realize that one really is in the centre of Africa . . ." As they walked, about twelve miles each day on the northern bank of the Nile, friendly tribes greeted them by throwing off their leopard skins and dancing naked in the dusk.

Theodore Roosevelt, one of the great naturalists of his time, led a hunting safari to Africa at the end of his second term in office as President, and his political opponents wished the "animals might bag him first." The expedition had been commissioned by the Smithsonian Institute to collect big game, birds, reptiles and plants for the National Museum in Washington, where most of the collection can be seen. He collected 296 animals of seventy different species, saying that he needed so many to complete family groups of animals for the museum display. He had two hundred porters plus gun bearers, tent boys, soldiers and syces (people who look after horses), a huge tent with a canvas bathtub and an enormous American flag waving in the breeze.

The Duke of Windsor, then the Prince of Wales, covered thousands of miles hunting and photographing wildlife in Africa in 1928 and 1930. He was charged by an elephant with only one tusk, but before he could reach for his gun one of the white hunters in the group shoved him out of the way of the elephant's tusk which was coming at him "like a gigantic sword" and shot and killed the beast.

In the 1920s it became fashionable for European and Indian royalty to go on safaris, just as it became fashionable in the 1970s for Americans to go on camera safaris.

An early figure on the East African scene who typified the adventuresome, educated, Victorian eccentric was Ewart Grogan. Wreathed in academic honors, he left Cambridge just before the turn of the century and set out to explore the world. When he reached New Zealand he fell in love with the daughter of a well-to-do rancher.

"What do you think you have achieved that makes you worthy of the hand of my daughter?" demanded the prospective father-in-law. "Go prove yourself, young man."

Right off the top of his head the youthful Grogan replied, "I will walk from Cape Town to Cairo." (5,000 miles.)

That was grand by the father, who figured they would never see *him* again. Obviously he wouldn't have the guts to go through with it, and if he did he would never survive.

Grogan caught the next ship to Cape Town, hired about thirty porters and set out. The first part was easy since it consisted of walking through already tamed South Africa—not that different from a stroll across the fields of New Zealand. But soon things changed, and he found himself entering the Africa of Livingstone and Stanley, of Speke and Burton. There were no proper charts, he had no means of knowing whether tribes in his path were friendly or cannibals, and the danger from wild animals increased the deeper he penetrated.

His porters caused tedious and irritating problems by deserting just at the moment he needed them most. He would then hire new ones who would travel with him only to the limits of their own tribal areas. Once again, he would have to negotiate with the next tribe.

His party was attacked frequently, forcing him to defend himself with his gun. There were stretches of waterless desert to be crossed and sharp volcanic rocks quickly tore the soles out of his boots. At other times he struggled through dense forests and the mosquitoes saw to it that Grogan no sooner recovered from one bout of malaria than he went down with another.

His adventures are too numerous to list here, and in any case he wrote them himself in his book *Cape to Cairo*. Suffice it to say that the journey took three years and that only one of his original porters stuck with him all the way. One incident that struck me as delightful was that when Grogan and his trusty porter finally approached Cairo a train suddenly appeared round the corner of a slight hill. Without hesitation the porter, who was by now proficient with a gun, flung himself into a firing position on his stomach and started to blast away at the new and unfamiliar menace, just as he had done with charging rhino and elephant.

To the amazement of Dad, Grogan presented himself once more in New Zealand, and even though it had been three years since they had heard a squeak out of him, the girl had waited. So they married—(and lived unhappily ever after?)

But how often do you hear romantic tales of that caliber nowadays? The next thing Grogan did was to move to Kenya. The railroad had just been completed, a few shacks were going up in Nairobi and the country offered just the kind of challenge suited to a man who was not merely physically brave and adventuresome but who was mentally equipped to comprehend the problems facing a young country.

He quickly became a member of the legislative body and had a particularly fine brain for finance. He was also capable of being highly unorthodox to make his point.

In those early days, when Nairobi consisted of little more than a main street and a railway station, gold prospectors were pouring into the country and staking out claims anywhere they chose. Grogan had pressed for legislation for the proper registration of claims, but no action was taken. One morning, the residents of Nairobi were astonished to see a shirt-sleeved Grogan with half a dozen Africans digging up the main street, making an enormous mess and blocking the road. When the police called upon him to stop and asked him what he thought he was doing, he replied that he had turned prospector, that he was looking for gold, and that he would stop digging when they showed him the law that stated he could not stake out anywhere he chose— including Nairobi. The legal registration of claims was processed within a few days.

Jock knew Grogan quite well and often used to chat with him. He remained active until the end and dabbled in politics until just before he died at the age of eighty-four. He was very far to the right in his political thinking and could not accept that Africans were going to govern Kenya. Having spanned Kenya's history from its first colonial days right through to independence, it is probably not surprising that he was unable to adjust in his latter years.

A colorful local family are the Allens. They are Romany gypsies and therefore are entitled to wear one gold earring, which Bunny Allen, a professional hunter, always does. (Perhaps he's rounded Cape Horn, under sail, too—the other thing entitling men to wear an earring.) Laughter follows the Allens everywhere and one brother even has the nickname of *Cheka,* which is "laughter" in Swahili. They are legends in a way, and a story about one of the clan is that one evening he was sleeping with a Maasai woman in her hut when the woman's husband walked in. Not because of intercourse with his wife, which in certain circumstances is permissible by Maasai custom, but because Allen had left his socks on or flouted some such convention, the Maasai thrust his spear through them both, pinning them to the floor together. The Allen family were delighted that if one of their members had to die it was in such a beautiful way.

Other people, usually missionaries, say things like, "Oh, my mother and father walked from the Congo to Ethiopia carrying me all the way."

This is 1,000 miles, and I know the American pioneers walked a long way, but they were mostly in groups, meeting only hostile Indians. But these people walked alone with not only hostile tribes but charging elephant, leopard, lion, pythons, scorpions, equatorial heat and tropical diseases to name just a few adversities.

Then there was the opposite of the suffering missionary types— the Happy Valley crowd. Happy Valley must have been where the originator of Peyton Place got her idea. The participants in Happy Valley activities were mainly bored and wealthy playboys and their playgirls from England.

I have been told that heroin was prevalent in those days—and that it used to come into the country in the ladies' talcum powder tins. In addition to drugs, there were swinging orgies. For example, for weekend parties (which were every weekend and lasted six days—one day to travel to the next party) after dinner the men would stand behind a sheet so they couldn't be seen, and insert their penises through holes which had been cut in the sheet, and the women on the other side would choose their bed partner for the night in this manner. There are masses of charming stories like that about Happy Valley, and I must say the tragedies that happened there might tempt one to say the gods grew very angry and punished them. There were no end of grisly and untimely deaths which would not be believed if you put them in a novel. In fact, the minute I finish writing this book I am going to start a novel based on the true story of the murder of Lord Errol, a case here that has never been solved.)

Jock's mother and father, while geographically part of the Happy Valley, were not part of all the goings on (except, of course, that's how Jock was born—he was chosen through a sheet) and in fact by the time they had built a house and settled in, most of the really hairy activity had died out. Jock has told me that as he used to drive with his mother to Nairobi from the Happy Valley she would point to farms and houses along the way, describing the people who used to live there and what had become of them. One was burned to death when he took time out from the parties to repair a tractor. He left his gin in the house but not his cigarette, and as he leaned over the gas tank the thing exploded.

Another died with his sister in a bush fire when he tried to rescue her after she was overcome by smoke and heat. (If you should ever get caught in a bush fire and you have a match or lighter, the answer is very easy. As the fire races toward you, blown by the wind, all you do is to start your own fire which will be carried away from you, blown by the same wind that is driving the main fire toward you. As your private fire spreads away from you, you follow it so that you are standing on the ground where everything has already been burned. When the big fire arrives there is nothing for it to burn and you are standing laughing at it in complete safety.)

Another neighbor, on the adjacent farm to where Jock lived, shot herself, but in style. She entirely filled a room with white lilies, poisoned her dogs, and left a note asking to be buried next to the dogs overlooking the river. Reclining on a chaise longue midst the funeral flowers she had picked herself, she put a bullet through her head. When they found her, her friends fortified themselves with gin and solemnly buried her exactly as requested. They then repaired to the house for more gin. After a while someone suggested that they should tell the police at the police station thirty miles away, and they were astonished when the policeman insisted that she be dug up again immediately for a post-mortem examination and an official verdict. When the question of foul play had been ruled out she was buried once more in the same spot. And that, of course, called for more gin.

Another of the neighbors shot himself accidentally while hunting, and yet another nearly survived an encounter with a wounded elephant. The technique favored by elephant who have it in mind to demolish a human is not to spike the victim with a tusk, but to club him with their trunk or to pick him up like a rag doll and then bash him on the ground or against a tree, after which they trample all over him just to make sure. This man survived being slapped to the ground and then had the presence of mind to lie on his side, exposing a minimum surface area to the trampling feet. Though terribly injured he survived and was taken to the hospital where he all but recovered, overcoming the worst injuries but finally succumbing to a relatively insignificant complication caused by his ordeal. Hardly any of the Happy Valley crowd died a normal dull old death.

Even Jock's father and stepfather met untimely ends. His father had been sick for some time, following a head injury received in a polo accident. Feeling worse than usual one day, and with severe stomach pains, he drove the 130 miles from his farm to see a doctor. An immediate operation was performed for appendicitis but it was too late—his appendix had burst and he died at the age of forty-seven of peritonitis.

Jock's stepfather, Arthur Miller (no connection with the playwright), was a daredevil—and a tremendously fine horseman. He lived for steeplechasing, show-jumping, racing and polo and he excelled at them all.

As a former cavalry officer, at the outbreak of World War II he joined an armored regiment but quickly accepted an assignment in West Africa because it meant riding a horse instead of an armored car. The Allies feared that the German campaign in

North Africa might involve bordering West African countries and a highly mobile mounted unit was formed to operate in roadless territory.

One day when Jock was about nine, his mother received a cable from the War Office stating that her husband had been drowned after being thrown from his horse while fording a river. For twenty years that was all she knew about his death. Then one day in England Jock was staying with friends for the week-end when one of the guests asked him, apologizing for the long shot, whether he had ever known an Arthur Miller in Kenya years ago. It turned out that the guest was actually with Jock's stepfather when he died and he described how it happened.

Leading his troop, Captain Miller reached a river that was in flood and a roaring torrent. He gave the order to ford it but the men and his junior officer—the one who was now telling Jock the story—hesitated and looked dubious. They could see that men and horses would be swept away and they were in no mood, since there was no battle, to risk their lives. Arthur Miller repeated the order, but the younger man declined to obey and when threatened with court martial shrugged and turned away. In a rage—he was very quick-tempered—the fearless Arthur Miller spurred his mount into the river, was immediately thrown from the horse onto some rocks and stunned. Within seconds he and the horse were swept away and drowned, and doubtless the others would have perished also had they followed.

In these early days, even during the 1930s when Jock was a boy, communications were still poor. He clearly remembers the days during the rainy season when roads were too muddy for a car and the only way to the nearest store and post office thirty miles away was by ox-wagon or on horseback, and twenty of those miles were across a great plain inhabited only by animals. As children, Jock and his sister learned to ride and to find their way through the forests and across the plains on horses, not as one might learn these things on a dude ranch or at summer camp, but as a part of everyday life, like crossing the street in heavy traffic. Learned in this way as a child, the techniques stick and remain a part of the person, so that he knows them without knowing that he knows them. We can drive miles through the bush where there is no track and where everything looks alike to me, and seven years later, returning to the same area Jock will say, "We'll reach that place where we camped in about ten minutes. Watch out for that large rock just after the clump of trees." The fact that he had spent as much time in New York as in the bush during the seven years since we were there does not seem to dull this and other mystifying semi-instincts which he has and which I know I will never acquire.

Not only was the road often impassable where Jock grew up, there was no telephone or radio either. The amazing thing, though, is the speed at which news travels by "the grapevine" in Africa. The romantic (Tarzan) concept of this phenomenon is that jungle drums beat out the news and messages flash from village to village, finally arriving at the chief. Well, that does happen, but only among certain tribes who are the exception rather than the rule. Shouting from the hilltops is more common, and anyone who has lived in Africa will have noticed how African voices carry, even when the speaker is just "chatting" to someone on the other side of the river as they draw water. The women, particularly, have shrill and penetrating voices even in ordinary conversation. The typical speaking voice of the African man has a soft yet resonant timbre that is really easy on the ear— much more attractive than most white male voices. (Beautifully formed hands is another almost universal characteristic of Africans—notice the next time you have a chance.) One afternoon when Jock's father shot a rhino that had been causing a lot of trouble in the area, he drove to the post office at Gilgil to send a telegram to the Game Warden in Nairobi more than a hundred miles away. By the time the cable reached him early the following morning, the Warden already knew all about the rhino incident, who had shot it, where and at what time, and he had learned all this from his cook, who had simply heard the news in a matter of hours on the tribal message system.

The Kalenjin group of tribes in western Kenya have an almost instant means of alerting several hundred thousand people in times of emergency. They shout from village to village and attract each other's attention with a kind of bugle made from buffalo horn.

A truly fantastic thing is the endurance of some of the nomads. The next time you walk from the living room to your garage which is attached to your house, drive to your office building, park in the basement and take the elevator up to your office, just think of Chief Lago, of the Rendille.

Jock met Lago in Marsabit in the middle of Kenya's northern desert area a few years after the chief performed an amazing feat following some emergency that happened in the Mount Kulal area near Lake Rudolf. Lago set out by himself on foot in the middle of the afternoon and walked just over a hundred miles to Marsabit in just under twenty-four hours. He never stopped. He walked all night and all day through blistering heat and other than being tired he was quite unaffected, waking up in fine shape after a night's sleep. Such African men are tough, are "men," and they know it. The passage from childhood to manhood is formalized in most tribes with a series of ceremonies and tests.

A Western youth can progress from childhood to the full status of an adult without ever undergoing any kind of "trial by fire" or proving of self. There need be no definitive line between man and boy and indeed in our society there are thousands of twenty-five or thirty-year old "boys" who have never experienced any ordeal which qualifies them as "men." There are exceptions, in that the draft can be regarded as an ordeal of a kind, even if the draftee does not go to the front line. Working on highway construction during the summer or hitchhiking through some foreign country on a tight budget definitely does not qualify—as anyone who has been drafted will testify. These remarks apply more to boys than girls, of course. The subject does not really concern "virility" or "manliness" in that stupid sense of being tough and "one of the boys," and drinking too much beer and being cool, man. Gentle, sensitive men can also have "graduated" in this sense, and although third parties may not recognize them they will surely recognize and give an unspoken salute to one another. (They are not better or worse, it is simply that in the area of having a certain knowledge of self, they are different.)

For Africans the process of arriving at recognized manhood is much more simple. There are initiation ceremonies and every young man, and in many cases young women, must submit to them. Most of the rites have months of preparation in their pure versions (in contrast to the diluted 1970s versions) and the Maasai, for instance, go through elaborate weeks of living with a small band of their peers in the bush without the succor of established elements of the tribe. As a culmination—a final test of endurance and disdain for physical pain—circumcision is very popular. The initiate, aged about fifteen to seventeen years old, must show no sign of feeling pain as the witch doctor or some tribal elder hacks away with a crude instrument—and bush surgeons are not renowned for their knowledge of anesthetics. One tribe has an added refinement in that immediately after the operation the subject must have intercourse successfully with a hole in the ground. Those who survive and pass these tests, which in practice is almost everybody since the psychological will to avoid a lifetime of disgrace and derision overpowers the urge to scream, definitely know they have passed. The separation of the men from the boys is from then on clear cut, is understood absolutely by the participants and by all members of the tribe.

Female circumcision in certain tribes is done for quite another reason. The clitoris is snipped off, not so much as a part of a test, though of course much ritual surrounds the undertaking, as to reduce the possibility of orgasm. The theory is that if married women derive no pleasure from intercourse they will have no reason to run around with other men. The "excuse" given is that the operation discourages immorality. Whew!

Fortunately the practice is dying out and the modern young lady in Nairobi, for example, would not dream of allowing her very womanhood to be desecrated in this manner. The clitoridectomy was always undertaken by an older woman with a team of assistants who were also women.

But how long ago was it that English knights went off to the wars with the only key to their wives' hideously uncomfortable chastity belt securely lodged in their pockets? And refined Victorian ladies were not supposed to enjoy "it" in any case. Am I glad I live right now!

Sometimes when you are driving through Maasai country a lean warrior will flag you down and ask for a lift—and he doesn't seem to mind where you are going. After fifty miles of desolate nothingness he may ask to get out and will set off at once in the direction you have just come from. All he wanted was the ride in the car.

But, of course, these days not all Africans are at home in the wilds. There is a segment of the population who have grown up in and around cities, who may from time to time ride "home" by train or bus to a relatively civilized rural area, and who never have and never will see an elephant. Two of the three men who work for us had never seen anything other than antelope and the occasional hyena until we took them through Tsavo Game Park on the way to Malindi. We got a strange vicarious kick, different in quality and degree from showing tourists around, as we introduced them to their own heritage of wildlife.

This, incidentally, is one of the problems with the whole question of conservation. Most of the present-day African population have no knowledge of the wildlife and couldn't care less about its survival. I don't say this disparagingly. A sense of aesthetic response to any subject has to be inculcated and is not necessarily natural to human beings. The governments are well aware of the economic advantages of a self-regenerating asset that requires little or no maintenance, other than protection, and for this reason—to attract the tourist dollar—they look after the wildlife. Only a few appreciate the animals for their own sake, but a new generation of African boys and girls who have been taken on school outings in buses into the game parks will begin to enjoy animals for the same reason that they may learn to like classical music or will travel deliberately to the Louvre. Like art and music—perhaps as a compensation for the lack of fine paintings and concerts in Africa—the animals in their scenically spectacular habitat can become the principal objects of appreciation on a high cerebral level.

Unfortunately, parallel with the appreciation of so-called higher things comes the introduction to a relatively virgin continent of the plastic and the tawdry, the neon and the chrome. Not a minute too soon Nairobi has been chosen as the site for the newly created United Nations Environmental Headquarters. Yes, the good and the bad will come to Africa from the rest of the world, but by being aware of the inevitability of the advance, there is an outside chance of being selective about which ideas and forms are to be adopted and which pitfalls can be avoided altogether. Environmental pollution is a graphic and easily understood example. By the time it becomes a problem in Africa, solutions will, hopefully, already have been devised elsewhere and can be applied before rivers are destroyed or the air is too foul to breathe. But political forms, attitudes, national and individual goals and accompanying standards and values are much more difficult matters over which to be selective and cautious.

Hemingway's son lives here permanently. Theodore Roosevelt's son and grandsons have been here on safari, and Churchill's son and grandson and granddaughter have all spent varying amounts of time in East Africa.

Doubtless they have found degrees of adventure and excitement, but some of the magic encountered by their forebears is surely missing—for they were here when this was Africa.

Of course not all people like that kind of "magic," and many would never consider coming over to Africa if they had to trek through the bush collapsing with malaria. Many of our friends who have been here have camped in the bush—but it has been highly organized. The men may even have walked a little to shoot birds or to photograph, but that is usually about the limit of their exposure to physical Africa. It is not the same now as it was in the days of Tarzan and Jane—and it is not even the same as it was when Jock was a child.

"Any fool can be *uncomfortable*," says Jock. The hard part has been making the more remote regions both accessible and safe. Happily, Africa can now be almost luxurious for anyone who wants it—even lone women in their eighties—and it is a source of great pride to safari organizers that it is possible to send even the frail and fastidious on a safari, and that they will return home fit and often rejuvenated.

Not so for a distant relation of Jock's who was married to a beautiful Russian princess and who came here on a safari in the very early days. Halfway through the trip, which they were doing on foot, he fell sick with malaria but she wanted badly to go on. With some porters and a gun bearer she set out, planning to pick him up on the way back ten days later. The porters reappeared but not his wife, and the stories they told about how she was devoured by a lion were both vague and varied. He never did get to the bottom of the tragedy, and when Jock used to stay with him forty years later in England he would still not talk about it. Jock thinks he suspected she was eaten by the porters, not the lion.

Even by the middle of the century there were still pretty weird things going on in East Africa.

In about 1950 in the Singida area of Tanzania (then Tanganyika), over a period of months a number of dead Africans were found in the bush who had apparently been clawed and mutilated by lion. This was most unusual because lion do not, in the normal course of events, eat or molest man. Some years before this rash of killings in Singida, there had been a number of babies kidnapped in the same area, but these cases remained unsolved. The reports of the man-eating lion therefore led the police to believe that the undetected "kidnappers" had been one and the same as the man-eaters. While the Game Wardens were fruitlessly searching for the man-eaters, the police became aware of a peculiar thing—all the victims who had been clawed to death were men, and in addition to the claw marks, from which they had obviously died, their testicles were missing. A thorough investigation was started by the police because no lion would ever consistently mutilate a person in this manner, and their enquiries led them to a witch doctor. The terrible facts that came to light were that the witch doctor needed human testicles for one of his magic potions, but he knew he could not go around openly murdering people to obtain them, so he devised the horrible solution of kidnapping little babies which he then raised as lion. He fed them on raw meat, trained them to walk on all fours, and attached steel claws to their hands and feet. He taught them to attack and kill at his command and always to bring the victim's testicles to him. Thus, both mysteries—the kidnappings and the strange deaths by man-eaters—were solved simultaneously.

I asked the policeman who told me the story, and who had been involved in the case, what had happened to the "Lion Men of Singida" as they came to be called. Did they have a trial?

"A trial?" he asked sadly. "They couldn't even stand up, much less talk. They shot them."

Of course the only person responsible for the crime was the witch doctor, and he was sentenced to death.

Popular twenty years ago in the Kisii district of western Kenya, and perhaps still going on today in remote corners, is a skull operation, a trepanning. Many of the inhabitants of this area are victims of terrible headaches, so the bush doctors study the part of the head that needs surgery, and then operate. Because of the pain—they have no anesthetics—the patient is held down and nettles (stinging plant leaves) are stuffed into his ears to distract the pain from one place to the other. Then the doctor, using a sharp tool known as an *omoyioni* removes part of the skull. This charming procedure may take up to twelve hours. The purpose of it is to release the evil spirits that caused the headaches in the first place, and once they have been allowed to escape the headaches go too, supposedly. A medical doctor told me the reason so many people in Kisii get headaches is because the hills are radioactive (which sounds as spooky to me as evil spirits). A Nairobi shopkeeper who knows more than twenty people in his clan who have had this primitive trepanning says they are "doing fine"—it took them each about six months to recover fully. Of course, the patient no longer has a full skull to protect his brain, but only a thin layer of skin. If ever in your wanderings you go to Kisii, you must not be surprised to see a few barefoot Africans with nothing on but a cloth wrapped around their bodies and a football helmet on their heads—the latter provided by missionaries to protect the skulls of those who have undergone this operation.

And tonight our dinner guest is an African brain surgeon who was trained at Johns Hopkins Hospital.

Zanzibar was still Africa when I saw it, but that was thirteen years ago and thirteen years can change many things—especially Zanzibar with its revolutions and massacres.

I seem only to remember the smell of cloves and the ceiling fan in our hotel room and that the entire time spent there was like watching a B-rate movie. My memory is pitiful, which has many advantages—I can read a book three times as if I had never read it at all and see films time and time again (and sometimes I can't remember who my first husband was.) But it is more than just not remembering Zanzibar. When too many things happen too quickly, and many new visions dance before your eyes, you simply cannot take them all in. I was also past absorbing by the time I got to Zanzibar. It was all so alien to me. At that time, I had had crash exposure to Africa, and open spaces and bush and animals and different tribes, and Zanzibar was another thing altogether—an island with a city and buildings and streets and an ancient culture with civilized Arabs—and it all just rolled off me.

This feeling of non-absorption has been described in its extreme form as cultural shock. It happens when changes are too swift, and there is too much to see and adjust to too suddenly. Jock told me that when he was in London he once volunteered

to show some visiting African soldiers around, since there were
not too many people in London who spoke Swahili. He took the
men, some of whom had never left their villages until a year
earlier when they enlisted, to Westminster Abbey and the Tower
of London, and they all rode on the Underground—which in
London means descending into the depths of the earth on an escalator to reach the trains.

Jock was expecting a great vicarious kick out of their wonder-
ment, but instead they were completely blog, not reacting to
anything. Finally, on the way home, as they started down yet
another escalator, there was a great shout of joy from the men,
followed by much laughter and pointing. They had spotted an
enormous picture of a cow on a billboard advertising Ovaltine,
and here at last was something to which they could relate, something familiar and comforting from their own world.

The interesting thing is that so-called civilized people are just
as subject to this feeling of desolate bewilderment when removed
from their environment, and we have had friends on their first
trips here who have been in a daze for a week—and who get oddly
withdrawn and silent—almost sullen sometimes.

There are classic stories about early Kenya which are always
told as gospel, but I have no idea if there is one iota of truth in
any of them. This kind of a story often reflects the discomfiture
of the "civilized" when confronted by the icy logic and literal
responses of the "primitive" at a time when this was Africa—
before the crazy ways of the crazy white men had been absorbed.

The first is about the bachelor who went into his kitchen and
found his cook straining the soup through one of his socks.

"Oh, you mustn't strain the soup through my socks," said the
man, and the cook, grinning, answered,

"Oh, don't worry, Bwana, it isn't one of your *clean* socks."

An early governor of Kenya was about to retire and he wanted
to give his successor the fanciest party in all of Kenya. He and
his wife planned and prepared for weeks. The thing his wife was

particularly anxious to have was a procession of servants carrying her superb meal into the dining room. A boar's head on a grand silver tray—complete with an orange in its mouth and parsley in its ears—was to be the first item borne in by the major domo, and the Africans, used to their own tribal pageantry and ritual, looked forward to enacting the white man's ceremony. Finally the night of the big event arrived, and as all the guests in their evening clothes were seated at an enormous banqueting table the governor's wife gave the signal. A hush fell over the party, the door opened, and there stood the head servant with the boar's head on the silver platter. But the orange was in the servant's mouth and out of his ears stuck the parsley.

Another is the story of the African riding in the back of an open truck that was taking an empty coffin from up-country to Nairobi. It started to rain, so he got into the coffin, closed the lid and fell asleep. A few miles farther on down the road, three Africans were hitchhiking, so the driver stopped and told them to climb into the back. After a while the man in the coffin awakened, and wondering if it were still raining, he opened the coffin lid and put his hand out to feel if there were any raindrops. The three new passengers jumped from the moving truck screaming, and one broke his leg.

Long ago Jock took an African, who had never seen the ocean before, to Malindi. At his first glimpse of the sea he stared a minute, smiled broadly, and said, "Oh, so this is where the sky meets the earth."

Another time Jock took a servant, who had also never seen the ocean, let alone the surf, with him to Malindi, but his reaction was quite different—he was not pleased with it at all and would not go near the "boiling water."

A place guaranteed to produce either cultural shock or fascinated disbelief in the visitor is Lamu. Jock and I had been there once about ten years ago, and we decided to go again before it is raped by the twentieth century. Lamu is an island north of Malindi which the Arabs claim dates back to the seventh century, and it certainly still looks and feels like the seventh century. The town, unlike any town we know, is an ancient stone maze of ruins which at the same time isn't truly ruined in the sense that it is still inhabited . . . just as it has always been. Suddenly you are tossed back into almost biblical times. There are no wheeled vehicles except for a few hand carts, which won't fit into many of the streets. The "streets," often no wider than three feet, are merely tiny crooked paths between the ancient stone houses. There are no cars, no bicycles—and no dogs because the Muslims on the island think dogs are unclean, though they are curiously unaware of the narrow open sewers down which glide banana peel, sheep entrails, and chicken heads. To get to Lamu most people take a chartered plane from Malindi or Mombasa, land on a grass strip on another island (there is no landing strip on Lamu) and cross to Lamu by boat.

If you go by car from Malindi, as we did recently, it is a three-hour drive through emptiness, broken only by the hand-pulled ferry across the Tana River. A rope is tied from one bank to the other so that half a dozen Africans can pull on it to guide the ferry across—a weirdly silent means of locomotion.

When you come to the end of the road, you park your car and get into a boat to cross to the island, deserting your car for the length of your stay. We knew enough not to leave anything in our car and to lock it tightly. We also paid someone to watch it for our three-day stay, so our only loss was the locked cap of the gas tank being wrenched off and most of the gas being syphoned out.

A thirty-foot Arab boat, the most unseaworthy I have ever seen and looking as if Sinbad the Sailor had abandoned it a thousand years ago, was to take us to the shore of Lamu a mile away. As we climbed in and saw a black, crusty engine in the middle of the boat clanking weakly and smoking away, we feared we wouldn't make it. We were almost right. The engine rattled and smoked and stopped in mid-crossing, and as we drifted picturesquely toward India, cautioning each other not to smoke or the boat would certainly blow up, an old Arab hung over the engine with a lighted cigarette dangling from his lips and fixed the fuel leak with Fels Naphtha soap by scrinching it around the pipe and binding it with old rags. Astonishingly, we reached Lamu. We climbed up the weathered jetty steps just as a bugle blew and everyone stopped and stood at attention, including our bewildered party, but we didn't learn why until later—it was for the lowering of the flag, a ceremony that happens every evening in Lamu at sunset. We took our first two steps on Lamu soil and were arrested. The police marched us to the station house on the sea front—we had no idea why and they didn't tell us, but they were very pleasant. At the jailhouse we learned we were there just to sign in—a sort of visitors' or guest-book formality. The sea front looks like an Arabian cowboy movie set (are there such things as Arabian cowboys?). In addition to the jail there are cannons, but no bars because public drinking in Muslim Lamu is out—just public mirarh eating instead, ignoring the Mirarh Prohibition Act with abandoned flair. You can't even get anyone to sell you their wares if it is the day the mirarh arrives. (Mirarh is a plant stem that is chewed for stay-awake energy—a sort of African No-Doz or speed. Many Africans feel sick much of the time because they are sick, and the mirarh gives them the energy needed to carry on. There is a terrible hangover from mirarh, we are told, and it is quite habit-forming and not at all good for you.) From the sea front we turned into the walled stone maze which is the city. I just know that the person who wrote *There Was a Crooked Man* must have composed it in Lamu—for there are crooked miles and crooked houses and crooked mosques—and crooked Arabs . . .

Friends of ours have bought a ruined house there, and are slowly "doing it up." The bats hang upside down from the twelve-foot ceilings or, worse, fly around bumping into you. Nothing is modern in Lamu—not even the bats. It seems they lack the radar of modern sophisticated bats. The walls of our friends' house still stand—more or less—they lean somewhat and have not seen paint for four hundred years (an accurate figure), and the rain doesn't come in—very much. A ridiculous problem was that their street is so narrow they were unable to get their refrigerator down it. While we were there two donkeys walked into their living room and dumped a load of sand for plastering and took away some rubble. They walked in single file, for two donkeys are unable to pass on most of Lamu's streets. In their house there are two stairways going out of the "living room"—one for the women and one for the men. The men wouldn't degrade themselves by walking up the same stairway as the women.

In the movies (there is one tiny movie house) the women are roped off from the men and there they must sit on one side in their *bouibouis* (black sheets wrapped around their bodies leaving only a slit for the eyes) while the men sit on the other. During the day you see mostly men and children in and around Lamu, for this is the Muslim wont, but after dinner when the men have finished eating, about 10 P.M., the women may go out.

But my favorite story about Lamu—which I could hardly wait to tell my very special friend in Baltimore, Anne Boucher, who was appointed Chairman of Maryland's Commission on Status of Women by the Governor—is that only the men in Lamu go to Heaven! They may invite their wives to join them there, but there has only been *one* woman from Lamu ever invited to Heaven and her tomb is right in front of our friends' house. Talk about chauvinistic pigs! And since we learned this, Jock keeps threatening me if I don't do everything exactly as he wants, "I won't invite you to Heaven."

Because I have a pathological loathing of bats we decided to stay at a local Arab hotel instead of the bats-infested house of our friends. We made for the "town square" which is the only open space in town, where the old fort still stands and where everyone gathers and buys coffee with ginger sprinkled in it. A town crier rang his bell and announced a meeting would be held by the district commissioner for the men that night to discuss a new school project. Does any other place in the world still have a town crier? Our "hotel"—a euphemism indeed—was right next to the whitewashed fort—which is now used as the jail, and our rooms looked right into the prisoners' cells. We entered the hotel from a tiny stairway on the street and climbed the cement steps into a stark whitewashed lobby, containing only an unpainted wooden kitchen table at which stood a twelve-year-old boy ironing sheets. I asked if he ironed there a lot and he told me, "All the hours of the days."

We staggered about the different levels of the hotel shouting *Hodi* (which is "yoo hoo" in Swahili, but which is a must to say. If a thief comes into your house and steals from you, the greater sin by far than stealing is the fact that he didn't say *Hodi*). Finally, an Arab in his long white robe and white embroidered beanie cap (the uniform of the men in Lamu) appeared saying *Karibu* ("come on in"—the response to our *Hodi*) and ushered us to our rooms which were about eight feet square, had two beds and one table, one hanging light bulb and two spiders. What else do you need—three spiders? A private bath. Surprise, surprise— we had a private bath, for which we paid heavily, and what do you know?—another spider. A room without bath is $1.42, but with a private bath and breakfast—which we chose because we are the last of the big-time spenders—was $3.85. We had a wash basin, a toilet and a "shower." The shower was just a fixture on the wall, and the water sprayed all over the entire bathroom—it is the only bathroom I know where you can sit on the john and take a shower at the same time. After your shower you wade over to the basin and brush your teeth with Coke because it's risky to drink the water. The walls of this hotel were proper walls—they reached to the ceiling, unlike the cubicles in the hotel we stayed in on an earlier visit to Lamu. There you could stand on your bed and peer over to see who was in the next room, which was very nice if you were curious as to who was in there or what they were doing. On that trip a friend went into the bath at the end of the hall to take a shower and as she stood under it and turned the knobs the water came bursting out beautifully for half a minute, but suddenly stopped. She twiddled and fooled with the taps and then glanced up to see if something was plugging up the shower spray and saw a man hanging over the top of the wall with a watering can—he had just come back with his refill after his first go. The owner swore he was blind, but . . .

(It must have been in just such a hotel that "Hippo" performed his fabulous act of retribution.

(Hippo is an elegant and fastidious Egyptian friend of our friend Esther Burton, and once when he was traveling through Egypt he had to stay in a really grotty hotel because the good ones were booked. Worse, he had to share a room with a stranger—no singles and no empty doubles. In the morning Hippo was awakened by the other man, a scruffy Egyptian peasant, getting out of bed. He opened one eye and peeped at him but pretended to be still asleep so he wouldn't have to talk. To his astonishment he saw the old man go to his, Hippo's, toilet case, take out his razor, shave with it, and leave the blade in the razor full of hairs without washing it. Appalled but fascinated, Hippo then watched his roommate take his toothbrush from the toilet case and brush his teeth with it. When this was finished, Hippo pretended to awaken, stretched, and ordered coffee and a large basin of hot water. When it arrived, Hippo squatted over it right in the center of the floor, so the other man could not possibly miss it, and with his toothbrush he carefully scrubbed his rectum, apologizing, "Sorry about this, but my doctor told me it is the best thing for my hemorrhoids and I have to do this every morning.")

Next to our room in Lamu and overlooking the prison yard was an open balcony which had a few chairs and a table covered with oilcloth where we ordered our supper which came, unfortunately, very quickly. The entire meal was an awfulness. The rice looked and tasted like glue with rooster curry on top of it. Just as we finished Jock decided chickens don't have rib cages attached to spinal columns, or something very technical and convincing like that, and we agreed we must have had curried rat or cat or bat and someone swore they found whiskers in theirs. Perhaps the Muslims were trying to get even with us Christians because hundreds of years ago when the Portuguese settled in East Africa they would keep any Muslim chicken that wandered onto their territory rationalizing that ". . . the chickens wanted to be Christians."

To digress a moment, a friend of ours was having dinner at a very elegant Chinese restaurant in Geneva and got a bone stuck behind her front upper teeth which she could not get out politely behind a napkin or even by yanking at it in the ladies' room. At 11 P.M. her husband called their dentist who said he would open his office and meet them there in ten minutes. They excused themselves from the dinner party and when the dentist got the bone out he asked what she had been eating. She told him it was the fancy expensive Peking duck which was this restaurant's specialty. He looked puzzled and asked if he could send the bone off for identification. It came back "frontal mandible of rat." They reported this alarming news to the health department who went to the restaurant and found they were breeding rats in the basement. The cellar was absolutely filled with rats that had been raised on the garbage of the restaurant's leftover food. I suppose there is nothing unhealthy about eating a rat raised in captivity, but it certainly is misrepresentation to serve it as duck and it offends the hell out of me. I, for one, will never order duck in a Chinese restaurant.

But back to Lamu. Other than curried cat, you can eat "roasted Arab on bicycle spokes" as a helpful member of our party described it. Along the twisted streets there are dirty and chipped enamel "dog bowls" filled with anemic-looking meat covered with what you first think is raisins, but then they fly away. You buy this, if you have the stomach, and they shove the meat onto the bicycle spoke and roast it right on the street corner—sort of a shish-kebab which I am told is delicious.

As we were going to bed I realized I had forgotten my bobby pins and having my hair hanging around my face when I sleep bothers me, so at 10:30 P.M. I suggested to Jock that we go out and buy some bobby pins. We both laughed at the absurdity of this and then went out and bought some bobby pins. We trotted down the hotel stairway into the tiny dark streets which we expected to be all sinister with just a few people lurking in doorways doing sordid Arab things, but not a bit—the place was alive—bubbling with Middle Eastern music and the chatter of the women who were doing their shopping in the crowded stores.

After a fine night's sleep in tablecloths (they ran out of sheets) we were awakened at 4:30 A.M. to say our prayers. Another town crier acts as the community alarm clock and soon after him the muezzins call from minarets to summon the faithful to the mosques. Then the school children start to squeal and holler in the playground—school is open on Sunday too. Lamu has got to be the noisiest city in the world. Much noisier than New York— from 4:30 A.M. to 9 A.M., at any rate. You give up trying to sleep and by 7 A.M. there we were walking around Lamu, and by 7 P.M. we were still walking, since there are no taxis, buses, cars, roller skates, bicycles—just feet, and we could barely make it to the oilcloth table for dinner for more curried cat. Lamu is like Venice in that you can take a boat to get from A to B along the waterfront, so at noon we chugged down to the one tourist hotel at the end of Lamu island, hoping to get a boiled steak or some other delicious English food. We asked the boatman to wait, but he got sleepy so he went home and never came back, and we were stranded about three miles up the beach. Since we had no choice, we walked back. We asked at the hotel if they ever walked to town and they said yes, but every time they did someone fell into the ocean. We learned what they meant. There are many parts along the walk back, when the tide is up—which it was—where you have to wade through the sea up to your waist. And then we were back to the 8,000 people who crowd into the tiny town, and the rancid smell of shark oil and the open sewers and the donkey dung which covers the streets. I fear I am too much a contemporary person to enjoy staying in Lamu for more than a few days. I guess I am not detribalized enough to throw off my American sterilization atti- tudes . . . I have a sanitation hang-up—I like closed cess pits and flushing loos and all those kinds of utilities. Lamu is just too dirty and too uncomfortable for me to exist in for any length of time. Also, I would not want to live in a historical monument which Lamu certainly is—and long may it stay that way. What a tragedy if they modernize Lamu—Allah forbid. A Texan has just bought a marvelous old building on the sea front and is converting it into a hotel—retaining all the Lamu flavor that he can. Mostly he has done a good job, but with unforgivable bad taste he has installed a swimming pool in a small yard and instead of sticking to traditional rectangular forms which make Lamu into a modern painting of almost colorless textured cubes, he has made the swimming pool kidney-shaped and bright turquoise—a crass modern abortion in such a setting. May romantic Lamu be protected from such insults. May it remain for the people of Lamu as it has been for a thousand years. Let tourists step back centuries and marvel. Let them go there too to make all their wishes come true, because on the outside wall of the Riyadah mosque it is written in Arabic:

> He who abides here gains his final goal.
> And those who visit get their wishes too.

It is my wish that you, Africa, will not pave the bush. The improvement of roads with tarmac means faster travel, but can't we have something left that is slower—just because it is nice to be slower sometimes? Anticipation is a major source of joy. Was it Somerset Maugham who once said, "The reach is greater than the grasp," and often it is *as* great anyway. Air travel is all the expedient things we know it to be, but I never felt as if I were "in Africa" as much as I did after taking thirty-three days to sail here once from New York. Your mind has time to catch up with your body, and you have time to look at the emptiness and to hear the nothingness. Perhaps this is what draws people to the sea. The bush is like the sea—untouched and unspoiled—yet able to be crossed or passed through. I know of no ocean that has been turned into a Disneyland, and let's hope that that day can be staved off in the bush too.

It is also my wish that you, Africa, will keep such things as the ferry we have to take on our way to Malindi. It is a terrible nuisance, this ferry, which is like the Toonerville Trolley, for frequently it breaks down and we have to wait there for an hour—once even for five hours. Hot and tired and impatient after 350 miles of driving we board it and find ourselves drifting aimlessly

toward Arabia—and no one seems to know how to turn the
ferry around, or else they can't get it "docked" straight and we
have to drive our car into the salt water. Yet despite all this I
would hate to see a bridge over the inlet because there are so
many bridges in the world and so few ferrys. Like much else,
ferrys are an endangered species too.

Oh, Africa, please keep a few samples of what you were when
you were Africa instead of leaving us with just memories.

It is good that you now have your own brain surgeons and
Nairobi grows up in the air and becomes more sophisticated. But
you also have Colonel Sanders' Kentucky Fried Chicken, and
there are automobile horns that play a corny scale on four notes
and there are Tigers in Tanks (yes—still). Oh, Africa! What
have we done to you? How long will it be before your golden
plains are paved and your game paths are eight-lane highways?
Is all the progress really progress? Will your people all be happier
when they live in high-rises and have six different pairs of shoes
each? Will the supermarket be as much fun, such a social occasion, as the fruit and vegetable market under the big tree? Is there
an answer to these questions? Is there any point whatsoever in
asking these questions?

Almost certainly both the good and the bad will come to you
from the outside world. Please be selective and avoid the pitfalls—
just keep your eyes skinned, dear Africa, keep your wits about
you, and good luck—you'll need that too.

It has been said by The Little Prince, "You have to be a caterpillar before you can be a butterfly." But dear Africa, you were
born a butterfly—don't turn into a caterpillar now. And if you do,
I won't invite you to come to Heaven with me.

Appendix

Johannesburg Consular District

A.F.I.A., New York, N.Y.

Abbott Laboratories, North Chicago, Ill.

(Adams Brands), Warner-Lambert Pharmaceutical Co., Morris Plains, N.J.

Addressograph-Multigraph Corporation, Cleveland, Ohio.

(AFAMAL-Quadrant), The Interpublic Group of Companies, Inc., New York, N.Y.

(Africa Triangle Mining), U. S. Steel, Pittsburgh, Pa.

Allis-Chalmers International, Milwaukee, Wis.

American Abrasives Inc., Westfield, Mass.

Ayerst Laboratories International, New York, N.Y.

American Express Company, New York, N.Y.

American Motors Corp., Detroit, Mich.

Ampex Corporation, Redwood, Calif.

Arthur Andersen & Co., Chicago, Ill.

(Anikem) Nalco Chemical Co., Chicago, Ill.

Applied Power Industries, Milwaukee, Wis.

Armco Steel Corporation, Middletown, Ohio.

J. C. Allen, Wilmot, Ill.

(Artnell Intl.) Rockwell Mfg. Co., Pittsburgh, Pa.

Automated Building Components, Inc., Miami, Fla.

Avis-Rent-A-Car System, Inc., Garden City, N.Y.

Bechtel Corporation, San Francisco, Calif.

(Big Dutchman), United States Industries, New York, N.Y.

The Black Clawson Company, New York, N.Y.

Booz, Allen & Hamilton International, Inc., New York, N.Y.

Borden, Inc., New York, N.Y.

Born Engineering, Tulsa, Okla.

Bristol-Myers Company, New York, N.Y.

Bucyrus-Erie, South Milwaukee, Wis.

Burroughs Corporation, Detroit, Mich.

The Butterick Co., Inc., New York, N.Y.

J. I. Case Company, Racine, Wis.

Caterpillar Tractor Co., Peoria, Ill.

Champion Spark Plug Company, Toledo, Ohio.

Chesebrough-Pond's Inc., New York, N.Y.

Chicago Bridge & Iron Company, Oakbrook, Ill.

(Chrome Corporation), Union Carbide Corp., New York, N.Y.

Chrysler Corporation, Detroit, Mich.

The Coca-Cola Export Corp., New York, N.Y.

Colgate-Palmolive International, New York, N.Y.

P. F. Collier, Inc., New York, N.Y.

(Collier-Macmillan), The Macmillan Co., New York, N.Y.

Collins Radio Company, Cedar Rapids, Iowa.

Columbian Carbon International Div. of Cities Service Co., New York, N.Y.

Combustion Engineering Inc., New York, N.Y.

Computer Services Corp., Los Angeles, Calif.

Clipper Manufacturing Co., Kansas City, Mo.

Continental Grain Company, New York, N.Y.

Control Data Corp., Minneapolis, Minn.

Crane Co., New York, N.Y.

Crown Cork & Seal Co., Inc., Philadelphia, Pa.

Cutler Hammer International, Milwaukee, Wis.

Dean Export International, Ltd., Long Beach, Calif.

(Derby & Co.,) Englehard Minerals & Chemical Corporation, New York, N.Y.

Diners Club, Inc., New York, N.Y.

Dodge & Seymour, Limited, New York, N.Y.

Donaldson Co., Inc., Minneapolis, Minn.

Dow Chemical International, Midland, Mich.

Dubois Div. of W. R. Grace & Co., Cincinnati, Ohio.

Dun & Bradstreet International, Ltd., New York, N.Y.

(Dunlop Ozite) Ozite, Inc., Libertyville, Ill.

Emergy Air Freight Corporation, Wilton, Conn.

Encylopaedia Britannica, Inc., Chicago, Ill.

Endo Drug Corporation, Garden City, N.Y.

Englehard Hanovis, Inc., Newark, N.J.

Englehard Mineral & Chemical Corp., Inc., Newark, N.J.

Esso Africa, Inc., affiliate of Standard Oil (New Jersey), New York, N.Y.

J. A. Ewing & McDonald, Inc., New York, N.Y.

F. M. C. Corporation, San Jose, Calif.

First National City Bank, New York, N.Y.

Fairbanks Morse Int., Inc., Glen Rock, N.J.

Farrell Lines, Inc., New York, N.Y.

Ferro Corporation, Cleveland, Ohio.

(Fiberglas) Owens-Corning Fiberglas Corp., Toledo, Ohio.

(Fordom) Walter E. Heller International Corp., Chicago, Ill.

Fram Corporation, Providence, R.I.

(Friden) The Singer Co., New York, N.Y.

The Jeffrey Galison Manufacturing Co., Columbus, Ohio.

Gardner-Denver Co., Quincy, Ill.

The Gates Rubber Company, Denver, Colo.

General Tire and Rubber Co., Akron, Ohio.

A. J. Gerrard & Co., Des Plaines, Ill.

Gilbert & Barker Mfg. Co., Greensboro, N.C.

The Gillette Company, Boston, Mass.

Grant Advertising International, Inc., Chicago, Ill.

Grolier, Inc., New York, N.Y.

Gulf Oil Corp., Pittsburgh, Pa.

Harnischfeger Int. Corp., Milwaukee, Wis.

Heinemann Electric Co., Trenton, N.J.

Helena Rubinstein, Inc., New York, N.Y.

Hewitt-Robins, Inc., a Div. of Litton Industries, Stamford, Conn.

Hewlett Packard, Palo Alto, Calif.

Hochmetals, South American Minerals & Merchandise Corp., New York, N.Y.

Honeywell, Inc., Minneapolis, Minn.

The Hoover Co., North Canton, Ohio.

Hyster Co., Portland, Ore.

Industrial Chemical Products, Amchem Products, Inc., Ambler, Pa.

Ingersoll-Rand Co., New York, N.Y.

Insurance Co. of North America, Philadelphia, Pa.

IBM World Trade Corp., New York, N.Y.

International Flavors and Fragrances, Inc., New York, N.Y.

International Harvester Co., Chicago, Ill.

International Ore & Fertilizer Corporation, New York, N.Y.

The Jeffrey Company, Columbus, Ohio.

(John Deere) Deere & Company, Moline, Ill.

Johns-Manville International Co., New York, N.Y.

S. C. Johnson & Son, Inc., Racine, Wis.

Joy Manufacturing Co., Pittsburgh, Pa.

King Resources, Denver, Colo.

Kaiser Jeep International Corp., Toledo, Ohio.

The Kaiser Trading Co., Oakland, Calif.

(Keagrams, Ltd.) Baxter Laboratories, Chicago, Ill.

Kellogg Company, Battle Creek, Mich.

Kelly-Springfield Tire Co., Cumberland, Md.

The Kendall Company, International Division, Boston, Mass.

Kidder, Peabody & Co., Inc., New York, N.Y.

Kimberly-Clark Corp., Neenah, Wis.

(Kodak) Eastman Kodak Co., Rochester, N.Y.

Lakeside Laboratories, Inc., Milwaukee, Wis. (subsidiary of Colgate-Palmolive Intl.)

E. J. Lavino & Co. Div. Of International Minerals Chemical Corp., Philadelphia, Pa.

Lease Plan International Corp., Great Neck, N.Y.

Leo Burnett Co., Chicago, Ill.

(Le Carbone) The Carbone Corp., Boonton, N.J.

(Ledlab) Cyanamid International, Wayne, N.J.

Eli Lilly and Company, Indianapolis, Ind.

The Lovable Company, New York, N.Y.

Merck Sharp & Dohme International, New York, N.Y.

(Maister) International Telephone & Telegraph Corp., New York, N.Y.

Masonite Corporation, Chicago, Ill.

Max Factor and Company, Inc., Hollywood, Calif.

McGraw-Hill, Inc., New York, N.Y.

(McKinnon Chain) Columbus McKinnon Corp., Tonawanda, N.Y.

Metro-Goldwyn-Mayer., Inc., New York, N.Y.

George J. Meyer Co., Milwaukee, Wis.

Mine Safety Appliances Co., Pittsburgh, Pa.

Minnesota Mining & Manufacturing Co., St. Paul, Minn.

Monsanto Company, International Div., St. Louis, Mo.

(Montrose) Allied Chemical Corp., Ltd., New York, N.Y.

Motorola, Inc., Chicago, Ill.

Muller & Phipps International Corp., New York, N.Y.

National Cash Register Co., Dayton, Ohio.

(National Packaging Co., Ltd.) St. Regis Paper Co., New York, N.Y.

Nordberg Mfg. Co., Milwaukee, Wis.

Norton Company, Worcester, Mass.

Otis Elevator Company, New York, N.Y.

(P. E. Consulting Group) Kurt Salmon Associates, Inc., Washington, D.C.

(Palabora) Newmont Mining Corp., New York, N.Y.

Pan American World Airways, Inc., New York, N.Y.

Pioneer Parachute Co., Inc., Manchester, Conn.

(Paragon) Keylite Chemicals, Los Angeles, Calif.

Parke, Davis & Company, Detroit, Mich.

The Parker Pen Company, Janesville, Wis.

Pepsi-Cola Company, New York, N.Y.

Permatex Co., Inc., West Palm Beach, Fla.

Pfizer International, New York, N.Y.

(Placid Oil) Hunt Oil, Dallas, Tex.

(Platex) International Playtex Corp., New York, N.Y.

Plough, Inc., Memphis, Tenn.

(Potter & Moore) DeWitt Drug & Beauty Products, Inc., Great Neck, N.Y.

Preload International Corp., Springdale, Conn.

Proctor & Gamble Company, Cincinnati, Ohio.

Publicker International, Inc., Philadelphia, Pa.

Richardson-Merrell, Inc., New York, N.Y.

Revlon, Inc., New York, N.Y.

Richelieu Corporation, Inc., Long Island City, N.Y.

H. H. Robertson Co., Pittsburgh, Pa.

(Ruffel) Smith, Kline & French Laboratories, Philadelphia, Pa.

Schering Corporation U.S.A., Bloomfield, N.J.

Scripto, Inc., Atlanta, Ga.

G. D. Searle & Company, Chicago, Ill.

Simplicity Pattern Co., Inc., New York, N.Y.

The Singer Company, New York, N.Y.

A. O. Smith Corporation, International Div., Milwaukee, Wis.

(S. A. Cyanamid) Cyanamid International Corp., Wayne, N.J.

(S. A. Gen. Elec.) I. G. E. Export Div., General Electric, New York, N.Y.

(S. A. Paper Chemicals) Tenneco Chemicals, Inc., New York, N.Y.

(South Atlantic Cable Co.) International Telephone & Telegraph Corp., New York, N.Y.

(Southern Cross Steel) Eastern Stainless Steel Corp., Baltimore, Md.

Sperry Rand International Corp., New York, N.Y.

Squibb Beechnut Corp., New York, N.Y.

Stein, Hall and Co., Inc., New York, N.Y.

Tampax, Inc., New York, N.Y.

J. Walter Thompson & Co., New York, N.Y.

Timken Roller Bearing Co., Canton, Ohio.

(Titan Industrial Corp.) Pantheon Industries, Inc., New York, N.Y.

Tokheim Corp., Fort Wayne, Ind.

(Transalloys) Air Reduction Company, Inc., New York, N.Y.

Trans World Airlines Inc., New York, N.Y.

(Tuco) The Upjohn Company, Kalamazoo, Mich.

20th Century-Fox Films Corp., New York, N.Y.

Unimark International, Chicago, Ill.

Union Carbide Corp., New York, N.Y.

Uniroyal Inc., New York, N.Y.

United Artists Corp., New York, N.Y.

The Valeron Corp., Berkley, Mich.

(Valvoline) Ashland Oil & Refining Co., Ashland, Ky.

Van Dusen Aircraft Supplies Export Div., Inc., St. Louis, Mo.

The Vendo Company, Kansas City, Mo.

(Wabco) Westinghouse Air Brake, Pittsburgh, Pa.

Wendell C. Walker & Associates, New York, N.Y.

Warner Bros., International Corp., New York, N.Y.

Watkins Products Inc., Winona, Minn.

(Gordon Webster & Co.) Standard Pressed Steel Co., Jenkintown, Pa.

(Western Knapp Engineering) Arthur G. McKee, Cleveland, Ohio.

Westinghouse Electric International, New York, N.Y.

(Whitney Murray) Ernst & Ernst, Cleveland, Ohio.

(Whitehall Products) American Home Products Corp., New York, N.Y.

White Motor Corp., Cleveland, Ohio.

W. A. Whitney Co., Rockford, Ill.

Wyeth International Limited, Philadelphia, Pa.

Arthur Young & Company, New York, N.Y.

Cape Town Consular District

Atlantic Richfield Co., New York, N.Y.

(Armour) International Packers, Ltd., Chicago, Ill.

(Ault & Wiborg) Inmont Corp., New York, N.Y.

Joseph Bancroft & Sons Co., Wilmington, Del.

(Barlow) Oshkosh Motor Truck Co., Oshkosh, Wis.

Beckman Instruments, Inc., Fullerton, Calif.

The Black and Decker Mfg. Co., Towson, Md.

Burlington Industries, Inc., Greensboro, N.C.

Caltex Petroleum Corp., New York, N.Y.

(Chamberlain's) Warner Lambert Pharmaceutical Co., Morris Plains, N.J.

Connel Bros. Company, San Francisco, Calif.

(Gabriel) Maremont Corp., Chicago, Ill.

J. Gerber & Co., Inc., New York, N.Y.

Getty Oil Company, Los Angeles, Calif.

W. R. Grace & Company, New York, N.Y.

Eastman Kodak Company, Rochester, N.Y.

Koret of California, Inc., San Francisco, Calif.

Mobil Oil Corporation, New York, N.Y.

(Mono Containers) J. C. Allen, Wilmot, Ill.

(O'Okiep Copper Co.) Newmont Mining Corporation, New York, N.Y.

(Phoenix Assurance Co., Ltd.) Continental Insurance Co., New York, N.Y.

(Royal Baking Powder) International Standard Brands, Inc., New York, N.Y.

The Scholl Manufacturing Co., Inc., Chicago, Ill.

(Servac Laboratories) Miles Laboratories, Inc., Elkhart, Ind.

(Sacony) Mobil Oil Corp., New York, N.Y.

(South Africa Preserving Co.) Del Monte International, San Francisco, Calif.

(E. R. Syfret) Arthur Young & Co., New York, N.Y.

(Tidal Diamonds) Getty Oil Company, Los Angeles, Calif.

(Tsumeb Corp.) American Metal Climax, Inc., New York, N.Y.

Tupperware Home Parties, Orlando, Fla.

(Vitreous Enamelling Corp.) Symington Wayne Corp., Salisbury, Md.

Wilbur-Ellis Company, San Francisco, Calif.

Cape Town Consular District
(*Eastern Cape Province*)

Berkshire International Corp., Reading, Pa.

Borg-Warner Corporation, Chicago, Ill.

E. C. De Witt and Co., Chicago, Ill.

Firestone Tire and Rubber Co., Akron, Ohio.

Ford Motor Company, Dearborn, Mich.

General Motors Acceptance Corp., New York, N.Y.

GM Overseas Corp., New York, N.Y.

The Goodyear Tire & Rubber Company, Akron, Ohio.

Johnson & Johnson, New Brunswick, N.J.

Phillips Petroleum Co., Bartlesville, Okla.

(Rexall Drug Co.) Dart Laboratories, Inc., Los Angeles, Calif.

Rockwell Manufacturing Co., Pittsburgh, Pa.

(Thompson Ramco S.A.) TRW Inc., Cleveland, Ohio.

Durban Consular District

(Amalgamated Packaging) St. Regis Paper Co., New York, N.Y.

American Bureau of Shipping, New York, N.Y.

Anderson Clayton & Co., Houston, Tex.

(Anikem) Nelco Chemical Co., Chicago, Ill.

(Barlow, Weyerhaeuser) Weyerhaeuser Co., Tacoma, Wash.

Beech-Nut Life Savers, Inc., Canajoharie, N.Y.

Carnation Co., Los Angeles, Calif.
Coca-Cola Export Corporation, New York, N.Y.
Corn Products Co., New York, N.Y.
(Diamond H. Switches) Oak Electro Netics Corp., Crystal Lake, Ill.
(Duroplastic Pentz Industries) Engelhard Hanovia, Inc., Newark, N.J.
(Gamlen) Sybron Corp., Rochester, N.J.
General Foods Corp., White Plains, N.Y.
The Lubrizol Corp., Wickliffe, Ohio.
Lykes Bros. Steamship Co., Inc., New Orleans, La.
Mobil Petroleum, Inc., New York, N.Y.
Moore-McCormack Lines, Inc., New York, N.Y.
Rheem International, Inc., New York, N.Y.
(Robertsons) Corn Products Company, New York, N.Y.
Sterling Drug, Inc., New York, N.Y.
(Triton Chemicals) Rohm and Haas Co., Philadelphia, Pa.

*United States firms not separately incorporated in South Africa but
having direct factory of company representative*

Boeing Company, Philadelphia, Pa.
Clark Equipment Co., Battle Creek, Mich.
E. I. Du Pont De Nemours & Co., Inc., International Dept., Wilming-
    ton, Del.
Kaiser Exploration, Oakland, Calif.
Singer Sewing Machine Co., New York, N.Y.
United Aircraft International, Inc., East Hartford, Conn.
United States Steel (New York), Inc., New York, N.Y.

The address of the South African Institute of Race Relations: Auden
House, 68 DeKorte Street, Braamfontein, Johannesburg, Republic of
South Africa.